Studia Fennica
Litteraria 6

The Finnish Literature Society was founded in 1831 and has from the very beginning engaged in publishing. It nowadays publishes literature in the fields of ethnology and folkloristics, linguistics, literary research and cultural history.

The first volume of Studia Fennica series appeared in 1933. Since 1992 the series has been divided into three thematic subseries: Ethnologica, Folkloristica and Linguistica. Two additional subseries were formed in 2002, Historica and Litteraria.

In addition to its publishing activities the Finnish Literature Society maintains a folklore archive, a literature archive and a library.

EDITORIAL OFFICE

Hallituskatu 1
FIN-00170 Helsinki

Nodes of Contemporary Finnish Literature

Edited by Leena Kirstinä

Finnish Literature Society · Helsinki

Publication has undergone peer review.

This work has been published with the financial assistance of FILI
– Finnish Literature Exchange and the Jenny and Antti Wihuri Foundation.

ISBN 978-952-222-359-3
ISSN 1458-5278

www.finlit.fi/books

Hansaprint Oy
Vantaa 2012

Table of Contents

Foreword

*N*odes of Contemporary Finnish Literature is the sixth volume of the series of Studia Fennica Litteraria published by the Finnish Literary Society since 2003. It is a subseries of Studia Fennica, which was established in 1933. The series includes six thematic subseries: Anthropologica, Ethnologica, Folkloristica, Historica, Linguistica and Litteraria.

The goal of Studia Fennica Litteraria is to offer an internationally refereed English-language publication for studies on Finnish literature. The scope of the series is comparative and international. It aims to create a dialogue between Finnish and European literatures.

The volumes previously published in Studia Fennica Litteraria are as follows:

- *Changing Scenes. Encounters between European and Finnish Fin de Siècle* (Ed. Pirjo Lyytikäinen 2003)
- *Women's Voices. Female Authors and Feminist Criticism in the Finnish Literary Tradition* (Ed. Lea Rojola & Päivi Lappalainen 2007)
- *Metaliterary Layers in Finnish Literature* (Ed. Samuli Hägg, Erkki Sevänen & Risto Turunen 2008)
- *The Emergence of Finnish Book and Reading Culture in the 1700s* (Ed. Cecilia af Forselles & Tuija Laine 2011)
- *Aino Kallas. Negotiations with Modernity* (Ed. Leena Kurvet-Käosaar & Lea Rojola 2011)

Nodes of Contemporary Finnish Literature has a dual aim. On the one hand, its purpose is present to the reader some phenomena of recent Finnish literature and sketch some possible directions for future literary history; on the other hand, it also brings to the fore some young Finnish scholars in literature. The anthology could be a manual for students learning the Finnish language or studying Finnish culture at universities; in addition, it could make these literary phenomena accessible to others who are interested in these issues.

This anthology owes much to the Jenny and Antti Wihuri Foundation and to the Finnish Literature Exchange (FILI) which have granted funds for English translations and language checking. Thanks also to the Finnish Literary Society and its publication council for accepting it to the series of Studia Fennica Litteraria and for publishing it. The greatest of thanks to the authors of the articles, and to those who have helped with the English language revision and translation: Ph.D. Marlene Broemer; M.A. Michael Dutton; M.A. Susanne Kalajaiye; M.A. Pamela Kaskinen; M.A. Anne Langendorfer; M.A. Jennifer Nelson; B.A. Susanna Siitoin; Ph.D. Maija Kalin, the former director and M.A. Sirpa Vehviläinen, the assistant of the Language Centre of the University of Jyväskylä.

In Helsinki 9.2.2012
Leena Kirstinä

Leena Kirstinä

Introduction

To write any historical presentations of contemporary phenomena is a challenging, if not impossible, task. The perspective might be too short to understand them and their true relationships. However, the risk has been taken, thanks to Brian McHale, who introduced his and Randall Stevenson's inspiring literary history project to the participants of the summer course at the University of Tampere in 2005. Its results have been published in the magnificent work titled *The Edinburgh Companion to Twentieth-Century Literatures in English* (2006). It represents a new way of thinking about literary history that has been undergoing changes since the Second World War.

The Edinburgh Companion to Twentieth-Century Literatures in English does not survey the decades, literary movements, or national literatures; rather it presents a 'spatial' literary history, mapping 'hot spots' – crossroads in space and time – around which the works and movements of literature can be seen to arrange themselves.

The traditional positivist paradigm of literary history has been criticised during the last half of the 20th century, because of its epistemological problems. The critics targeted literary histories, written in the spirit of nationalism and favouring canonised authors. They did not meet with approval, because they were normative and not historical; literature was separated from historical processes and connected with genial authors and their influence on others. Proponents of the New Criticism demanded competent literary analysis and interpretation.

New Criticism itself was interested in autonomous works, not in history. The premises of writing literary history needed then to be scrutinized, i.e. reception aesthetics paid attention to that literary reception and production should be taken into account. Structuralism promoted the idea to reflect on relations and to stop the flux of time in simultaneous moments. Post-structuralism found the way back to history via intertextuality, with the help of the chains of ideas, figures and tropes, used in literatures, that can be followed between times and places. This is where we are now.

Literatures as a network of relationships and communication seem to be traffic centres or smaller crossroads. Some works act like magnetic fields or form nodes. With the help of soft statistical data and by observing reception, one can try to locate such hot spots in literature. Obviously, every literary year has its own characteristics; some topics or matters attract more attention than others do, and some genre or stylistic traits rise to the fore. Literary prizes, based on the evaluations of expert readers, are signs that illustrate these trends. It is clear that the perspective from which literature is viewed by the observer influences her/his interpretations of the findings.

In this anthology, we study the situation in Finnish literature from the 1980s to the first decade of the new millennium. We want to observe the trends in Finnish or Finnish-Swedish language written prose, poetry or children's literature. Obviously, our volume offers a highly limited view of the subject. There are initial observations; we must be satisfied, if we can form a valid hypothesis of some current nodes in contemporary literature.

During the chosen period, there were many turning points in global political history. The collapse of the Soviet Union in 1991, the two world-wide economic crises, and the bombing of the WTC towers in New York, 11.9.2001, have all influenced Finnish literature. There were also changes that were important to Finland itself, such as accession to the European Union in 1995. We are also aware of huge nuclear catastrophes (Chernobyl, Fukushima), and the earthquakes and tsunamis in Thailand and Japan, although we do not take them as starting points for our articles. The determination of the first junction year that we consider – 1985 – is not due to Mikhail Gorbachev's reform politics, but to the outstanding literary phenomena, which took place simultaneously at that time.

We will focus on the period from the 1980s onwards, because the 1980s was the decade when the modern really met the postmodern in Finland in different ways. There were ruptures and mixtures of modernism and postmodernism. There are sparkling bubbles in style and rebellious themes that led to new kinds of writing. Their connection with postmodernism was much discussed, especially after 1987, when Markku Eskelinen and Jyrki Lehtola published their pamphlet, *Jälkisanat: Sianhoito-opas* (Epilogue: Guide to Raising Pigs). These young men argued fiercely that Finnish literature and its research were out-of-date because of a continued fascination with and appreciation of mimetic realism. The debate was refreshing; however, their accusations were only partly correct, as the poetics of late realism and the modernism of the fifties were in the process of being renewed (see Anna Helle 2009).

As a sign that something new was coming, the most precious prize for literature, the first Finlandia Prize, was bestowed on Erno Paasilinna, a satirist, whose genre is one of the most weakly developed prose forms in the Finnish language. His satirical work *Yksinäisyys ja uhma* (Solitude and Obstinacy) beat out the competition from established modernists in poetry, Bo Carpelan and Paavo Haavikko, and the new realists in prose, Veronica Pimenoff and Joni Skiftesvik.

1985 – the Crisis of Mimesis

The year 1985 points to changes even more clearly, when the following novels appeared: Leena Krohn's *Tainaron. Postia toisesta kaupungista* (*Tainaron. Mail from Another City*); Jörn Donner's *Far och son* (Father and Son); Matti Pulkkinen's *Romaanihenkilön kuolema. Tarua ja totta eli ihmisen kuvaus* (The Death of the Character. Legend and Truth or the Description of a Human Being), and Rosa Liksom's collection of short stories, *Yhden yön pysäkki* (One Night Stands). Krohn, Pulkkinen and Donner were also candidates for the Finlandia Prize. One common trait in these works is the epistemological questions that were raised: what is true in fiction, what relation does fiction have with reality and what is fiction's reality? The question of representation has an important influence on their narrative strategies, and structures. The reader takes the subject position of the *I*-narrator, her/his identity and selfhood. The writing and speaking *I*-person conquered the central station in the above-mentioned prose works. They also share the world-view of disillusionment.

Leena Krohn abandoned everyday kitchen realism at the beginning of her career when writing children's literature, which allows the use of fantasy (*Vihreä vallankumous*, 1970, The Green Revolution; *Tyttö joka kasvoi ja muita kertomuksia*, 1973, The Girl who Grew and Other Stories). She started to unify ontologically and epistemologically different materials, both fact and fiction, to her narratives. Her novels came to resemble collections of short stories, like her *Pereat mundus. Romaani, eräänlainen* (1998, Pereat mundus. One kind of novel) in which every separate episode features a character named Håkan, although he is always different. The Swedish name, Håkan has a connotation of a harmless but stupid person. Similarly, Krohn used the phrase, *Pereat mundus* which refers to a Latin phrase "Fiat justitia, et pereat mundus" and to its famous user Immanuel Kant. Kant paraphrases it as "Let justice reign even if all the rascals in the world should perish from it". This intertextual device creates peculiar humour in this apocalyptic novel where everyone is frightened and waiting for the end of the world.

Tainaron was Krohn's breakthrough in prose. It is a travel book and epistolary novel; it consists of extraordinary letters, sent to an unknown recipient by a female traveller when visiting the world of the insects. *Tainaron* connects – as is typical in Krohn's work – the visible and invisible, the real and imaginary, and the human and Nature. She does not write science fiction, but philosophical allegories similar to those written by Italo Calvino. Thanks to Leena Krohn, fantasy in the broad sense of the word, has become accepted as an important part of the contemporary literary canon in Finland, and science fiction has risen in value because of the ecological themes with which Krohn has dealt in several works. She has, then, successors in writing postmodern allegory, such as Maarit Verronen and Risto Isomäki, who writes speculative prose.

Krohn very often examines in her *oeuvre* the ephemeral nature of selfhood and the continuous metamorphosis of identity. Identity is also problematized by Jörn Donner in *Far och son*; he especially focuses on the Finnish-Swedish identity of a solid *I*, which is represented to be weaker than before. The title of the novel suggests that there is a bond between the father and the son, and it is just that bond for which the son is longing, because he has not known his father who has died before his birth. The main person who resembles the real author is seeking himself in trying to write a novel in which he represents himself by another name as a fictive character of the manuscript. The Finnish-Swedish identity seems to have become postmodern, an empty place without a centre. In the next two decades, the so-called "cyclope novel" with its monologue style of narration was sidelined by the new generation of Finland-Swedish writing prose authors, such as Monika Fagerholm, Pirkko Lindberg, Fredrik Lång, and Lars Sund, to name a few, who learned to use metafictional and self-reflective strategies.

Continuing the change from realism in Finnish language literature of the 1980s, Matti Pulkkinen's novel, *Romaanihenkilön kuolema* was labelled as postmodern. The authorial voice in the text itself describes the novel as "literarily bankrupt" and an "unfinished draft of an autobiographical anti-novel". At the beginning of the novel, the reader learns that this author, much like Pulkkinen himself, has published a book called *The Power of the Word*, which has received the literary prize granted by the Nordic Council. During the celebrations in Stockholm, Finland has suddenly been occupied by the Soviet Union, and the author determines that he will not return to his country. The frame of the novel is mere fantasy and suggests the genre of dystopic utopia. What the reader is reading are fragments, unbound pages and notebooks left behind in Finland on the bench of a small town park, that were found, edited and commented upon by a literary researcher who represents himself as "Makkonen", an old friend of the author, a fact confirmed by the manuscript itself.

Romaanihenkilön kuolema is a self-reflective metafiction that kills at the end all of its central figures, the author and the reader, in spite of the fact that they are paradoxically immortal on the pages, which is quite the opposite of the real reader's situation, as "Makkonen" is mocking. The novel contains essay-like passages and aphorisms on writing and reading. In its poetics, it tries to apply real politics to the novel form, as the author says. It is partly a book about travel to Berlin and Africa; its illustrations come from the journey to Germany. The newspaper pictures represent tragic events when people were trying to cross the wall (*die Mauer*) from the east to the west. In a sense, the novel is a political essay that criticises especially Soviet politics, the Finns' overly sympathetic attitude toward the Soviet Union (*die Finlandisierung*) and their naïve belief in development aid to Africans. The *I*-figure, the narrator, by means of whom "the world is written itself", continually exceeds the borders of reality and fiction speaking of living and dead artists, politicians and authors. Pulkkinen's novel is a genre-blending type of fiction; according to the narrator, the novel as a genre is omnivorous like a pig. To this poetical definition, the young writers, Eskelinen and Lehtola, showed their admiration in the subtitle of their polemical book *A Guide to Raising Pigs*.

Contrary to the important critics' expectations, *Romaanihenkilön kuo-lema* was not awarded the Finlandia Prize that year; rather, it was granted to Donner's anti-autobiography *Far och son*. After that, the prize was given only to poetry, until 1990 when the novel was again rewarded. In 1992 Leena Krohn' fantasy (*Matemaattisia olioita tai jaettuja unia*, Mathemathical Beings and Shared Dreams received it); then the rules of the competition were changed, so that only novels could be considered. The Union of Finnish Publishers, which finances the prize, wanted to promote the novel, the best-selling and most popular genre.

Krohn, Donner and Pulkkinen represent subjective *I*-narration and play with the relationship between language and reality, each having their own purpose and method. The post-structuralist idea of language, denying the transparency of language or its ability to evoke reality, was worked through in many forms of *I*-narration during the following decades. In 1985, Rosa Liksom questioned even the reality of authorial identity by using a pseudonym. Her coming to the literary stage was a performative act: there were ten young women wearing uniforms and fur hats, among them the author, when the announcement of her first book was made. The author was not dead, as Roland Barthes would put it, but hiding, which of course, increased the media's interest in her. It was some years before her real identity was revealed to the public: Anni Ylävaara (b. 1958) in Ylitornio, Lapland, Finland, studied anthropology at the University of Helsinki, lived in, among other places, the free city of Kristiania in Copenhagen. Her pseudonym comes from that time. She is named Rosa after Rosa Luxemburg, the German revolutionary from the beginning of the twentieth century. The Swedish word *liksom* means both 'like' and 'as if' in English. She used it when she was searching for the right word in Swedish.

Rosa Liksom created in *Yhden yön pysäkki* and in the following collection of novels *Unohdettu vartti* (1986, The Forgotten Quarter), a new kind of poetics, with her shortcuts. The intrigue is structured in episodic screens as in comic strips. Her stories depict without illusion young people who are trying to find some place to stay overnight, in the railway station in Helsinki or in other halls of European cities or in Lapland. The sections of her shortcuts are geographically indicated by the term, "67 northern latitude". Those who come from the north are allowed to use their own colourful dialect, due to Liksom's sometimes grotesque humour. They tell their unembellished life stories openly as if to a microphone, held out by an anthropologist. Her first novel, *Kreisland* (1995, Graceland), is also written as if it had been recorded by an interviewer. Mythical figures by their miraculous birth, Impi Agafina and Juho Gabriel as well as the seer, Mikri Vuoma, relate Lapland's historical development and at the same time Finland's history as they have experienced it from the creation of the northern hemisphere to the time of the Russians' space flights. *Kreisland* is a Lappish epic and at the same time an indirect parody, not only of Elias Lönnrot's *Kalevala* (1849), but also of the whole genre of national epics. Liksom's special ability is to parody cultural-ideological discourses – religious, communist, capitalist – which the northern people, living between the west and the east, have been obliged to learn over the centuries in order to "develop themselves"; the word is put between parenthesis by the ironic novel itself.

Rosa Liksom vivifies a new orality in fiction, a phenomenon that was born paradoxically at the same time as electronic media developed (see Walter Ong 1988.) New oral narration pretends to be like narration around the campfire. Good examples of it are talk shows and other kinds of direct radio programs carried out by telephone conversations between the journalist and listeners. Big Brother-type TV programmes, which have also increased in Finland from the 1990s onwards, are another example of a creation that mimics campfire speech. Imitating spoken language in fiction is known everywhere in late-modern, Western prose (see, Monika Fludernik 1996), but it was very new and that is why it is still astonishing in Finland. Written Finnish is a somewhat new phenomenon. It was developed very quickly in the 19th century when Finnish had become the official language in 1863 and when it began to be taught at school on all levels. The use of dialect was allowed only in private communication. It did not belong to civilised speech manners, but the vocabulary of dialects gave its rich resources to be used properly in literature itself, but in written, not oral transcription. Liksom delivered dialect from purism's oppression, and later on, dialects have also been approved in serious poetry (Heli Laaksonen). Highly canonised works like *Kalevala* and parts of the *Bible* were translated into some dialects; Matti Pulkkinen expressed himself in public interviews using his North-Carelian home dialect.

Some kind of new orality can also be seen in the changing narrator's voices that seem like tracks side by side on a recording or a montage of different narrators' stories which resembles TV viewers changing channels with a remote. The father of this currently very popular technique is Hannu Raittila, who has written many radio plays. He has succeeded in giving to every person his/her own idiolect so that the reader can recognise when an old minister, a Hell's Angel, a car or sausage seller, an administrator of a sound reinforcement system, a member of a devout religious family or an academic researcher is speaking in his novel, *Ei minulta mitään puutu* (1998, I Lack Nothing).

1998 – Identity Discussion

The year, 1985, was a time of problematizing the poetics of realism, the codes of author, narrator, character, action and reader. The roles of author, narrator and reader are nearly interchangeable when writing or speaking alone takes the place of action and when nothing is happening outside the text. In the following decade, the primus motor in narratives does not really change; such concepts as identity, subjectivity and selfhood are still dominant. However, in 1998, there is a change in female writing, and social, national or international issues in literature.

The period from 1980–2000 meant first the explosion of individuality and subjectivity, the rebirth of individualism; Finnish cultural homogeneity was understood to be illusionary. Finland started to become a multicultural society because of the increasing number of immigrants coming, first from such African countries as Somalia. The resurrection of *I* meant that the omniscient narrator and objective observer were obliged to leave their positions in narration, or the author-like person was mixed with the story, as we have already seen. This meant that biographies, autobiographies, autofiction types of prose, memoirs, dairies, collections of letters, epistolary forms of novel, even e-mail novels were the most prominent genres. Some of them followed the rules of real biographies, in that the name of the author and the main figure was the same; some imitated the autobiographical genre and autofiction. Some authors such as Kari Hotakainen began to mock the publisher who wants the author to write intimate confessions, even though he has nothing to tell. He plays with the conventions of autobiography in his metafictional novel, *Klassikko. Omaelämäkerrallinen romaani autoilevasta ja avoimesta kansasta* (1997, The Classic, An Autobiographical Novel about a Driving and Open Nation). Inside, there is another book, which is the writer's dairy from his early career as a poet, titled "It was nice to live, but difficult to keep silent".

The subjective focalisation of narration had also a function to empower the search for new strategies to express such social issues as womanhood, women's human rights and female biological and physical existence. First-person narration signalled the rise of a new kind of feminism. The first hot spot of *I*-writing was *Sonja O. kävi täällä* (1981, Sonja O. Was Here), a description of student bohemians of the 1970s, by Anja Kauranen (from 1997 onwards Anja Snellman). It was a critical and commercial success; its innovative feature is that the writer and the principal character is a young woman who had appropriated the old freedoms of men, as George C. Schoolfield (1998) put it. The novel has in its title already a reference to Pauline Reage's pornographic novel *The History of O* (*Histoire d'O* 1954), the sadomasochistic situation of which Kauranen turns upside down. *Sonja O.*, confessions of Donna Juan, paints the Strindbergian fight between the heterosexual man and woman. *Sonja O. kävi täällä* was a turning point toward more courageous and, strictly speaking, female writing.

The doctrine of the eighties – the personal is political – was realised in an anarchic-feminist way by Anja Kauranen in her novel, *Pelon maantiede* (1995, The Geography of Fear). In order to defend women's human rights against masculine hegemony, an academic group of assaulted women from the Department of Women's Studies begins to plan aggressive acts of revenge against men and to conquer for themselves the frightening places of city space. Pirkko Lindberg, writing in Swedish, made visible the inequality of the sexes in culture and society by rewriting Voltaire's famous novel, *Candide*. As its predecessor, her *Candida* (1997) is a many-sided pamphlet of its time. The heroine of the novel is a young girl beginning her life as a servant in a 20th century, upper-class family. In many works, Anna-Leena Härkönen has described difficulties in female sexuality in *Akvaariorakkaus* (1991, Love in an Aquarium) and in motherhood in *Heikosti positiivinen* (2001, Slightly Positive). Maria Peura made her breakthrough by handling paedophilia in her first novel, *On rakkautes ääretön* (2001, Your Infinite Love) at the same time as everywhere in the world there was sensational news about child abuse.

The year, 1998, then means a change in Finnish feminist literature, although a similar tone as before persisted. It was understood that it is not an easy task for both sexes to grow up, because both of them must become accustomed to their physical existence and the outside world with its demands. Positive models or figures to deal with these issues were needed. Monika Fagerholm and Sirpa Kähkönen present feminist thinking without hostile attitudes to men. Fagerholm's *Diva* (1998) empowers a young girl in her identity project by means of magical realism. Described in Naturalism the fate of a poor country maid was to be spoiled in the city. Kähkönen saves her life in her *Mustat morsiamet* (1998, The Black Brides). Black brides – a peasant woman's wedding dress was earlier black – are not ruined; the seductive city life does not crush their hopes totally, because the city gives them opportunities to reach full citizenship, when they can earn their own living, and become the managers of their own lives. They have courage enough to express themselves in their own language, in this case in the eastern Finnish dialect. Kähkönen has written a sequel to her micro-history of *Mustat morsiamet*, now five volumes, in which she shows how women have endured the wartime difficulties thanks to their mutual solidarity.

In the overflow of female voices, it was first impossible to separate men's objections. Men write back! In 1999, manhood became a central theme in several collections of short stories such as Juha Seppälä's *Suuret kertomukset* (The Great Narratives); Hannu Raittila's *Miesvahvuus* (Men Strength); and Jyrki Vainonen's *Tutkimusmatkailija ja muita tarinoita* (The Explorer and Other Stories). Novels like Kauko Röyhkä's *Ocean City* and Markku Karpio's *Naisten mies*, (The Ladies' Man), are other examples. The main question was, how to be a man, not how to become a man. As a prime example of this discussion, is Kari Hotakainen's successful novel, *Juoksuhaudantie* (2002, The Trench Battle Road), which was awarded the Nordic Council Literature Prize. It makes visible what a man's life is after the women's fight for freedom and shows how a Finnish man fights for his own identity on two fronts: at home and in the society of the market economy.

The humour of Hotakainen's novel, *Juoksuhaudantie*, is signalled by its title, which refers to a street in a Helsinki suburb, constructed by ex-service men after the Second World War and the main character's definition of himself as a home-service man. He is now the Home Angel, submitted to serve his wife. In this position, he makes a big mistake, when he once hits his wife. This thoughtless act ruins his personality. The novel describes in a tragi-comic way his desperate campaign to get back his family, especially his daughter, by means of a single-family home, which he begins to seek. His situation is hopeless, because his wife and the entire social system seem to be against him.

In the Finland-Swedish novel, *Den finska mannens sorg* (The Finnish Man's Sorrow 1996), Fredrik Lång lets the fellow sufferer of Hotakainen's hero speak, also in the first person, about his suffering from the female emancipation in Strindbergian self-pity; for him his wife's longing for her own space is like a form of adultery. The coherence of the Male ego has been broken into pieces; they are remembering, experiencing, hoping, dreaming, and hating narrators who cannot collect themselves in spite of their eagerness to tell their stories. Kristina Carlson's novel, *Maan ääreen* (1999, To the Edge of the World) explains why it is so. Her hero is the forefather of the man who relates the tale, but is unwilling to tell the truth, because of self-deception. He is Lennart Falk from the nineteenth century, seeking his Fortune from Siberian coal fields, by any means, and with the help of women. This man of modernisation understands, at last, that narratives do not unify his selfhood, because no one is one, but many, and different stories are told according to who is listening. One can shape one's identity in general or to oneself, because human nature is not a clearly pre-determined unity, but one should be aware of one's own motives.

Did Community Disappear When the Individual Stepped Forth?

The foregrounding of the individual raised the question, if literature still had a common agenda in society. There are no more social classes or class struggle, it was said; communities consist of heterogeneous groups; even the poor and the rich include culturally different people. The detective genre was called a type of postmodern social novel, because social issues were found in this type of writing. Its popularity was increasing all over the world. Finnish crime literature by Leena Lehtolainen and Matti Rönkkö was successful in the wake of the famous Swedish authors like Henning Mankell and Liza Marklund. However, some authors such as the Finnish-Swedish author Kjell Westö believed, that it was possible to open the door from private experiences to general moral and social reflection and even to consolation (see Joni Pyysalo 2000).

Westö realized his ideas in *Drakarna över Helsingfors* (Kites Above Helsinki), which describes the social development in the Finnish society from the sixties to the economic crises of the nineties from the point of view of the Bexar family's sons. He also fulfilled the long-lasting wish of the Finnish-Swedish minority to have an identity saga like the one that Väinö Linna had given to the Finnish-speaking majority in the trilogy, *Täällä Pohjantähden alla* (1958–1962, Here Under the North Star). That was *Vådan av att vara Skrake* (1999, The Misfortune of Being Skrake) and its sequel (2006, *Där vi en gång gått*, Where Once We Walked). These novels give a century's historical perspective on the language minority that was born from peasants and fishermen on the western coast of Finland and immigrants from Sweden, Germany, Scotland, Russia and other European countries. During the nineteenth century, this part of the population took part in forming Finland as a nation. Westö proves that the Swedish-speaking minority does not differ too much from the majority in their mentality. This difference can be expressed by comparing the family name Skrake with the Finnish name Koskelo which one member of the family has taken as his name because he has married a Finnish-speaking woman. Both words refer to a water bird, merganser, but in Finnish the name sounds softer than in Swedish. Westö's mission is also to convince the public that not all Swedish-speaking Finns belong to "bättre folk" (better people) as is a common misconception.

In 1998, Juha Seppälä's novel *Sydänmaa* (Wilderness), Hannu Raittila's *Ei minulta mitään puutu*, and Sirpa Kähkönen's *Mustat morsiamet* were traffic signs to rethinking national identity. There were two reasons for this re-evaluation of Finnish identity: one was Finland's membership in the European Union, which animated general discussion about Finnishness, and the other was depression in economics; after that no one repeated the slogan, 'It is a Lotto prize to be born as a Finn'. Rather, what was needed was to revive the old Finnish spirit, i.e. all of these qualities – perseverance, diligence, unselfishness, which could be found in classical literature as in Johan Ludvig Runeberg (1804–1877), suggested the prime minister, Esko Aho's committee of philosophers. Their ideal figure was created by Runeberg's well-known poem about Paavo from Saarijärvi, who fights with Nature from year to year on his ice-bound farm.

Contemporary authors did not agree with the idea of returning to National Romanticism; Juha Seppälä's novel *Sydänmaa* does not believe in the idealised happiness of a hard worker. Working like a slave in the woods in order to earn a subsistence living hardens the body and the soul of the tenant farmer, and the beauty of Nature, admired by romantic poetry, does not ease the burden of work. The economic success, reached at last, which is a typical trait in the Finnish family novel, does not compensate for the lack of emotional happiness (see Lajos Szopori Nagy 1986). A shared heritage from father to daughter and from mother to son is spiritual coldness, even though they no longer suffer from hunger. In his next novel, *Suomen historia* (2000, Finnish History), Seppälä not only dissects the Finnish success story, remembered as mere personal suffering during the Civil War and the Second World War, but goes further by carnevalizing all history writing.

If Seppälä's *Sydänmaa* is a sarcastic comment on national history, Hannu Raittila's novel *Ei minulta mitään puutu* is the opposite; Raittila unifies the history of earthly and spiritual development in a humorous way. The grand old man of the Leinonen family is a very effective entrepreneur; he electrifies the country during the daytime and in the evenings, he arranges meetings in order to propagate fundamental Christianity. The problem of the *homo faber* family Leinonen is that they do not know when to stop their projects until it is too late. As a positive vision, the novel argues that it is a trait of Finnishness that at the moment of danger, the believers and pagans will find a common base and start to work together.

Like Sirpa Kähkönen, Mikaela Sundström creates female characters who demonstrate women's mutual solidarity in her novel *Dessa himlar kring oss städs* (1999, Around Us All These Heavens Remain). It describes almost the same hundred years' period as other mentioned family novels, but now the family comes from nowhere, from a small village in south eastern Finland. It is read as a continuation of the tradition of *hembygd*-literature (native place), which encourages the development of the Swedish-speaking country-side as before, but now with the help of women's power.

The new Millennium also opened the pages of new kinds of historical novels that approach history with suspicion and provocation. Jari Tervo questioned President Urho Kekkonen's political ethics in his novels *Myyrä* (2004, The Mole) and *Ohrana* (2006, Protection). Ulla-Lena Lundberg had courage enough to write about almost mythical themes such as the Winter War and the Continuation War in her novel *Marsipansoldaten* (2001, The Soldier of Marzipan), because Väinö Linna's national war novel *Tuntematon sotilas* (1954, *The Unknown Soldier*) was a kind of sacred work. *Marsipansoldaten* refers in its name to the phrase 'the army is marching with its stomach' as does also the bilingual Finnish army with the delicious food packages, sent from the starving home front to the dear boys 'there somewhere far away'. Göran and Frej Kummel are Finnish-Swedish counter-parts to Väinö Linna's second lieutenant Vilho Koskela, icon of democratic leadership in army. The brothers Kummel are also well approved by the soldiers, because they learn to speak better Finnish and do not differ negatively from others – there was still language racism in the Finnish army during the wars. The Kummels can enjoy outdoor life in the Carelian woods and organise cultural activities, sports and choir events, even theatre performances for the prevention of boredom during the position (stabilized) war.

Marzipansoldaten judges, as does *Tuntematon sotilas*, all war enthusiasts and the nationalist arguments on behalf of the war, i.e., to deliberate the so-called kindred nation, whose Finnish language sounds quite different from that they have learnt. Lundberg brings the uncomfortable front life with vermin physically near the reader, along with young men's inner life, their selfishness, naivety, and friendship. She dares to wonder at the absurd operations from the Finnish side and admire the competence of the equipment of the Russian Army, which was usually mocked at that time. Now, also historians agree with Lundberg's realism.

The recent war novels have detached themselves from front-line battles; Tuomas Kyrö's *Liitto* (2005, Union) and Sanna Ravi's *Ansari* (2007, Hothouse) both criticise the home front's ardent nationalism, expressed in militarist discourse and behaviour. The parody of nationalism goes even further in Miika Nousiainen's novel, *Vadelmavenepakolainen* (2007, Raspberry Boat Refugee). The odd title is explained. Its main character, Mikko Virtanen, declares himself to be a transvestite of nationality. He has determined to become Mikael Andersson, a modern, soft and sympathetic, complete Swedish man, when as a child, he first eats the raspberry boat sweets on a cruise to Stockholm. He considers his own father to be the wrong role model, because every Friday he drinks too much and hopes that the Swedes do not win in ice hockey. Everything is in order in his Finnishness, looking from the outside, but not from inside. He feels himself inwardly uncomfortable, because he recognises that he was born and raised to the wrong nationality, to the feeling of Finnish inferiority. Here Nousiainen discusses Benedict Anderson's theory of imagined communities, which are created and maintained by unconscious and/or conscious tropes, and narratives (see Anderson 1983).

Therefore, we have seen that the year 1998 activated an important theme of national identity from a historical perspective, because multicultural Finland was shaping itself. The novel also became interested in contemporary social reality without historical background. Just as in earlier, western realistic literature, the social tensions are situated in a family crisis. Mari Mörö's novel, *Kiltin yön lahjat* (Good-Night Gifts), which was awarded the Runeberg Prize, has a social thesis, but it is expressed only between the lines. It focuses on figures from two marginal groups of human beings in contemporary Finnish society: an almost abandoned child and a small-time criminal. Through these two focalisations, the reader watches in a tragic and sometimes comic close-up, the encounter between a very nice, clever girl and a vodka smuggler. The grotesque realism, the smell of poverty, a man and wife with many starving children in wretched clothes as seen from the step of the miserable hut, was the style in earlier historical realism descriptions. Now the reader must enter the two-room flat as Viikki does and meet Siia, the 6-year old girl, daughter of a "strip-tease dancer", playing with her mice as her only companions, without proper food, waiting for the mother coming home, but in vain as usual. The good-night presents, haberdasher's goods, given as a compensation for lonely nights, lose their value in Siia's eyes at the end of the novel, when a child protection authority, asked to come by the empathetic smuggler, takes her away from home. It is left open, if this is good for the child, or not and what kind of future she will have.

In the same year Arto Salminen's novel *Varasto* (Storehouse), also appeared; its atmosphere is very sinister, because the warehouse workers feel themselves to be among enemies, not fellow employees. Frustrated people do not feel any empathy for one another; they only fear being dismissed. An even more dire picture of society is shown in Salminen's last novel, *Kalavale* (2005, a pun on *Kalevala*, the title of the national epic) about producing a Big Brother type of TV program. There are no freedoms or choices when living on the margins of society; individuals are obliged to do whatsoever for a living. That question is also put in Asko Sahlberg's novel, *Pimeän ääni* (2000, The Voice of Darkness). He extends the theme to the community of Swedish-Finnish emigrants. Emigration is not its main issue, but a subject position thematised by existential philosophy. An emigrant man discusses his actions and motives as well as individual responsibility with Meursault from Albert Camus's novel, *The Outsider* (1941, *L'Étranger*). His purpose is to eliminate the feeling of alienation.

The function of telling about oneself is cognitive; that is, it allows the speaker to take possession of traumatic experiences, share them with others and recover from them. This new confessional literature is called trauma literature, from which I shall mention a couple of examples. One of the most tragic matters can be a relative's suicide as shown in Elina Hirvonen's *Että hän muistaisi saman*, (2005, If He Could Remember the Same) or the whole family's homicide as in Markku Pääskynen's *Vihan päivät*, (2005, *Dies Irae*, Days of Hatred). Sofi Oksanen's *Puhdistus* (2008, Purge), made the author world-famous; it is a novel about the political trauma of a whole nation. The title refers to the purification of political opponents, to their violent deportations to Siberia, and to Aristotelian catharsis. The subject of *Puhdistus* was exceptional in both Finland and Estonia, because it was a politically incorrect topic in both countries as long as the fear of the Soviet Union stiffened the author's pen.

In Finland, *Puhdistus* can be seen as a sign of the enlarged geography of the Finnish written novel. In the Swedish language, Finnish prose had been international from its beginning about a century ago. Hannu Raittila, however, brought his engineers in the commedia dell'arte novel, *Canal Grande* (2001) to Venice, to save the famous city from sinking into the water. The Finlandia Prize candidates in 2008 (mentioned below) seemed to be exceptionally international, as to themes and geography. The list of these possible winners is as follows:

Olli Jalonen's novel, *14 solmua Greenwichiin* (Fourteen Knots to Greenwich) deals with a sailing competition between a British couple and their Finnish friends; it is a journey around the world along the zero median, made in the same type of ship as used in the century of the Enlightenment.

Katri Lipson's first novel, *Kosmonautti* (Cosmonaute) is a story about the shipwreck of a young man's dream to become another Yuri Gagarin at the end of the Soviet era in Russia. Arne Nevanlinna's *Marie* tells the life-story of a German, Jewish upper-class young woman from Elsass, and a Finnish doctor's wife, living in Helsinki, in a narrow-minded, class society that was suspicious of foreigners. Juha Seppälä's novel, *Paholaisen haarukka* (The Fork of the Devil) is an allegory about the global market economy, and Pirkko Saisio's *Kohtuuttomuus* (Immoderation) is a satire about the misuse of male hegemonic power.

Oksanen's *Puhdistus* was without doubt the best one of them, measured by the number of prizes it received: the most important prizes in Finland (the Finlandia Prize and the J. L. Runeberg prize), as well as the Nordic Literature Prize and the Prix Femina for the best translated novel of the year in France. *Puhdistus* is a novel about shame, its anatomy and heritage. It shows how private general and personal politics is. The war has the cruel face of a familiar person: the body is the stage of business, humiliation and falsehood and a helpless witness who tries to survive. It is a historical and feminist novel, a thriller, which looks back into the mirror, shows the present and the future, too. Its publication has crossed many boundaries. Sofi Oksanen made Finland and Estonia visible on the European literary map and brought them to attention in the USA.

Here I have tried to sketch out some crucial years of contemporary Finnish literature and the literary phenomena surrounding recent publications, and to draw a context to the nodes, which will be analysed more profoundly in this anthology. The following research articles will deepen the idea of how certain literary works, recognised as hot-spots, are nodes; we will see the contacts they have with other literatures and how they can be interpreted.

Pirjo Lyytikäinen analyses in her article, "Allegories of our World–Strange Encounters with Leena Krohn", the whole production of the author, but concentrates especially on *Tainaron* and the creation of its ethical, existentially toned world-view. She asks how postmodern allegory is constructed by mixing some genres, by episode structure and by tropes, which allows the narrator to gain knowledge from the odd, but human-like country of insects.

Under the title of "The Unbearable Darkness of Being. Subject in Asko Sahlberg's Fiction", Mika Hallila interprets the modern figure of the outsider in the works of the author, who has made his career after his emigration to Sweden. Hallila does not argue that the modern subject has become the postmodern, but studies what is happening to the modern subject in postmodern conditions.

Päivi Koivisto elucidates the phenomenon of the large I-narration family in her article titled "The Author as Protagonist: Autobiographical Narrative in Finland." She describes its poetic variations and functions during the two decades it has dominated the genre field.

Kristina Malmio argues in her article, "Phoenix-Marvel Girl in the age of *fin de siècle* – Popular Culture as a Vehicle to Postmodernism", that Monika Fagerholm's *Diva* is an important node in Finnish-Swedish written literature, because she writes against the Finnish-Swedish tradition. *Diva*, the main character is a 13-year-old girl, whose diary the novel pretends to be. It reveals to the reader how this girl, who resembles *Pippi Long-Stocking*, is growing up to be an empowered young woman. In *Diva*, Fagerholm transgresses the boundaries between children's and adults' literature.

Mari Hatavara asks in her article, "History After or Against the Fact? Finnish Postmodern Historical Fiction", how postmodernism in Finland has changed the writing and reception of the popular new historical novel. She analyses the relationship of the genre to referentiality, mimesis and historical truth in three metafictional novels: Juha Seppälä's *Suomen historia* (Finnish History), Ralf Nordgren's *Det har aldrig hänt* (It Never Happened), and Irja Rane's *Naurava neitsyt* (The Laughing Madonna).

Outi Oja's article, "From Autofictive Poetry to the New Romanticism. The Guises of Finnish Poetry in the 1990s and 2000s", deals with the subjectivity of lyrics, a very subjective genre. Her research object is metalyrical poetry, which has defined new tasks for poets.These can be seen in four clear tendencies: Contemporary Finnish poetry shows an increased interest in such genres as autofictive poetry and dramatic monologue. The role of the poetry and subsequently the role of the poetic speaker have changed in the age of Digital culture, and the aesthetics of romantic poetry has returned.

Päivi Heikkilä-Halttunen's "Idyllic Childhood, Jagged Youth. Finnish books for children and young people meet the world" gives a presentation of many nodes of Finnish children's literature. Writing for children seems to be as challenging as writing for grown-ups, and children's literature seems to undergo the same changes as adults' literature.

Jussi Ojajärvi studies in his article, "Capitalism in the Family. On Realistic Involvement after the Neoliberal Turn", the realistic novel at the end of the last millennium and its way to build a critical construction of social reality after the economic depression. He describes different types of commitment and takes two novels as examples: the Finnish-Swedish author Kjell Westö's *Drakarna över Helsingfors* (1996, Kites Above Helsinki) and Mari Mörö's

Kiltin yön lahjat (1998, Good-Night Gifts), in which the liberal market economy has naturalised as an essential part of family life, even having an effect on the children.

Markku Lehtimäki explains in his essay, "Shadows of the Past: Sofi Oksanen's *Purge* and its Intertextual Space", the textual network with which this internationally famous novel is attached. It will simultaneously prove that even in the era of e-mail and other electronic devices, the book is an equally important communicator between countries, continents and cultures.

Nodes of Contemporary Finnish Literature contains several kinds of links between the chosen authors despite the fact that they are not studied with the same methods. There are mappings of postmodern allegories, feminisms, historiographies, selfhoods, identities, intertextual relationships, realities, and phantasies. The articles show how different times and places are intertextually situated in individual authors' writing, and some years connected with certain places seem to be more noteworthy than others. Thinking literary history, under the guidance of Brian McHale, helps to outline and study recent tendencies by fastening them to their base.

As to actual topics in society and culture, there are no longer any taboos, not even in children's literature. One of the most important themes in the contemporary prose and lyrics seems to be the I and the other and one of the strategies to study the problem is estrangement, realised by tools of postmodern poetics. If asked how to solve it, there are not simple answers, however, the value of tolerance, community spirit and benevolence can be read between the lines.

References

Anderson, Benedict 1991/1983: *Imagined Communities: Reflections on the origin and spread of nationalism*. London: Verso.

Fludernik, Monica 1996: *Towards a 'Natural' Narratology*. London/New York: Routledge.

Helle, Anna 2009: *Jäljet sanoissa. Jälkistrukturalistisen kirjallisuuskäsityksen tulo 1980-luvun Suomeen*. [Traces in the words. The coming of post-structuralist notions of literature to Finland in the 1980s.] Jyväskylä: Jyväskylän yliopisto.

McHale, Brian & Stevenson, Randall 2006: On and About 1910. London. Introduction. In: Brian McHale and Randall Stevenson (eds.), *The Edinburg Companion to Twentieth-Century Literatures in English*. Edinburgh: Edinburgh University Press, 1–8.

Ong, Walter 1988: *Orality and Literacy: Technologizing of the Word*. London/New York: Routledge.

Pyysalo, Joni 2000: Nykyaikaa vastavirtaan. Kjell Westön haastattelu. [Against the Current. An interview with Kjell Westö.] *Parnasso* 4/2000, 375–384.

Schoolfield, George C. 1998: *A History of Finland's Literature*. Nebraska: University of Nebraska Press.

Szopori Nagy, Lajos 1986: *Suomalainen sukuromaani*. [The Finnish Family Novel.] Helsinki: SKS.

Pirjo Lyytikäinen

Allegories of our World

Strange Encounters with Leena Krohn

One of the directions taken by postmodernist literature was to transgress or ignore all demands of verisimilitude in creating its fictional worlds. The flourishing of fantasy (or "the marvelous", according to Tzvetan Todorov's coinage[1]) brought forth imaginative fictional worlds where the ties that still connected many modernist works to some variant of realism were severed. This trend in postmodernism induced the return of allegory in new forms. Brian McHale analyses the resurgence of allegory as an aspect of postmodernist poetics in his book *Postmodernist Fiction*. Generally, the often playful construction of tropological worlds in postmodernism produces allegories. In fantastic texts, tropes may be literalized, and this permits partial or wholesale allegories to emerge. McHale sees postmodernist allegories in terms of hypertrophied metaphors, which have become "contiguous with the limits of the text." In this variant "the explicit markers of the metaphor" are suppressed, so that it is the reader who must supply the interpretation in terms of a continued metaphor (1987, 140).[2]

McHale's approach offers insight into one technique of allegory which seems to fit some postmodernist allegories quite well, but which does not cover the whole field of allegory. What is important in creating allegory, rather, is creating "a blended space" where the mixing of various input spaces (or frames of reference) results in generating allegorical meanings.[3] Such spaces may emerge through continued metaphors but also through the old allegorical device of personification. The devices of blending are many, and permit a view on allegory larger than the old (often competing) theories emphasizing either the use of continued metaphor or personification.[4] In contemporary literature, virtual realities, robots, cyborgs and creatures with artificial intellect provide allegories with new images which are often more complex than old personifications of virtues and vices or the device of talking animals. A conspicuous and playful blending seems to fit the general atmosphere of postmodernism as a means of creating allegories, but this by itself does not explain – any more than McHale's approach – the role and functions of allegory in contemporary writing. I hope to further explicate this aspect through the following examination of the writings of Leena Krohn, and thus offer at least one answer to this question.

To situate Leena Krohn (b. 1947), who is well-known in Finland for her allegorical and often satirical fantasy novels, in the context of postmodernist allegory is not unproblematic but, if due attention is given to the differences between her genre and some more playful forms of postmodernism as well as to her reliance on modernist allegories and older traditions of allegory and satire, I think this context can provide an illuminating background to her work.[5] It is important to emphasize her sobriety of style compared to the most conspicuous forms of playfulness in postmodernist fiction, but her tendency to fabulate and use sci-fi-like fantasy, even if these elements also draw from the tradition of satirical allegory, brings her close to the allegorical trends in postmodern writing. Her works, however, do not go in the direction of indefinite parody which may question the whole form of allegory (e.g. Thomas Pynchon's works have sometimes been interpreted in this light[6]), and do not conceal their ethical and satirical objectives. Krohn's ethical and philosophical engagements are most openly expressed in her essays and public statements on socio-ethical issues, but her fictional works reflect the same concerns. Thus her public image as an author with a critical stance towards the direction contemporary life and culture has taken is doubly confirmed. In the domain of intellectually demanding but imaginatively engaging literature, she belongs to the most prominent authors in Finland and has enjoyed this acknowledged position since the 1980s. Along with her allegorical and satirical fiction and philosophically interesting essays, she has written a great number of what could be called children's books. These are not only intended for children but all lovers of fabulation and, in fact, expand the range of her allegorical writing to include more fairytale-like areas.

In this article I will explore Leena Krohn's allegorical world-making, and reflect upon its forms and themes in her novels, concentrating mainly on one novel only. In the two introductory sections I briefly delineate a general profile of Krohn's novels and sketch elements of the poetics of allegory she uses in constructing her fictional worlds. Then I turn to a more detailed analysis of Krohn's allegorical techniques and thematic, focussing on *Tainaron*, Leena Krohn's masterpiece of allegorical fantasy, which has been recently translated into English. The key constituents of *Tainaron's* allegorical world are discussed as a representative example of Krohn's art of writing.

Strange People, Grotesque Masques, Animals and Artificial Life

Krohn began her career in the 1970s but her breakthrough came with *Tainaron* (1985). This fantasy about insect-people living in the mysterious city of Tainaron is probably her most admired work. It is an epistolary novel, presenting itself as a collection of letters to a friend by a human visitor to this city of insect-people. (Montesquieu's *Persian Letters* seem to give an overall clue to its form.) Plunging into the world of insects in *Tainaron* shaped the strangely grotesque but lyrical style that Krohn later used in allegorizing more everyday settings. Her allegorical fantasy produced whole galleries of grotesque characters and masques that often turn her hometown, Helsinki, into a phantasmagoric place where characters from opera, fiction or fantasy mix with the city's somewhat more realistically depicted despondent citizens (e.g. the novel *Umbra* 1990). As her side characters, she shows a marked preference for grotesque or marginalized figures as well as cyborgs. Her collection of short stories *Matemaattisia olioita tai jaettuja unia* [Mathematical Beings or Shared Dreams], for which she was awarded the Finlandia Prize in 1992, introduces the reader to a world of virtual creatures and artificial life, but these enigmatic mathematical beings are matched in strangeness by the human characters of the stories.

An important milestone in Krohn's career was the satirical novel *Pereat Mundus* (1998) where she makes fun of the fears connected to the approaching millennium. Although the apocalyptic dystopias articulated by the characters are a target of satire, they mirror the pessimistic tone characteristic of Krohn's view of our contemporary culture. In this novel, Krohn returns to one of her favorite sources of inspiration, the short story *The House of Usher* by Edgar Allan Poe. In an interview with Matthew Cheney she explains her fascination with it: "I think our whole civilization is like The House of Usher. Every civilization has its end, and ours has already grown extremely fragile from its internal hostilities, its overpopulation and its thoughtless ways of using natural resources. We have built on sand. 'That once barely-discernible fissure' extends now 'from the roof of the building, in a zigzag direction to the base.'"[7]

Pereat mundus initiated a series of satires, all of which ridicule an array of phenomena characteristic of what Krohn herself calls "our own shattering, absurd world". In *Unelmakuolema* [The Death Dreamed] 2004 – this very ambiguous title meaning both the death that one dreams of (itself a many-sided notion) and the death of dreams (or loss of hope) – she satirizes the overall commercialization of contemporary culture by describing the emerging forms of a 'death-industry'. The title refers to a commercial institute helping those weary of life to commit suicide in a pleasant way. The novel, set in a dystopic (near) future, emphasizes the paradoxical and contradictory impulses of our time. There are those willing to ensure the resurrection of their bodies (and minds) with the help of an institute specialized in freezing bodies and promising to the old and rich who can afford it a second earthly life in the future, when the technology is perfected. Then there are those, even young people, who are willing to commit suicide because life is unbearable. But however bizarre the wish, there is, in this fictional world, always an enterprise to help, if you can pay. Your death is someone else's profit.

Krohn's texts are not easy to read and consequently her popularity tends to be limited to a niche audience, yet she has many faithful admirers and her prestige has only increased over the years. She has continued publishing fascinating, imaginative books in her own personal style without much regard to passing trends, although, as already mentioned, a satirical vein is more conspicuous in her latest novels. Her work has found its way beyond Finland as well, having been translated into 15 languages. Three novels from her earlier period have been translated into English by Hildi Hawkings. In 1995 the British publisher Carcanet released a translation of two of Krohn's books, *Doña Quixote* (1983) and *Gold of Ophir* (1987), in one volume, and in 2004 *Tainaron: Mail from Another City* was published in the United States by Prime Books. The latter gained critical praise[8] which led to the above-mentioned interview published on the web in 2005. The interviewer Matthew Cheney depicts his positive experience of the work, which made him contact the author: "I find few joys as marvelous as the joy of reading a book by an author whose name is entirely unfamiliar to me, and discovering the book to be a masterpiece. It's a rare occurrence, but one that happened recently with *Tainaron: Mail from Another City* by Leena Krohn". He also mentioned that the novel had been marketed and reviewed in forums that specialize in science fiction and fantasy, a connection that has also been made in Finland. Even if Leena Krohn has been surprised by this association, it is not far-fetched in the light of more inclusive views of sci-fi and fantasy.[9] These genres are often intimately connected with allegory, and, in Leena Krohn's case, it is clear that fantasy and sci-fi elements are used to create allegory and satire.

Episodes and Encounters

All Krohn's novels have the peculiarity of being built from short chapters resembling prose poems, which sometimes seem to enjoy an independence that is typical in collections of short stories rather than in novels. Episodes are not linked together by any kind of continuous plot. They are, on the surface, held together by the protagonist, the narrator or a given place (house or city). *Tainaron's* episodic structure is based on the unity of place and the nameless letter-writing narrator. This figure is exceptional among Krohn's usually heterodiegetic narrators who only use the protagonists as focalisers, but otherwise the episodes resemble those of Krohn's other novels.[10] *Tainaron's* episodes depict the narrator's encounters with strange citizens and her new experiences in the city, juxtaposing these with her memories from before coming to Tainaron. The plotline, if this term can still be used, follows the logic of inventory and combines image after image instead of action after action. In a sense this structure repeats the "progress" typical of older allegories: it is like a journey through a series of phenomena/places with encounters continually introducing new curious sidecharacters, whose roles in the story are (at least initially) enigmatic.

An episodic structure is typical of many allegories although it cannot be considered to be either a necessary or a sufficient condition for designating a work as an allegory. The episodic structure of epic poetry as well as picaresque novels can closely resemble the organization of an allegory. But when the functions of the structure are taken into account we can see here a recurrent element in allegorical fiction. Angus Fletcher already discusses the strange plot of allegories quite extensively (1964, 147–180), but it seems that a more developed view pertaining to this particular type of allegory can be obtained by adopting the idea of a hermeneutic plot. Tzvetan Todorov's essay on Conrad's *Heart of Darkness* defines what he calls a *gnoseological* plotline to distinguish Conrad's novel from adventure novels with their plots that depend on suspense and eventful sequences of action. Opposing the idea that Conrad's novel could be considered to belong to the genre of adventure stories he writes: "If there is adventure, it is not there where one thought it was: it is not in the action but in the interpretation which unfolds from the givens that are posited in the beginning" (Todorov 1978, 162).[11] The narrative of action is there only to allow for the deployment of a narrative of gaining knowledge (*un récit de connaissance*).

The quest for knowledge unfolds from sign to sign rather than from event to event.[12] The protagonist, the narrator or the reader follows a series of signs: all episodes in this kind of narrative provide these signs for contemplation and reflection so that there is no need for causal series of actions. Instead, the order of the (text) production called for is that of juxtaposed images and emblems that can be deciphered as parts of the overall interpretative (allegorical) frame of reference. There is a tendency towards repetition: all the images are metaphors referring to the same allegorical meaning. Todorov sees this type of narrative as a dramatized hermeneutic process. He himself does not connect this structure of *Heart of Darkness* with allegory in general (although, as Todorov acknowledges, Conrad's novel certainly is an allegory whatever else it is) but does, in fact, describe the process at work in all allegories that dramatize the "progress" of the protagonist towards some revelation of truth, to salvation and to self-knowledge. In modernist or postmodernist allegories the gnoseological process is still there, although the hope of attaining final results, definitive knowledge or even the truth about oneself is gone. In *Heart of Darkness* the heart or kernel is empty or remains dark without any light shining in the darkness, although the narratorfigure Marlow still gains knowledge about the human mind and its darker sides. In *Tainaron*, every episode introduces the narrator to phenomena that are to be deciphered in terms of their meaning as regards the (paradoxical) world-view the narrator is discovering and surreptitiously suggesting to the reader.

Signs, not People?

The protagonist of Krohn's *Tainaron* is a typical reflectorfigure who is not involved in the action but is a passive onlooker rather than a real participant in the events – if there are any. A sudden threat on her life occurring during a promenade at the beach puts her in a dangerous situation, and her role is that of a potential victim; she is not searching for adventures but only curious to see more things in Tainaron and is ignorant of the pitfalls related to insect life. In many of the episodes she is guided by Longhorn, a beetle-like inhabitant of Tainaron and the figure corresponding to Virgile in Dante's *Divina Comedia*; he is the one who answers all her questions and explains the nature of the city to this visitor from another world.

The protagonist is confronted with "signs" that appear mainly in the form of the other characters of the fictional world. The outward appearance of Tainaron's citizens contributes greatly to their emblematic nature; seeing, in a café, a waiter with "his mandibles protruding just like those of a dragonfly-grub" or, on the tram, sitting next to someone who looks like a leaf (*Tainaron*, 16), dramatically separates the supposedly human narrator from the world where she now lives. Emblematic meetings with "the Mimic", "the Surveyor" or the creatures who are modelled after burying beetles or termite queens all incite the narrator as well as the reader to interpret the creatures as signs.

In allegorical literature, characters either non-human or only quasi-human in whom grotesque or supernatural elements dominate are the preferred inhabitants of the fictional worlds. Even when they are human, allegorical characters tend to be static and thinly characterized, because it is their mission to function as signs rather than full characters. Allegorical texts, thus, foreground hermeneutic processes instead of human relations and create the peculiarly estranged and dream-like atmosphere that most full-blown allegories exude. In fact, this is one of the key issues in the poetics of allegory: rendering characters and events in a way that encourages the reader to disregard their realistic, psychological or social and historical nature permits and encourages reading them as signs.

When the overall setting remains realistic in some respects the conflict between realistic reading and allegorical significance tends to create ethical tensions. In Krohn's novel *Umbra*, for example, an ethical dilemma seems to be present in the story. The novel is an allegory of modern life set in an everyday setting and features a doctor as its protagonist, while the other characters are mainly various patients who consult him. The protagonist is seen as (and confesses himself to be) a bad doctor because instead of caring for and curing his patients (he does not really even believe in cures) he reads them as signs that reveal aspects of human life and suffering. Of course, the reader is not supposed to read the novel in a realistic register and Krohn includes resurrected fictional characters (like Don Giovanni and other figures from Mozart's opera of the same name) among the patients to restrain the reader from a realistic reading. Nevertheless, the ethical insufficiency of the protagonist is an important theme in this novel about an everyday hell on earth where most of the characters suffer from even worse ethical deficiencies than the protagonist. In general, it cannot be maintained that the allegorical level replaces or redeems the images used on the literal level. The many interpretations of *Heart of Darkness* where the possibility of a realistic reading seems to be left open show that creating ambiguities between allegorical and realistic readings is ethically problematic and, furthermore, that using problematic metaphors is not innocent even if the allegorical interpretation is chosen. There is no way out of the ideologically questionable images of Africa in Conrad's novel – even if we must recognize that Conrad was only repeating the *doxa* of his day. Even Krohn's politics of fantasy, so to say, can be considered in the light of *doxa*. In *Tainaron*, she recycles a *topos* about the otherness of insects.[13]

Estrangement in Modern Cities

One of the allegorical images again and again appearing in allegorical writing is that of a city (or a city-state), be it the Celestial City or New Jerusalem in some form or a modern Babylon, Sodom or Gomorrah resembling hell on earth. The utopian or dystopian city-state is either a wholly imaginary and faraway place (which then functions as an allegory of a real city or state) or a familiar and relatively realistically described actual city where strange things happen. In many modern allegories a real city provides the starting point for the description. Camus is ostensibly describing Oran but transforms it right from the beginning into a ubiquitous place. Another device is to allude to other cities when describing one that is recognizable as a real city; Joyce's Dublin comes to symbolize the whole world through its mythical framework and its allusions. Krohn's Tainaron combines features from real cities, ancient and modern, but this ubiquitous and omnitemporal place is further estranged from real places by bringing in the insects as a prior frame of reference.

The insect context largely derives from one particular hypotext. *Tainaron* is dedicated (among others) to the French entomologist J. H. Fabre (1823-1915). The function of this dedication is to point out to the reader the main source of many descriptions of the inhabitants of Tainaron: Fabre's *Souvenirs entomologiques* (*Insect Life*). Those familiar with Fabre's books will easily recognize most of the insects involved, but Krohn also gives her readers hints and some relatively straightforward explanations about the species in question. The inhabitants are not mere insects, even at the literal level of the narrative, but insect-people. These hybrid figures emerge from a combination of two frames of reference: the human is intertwined with the insect. This blend clearly differs from the device of talking animals and constructs a much more uncanny world. The (apparently only partial) insect appearance is combined not only with human behaviour and human-like consciousness but also with modern city life. The discreetly humorous aspect of many of these descriptions seems to reveal how easily we can imagine our fellow humans in comparable terms – the insect life gives us a unique view of the strangeness of humanity. These creatures are no fairytale figures.

In her essays, Krohn has written that insects are the animal order that is most strange and estranging to humans:[14] it is not possible to understand (in a demanding sense) insect life. In the light of this statement, her choice of insect characters to reflect the estrangement of human beings from one another and using insects as a literalized metaphor for humans becomes clear. Krohn transforms her characters into insects to change one's perspective on humans, thus making readers see their own world and their own existence in a new light.

The allegorical world of *Tainaron* is offered as an image of modern human life. We can interpret the nature of its inhabitants as an image of life which lacks the communality and meaningful contacts that could make the world a home. Of course, it is the narrator as an outsider – and supposedly a human being among insects – who experiences this strangeness. Consequently, the insectworld seems also to mirror her spleen[15] that causes her estrangement from herself as well as from others. Writing letters to a lost friend without ever getting an answer emphasizes the narrator's lack of human contacts but this narrative structure has allegorical dimensions as well. On the literal level this friend can be interpreted as her former lover, who has abandoned her and caused her to be exiled in a foreign city (or in her own city transformed into a strange world). At the same time, the relationship becomes an allegory of everyone's existential loneliness, and the recipient of the letters in his "God-like" silence, a symbol of God's absence from the world. When the narrator wonders if the recipient is still alive, this too is a double vision.

Metamorphosis

The insect-life frame of reference brings into view the phenomenon of metamorphosis with its metaphorical potentialities pertaining, especially, to ideas of identity and change.[16] The narrator mentions this aspect of insect life as the most estranging thing about the inhabitants of Tainaron:

> The hustling forest of antennae and pedipalpi in the streets at rush-hour is certainly an extraordinary sight for people like us, but most difficult of all is to accustom oneself to a certain other phenomenon that marks the life of the majority of the inhabitants here in the city. This phenomenon is metamorphosis; and for me, at least, it is so strange, to my very marrow, that even to think about it makes me feel uncomfortable. (*Tainaron*, 33)

The presumably human narrator, who has for unknown reasons landed in the "other city" of Tainaron, juxtaposes this sudden change and the "two or many consecutive lives" that the inhabitants of Tainaron live, with the gradual change of "us" – changes in herself and in the recipient of her letters who lives in the "normal world". The issue of metamorphosis thus leads the reader away from the literal (from the description of insects) to the idea of change that haunts the narrator, and that is enmeshed with questions of identity. The change rendered through the Tainaronians' metamorphosis is so radical that the narrator can no longer see them as the same individuals. However, the citizens who emerge in new, unrecognizable shapes are not strangers to themselves; they are glued to their former lives by memory.

The narrator's initial shock over metamorphosis reflects her idea of identity as something immune to change. These questions haunt the narrator when she meets various strange citizens of the city. The problems of change and uncertain identities are, in the end, only loosely connected to insect metamorphosis. The most shocking figure with respect to the narrator's initial idea of the constancy of the self is the Mimic. This figure (who is of no particular species) has a chameleon-like ability to imitate whatever it meets. It has no personality or identity of its own. Krohn juxtaposes a more classical idea of identity with a postmodern one, so to say. The paradox of being someone without being someone is not solved, and cannot be solved, but this is a paradox that produces many images and frequent dramatizing in Krohn's works. In *Tainaron*, it is also connected to Eastern religious thinking, as one of the episodes, "King Milinda's question", makes evident with its reference to an old Buddhist text that keeps questioning about identities.[17] The novel is more about visualizing the questions than providing (definitive) answers to them. And there is a development in the attitudes of the narrator. By and by, the question is raised of whether there is any great difference between insects' sudden change and the more gradual change that occurs in humans: even if the outer shape of humans remains more or less the same, the self may not. The self can endure radical metamorphosis, and particularly in human life it is essentially the memory that binds past selves to the present. This is one main aspect of the 'progress' in the plotline of the novel: it is located in the process of gaining knowledge rather than in chains of events.

The allegorical meaning of the insects' metamorphosis extends to encompass another, even more dramatic dimension of change. In the sixth letter, where the initial puzzlement about metamorphosis is expressed, the narrator describes the cicadas:

> There are also those who withdraw into total seclusion for as much as seventeen years. They live in tiny rooms, no more than boxes; they do not see anyone, do not go anywhere, and hardly eat. But whether they sleep or wake there, they are continually changing and forsaking the form they had before. (*Tainaron*, 34)

After those seventeen years, these "hermits" come out and live one summer in the sunlight, just "celebrating". This description of the cicadas' monastic life awes the narrator; nevertheless, she also confesses feeling envy. She would like to curl up in a pupal cell, to be free of the past, and be reborn. In the light of the knowledge about personal identity that the narrator learns to accept, her idealistic wish connected to metamorphosis, namely to be freed from the past through a stay in a womb-like cell, does not really seem to apply to the Tainaronians: if they remember, they cannot be free of the past. This indicates the presence of other dimensions to the allegorical meanings of metamorphosis.

At the centre of the idea of metamorphosis in Krohn's novel is the notion of death, which is stubbornly connected with the hope of being reborn but also subjected to the knowledge of natural processes where the cycle of life and death is seen as a constant transformation of living matter into dead matter and dead matter into new living matter, but which leaves unanswered the yearning for individual immortality. Thus metamorphosis is connected to the theme announced in the enigmatic title of the book.

A City at the Gate of Hades

That the inhabitants of Tainaron live on the brink of death is hinted at by the name of the town – and the title of the book. In ancient mythology, Tainaron, a geographical place in the real world, on the Peloponnesian peninsula in Greece, was one of the entrances to Hades. Living at the gateway to the underworld reflects the philosophical perspective from which life is seen in *Tainaron*. This fundamental element of Krohn's allegory, which resonates from the title, is explicitly brought forth in the episodes.

The fragility of life in Tainaron is reflected upon several times and the threat of death is thematized in emblematic scenes. The whole city is built on a place where only a thin crust separates it from the destructive forces beneath: earthquakes can occur, as experienced by the narrator. The winter, seen lurking in wait in a mysterious huge cloud already at the end of summer, also announces and means death. When it comes, the whole city becomes desolate, its inhabitants disappear one by one, and the narrator loses her guide, Longhorn, but remains in the dying city. This is the second main line of 'progress' in the story. Early on, at the beginning of the text, we are reminded of the biblical idea that we will gain full knowledge after death, when we will see God "face to face". This idea that the process of knowledge is completed only in death seems to haunt the protagonist. Her ambiguous oscillation between understanding natural processes and the wish to be reborn, between her implicit deathwish taking the form of a desire to return to womb-like conditions and her wish to live and even be immortal, illustrates the human predicament but remains an unsolved question at every level.

When facing a concrete threat on her life the narrator chooses to save herself. In the episode entitled "Sand", she wanders to the seashore to see the beach of Oceanus. (The sea surrounding Tainaron is given the ancient name of the Oceanus Sea which, in Greek mythology, surrounded the entire world.) On the sand dunes she almost falls into a trap, a pit with a hole in the middle hiding a monster of death. The sand under her feet, like the sand in an hourglass, begins to shift and she must make an extreme effort to jump out; she succeeds, but has time to see the claw of the monster in the hole. The explanation of the source of this allegorical image is given at the end. When writing a letter describing this event to her friend back home the narrator compares herself with an ant:

> At this moment I could be hollow, as empty as the ants from which ant-lion grubs suck the innards and vital fluids. In writing this, I am a little ashamed, as if I wanted to disturb you by telling this; but it is true, after all. (*Tainaron*, 65)

The pits in the sand, one from which she escapes at the last moment, are equated with the holes that antlion grubs make to catch ants for their food. The narrator also reflects upon the fact that she cannot remember having seen the sea that must have been there. The last sentence of the letter summarizes her experience: "The skuas must have shrieked then, too, and the waves roared, but I, absentminded, saw nothing but the sand and the claw…." (*Tainaron*, 65). The presence of threatening death makes everything else disappear from the horizon of the human mind. On the allegorical level, the scene as a whole dramatizes normal careless living (everyday human life, "forgetful" of mortality)[18] in the shadow of ever-present but still surprising and unexpected death, and suddenly awakening to realize its presence. The narrator's instinctive reaction to save herself resonates with an intertext that describes the inevitable death awaiting its protagonist whose death also symbolizes the death of a whole era of history. To a reader familiar with Krohn's preferred intertexts this episode in the sand clearly echoes the deathscene of the protagonist in Giuseppe Tomasi di Lampedusa's novel *Il Gattopardo*, bringing into view its reflections on human life and mortality.[19]

The theme of death is approached in another vein in the episode "Like Burying Beetles", where the narrator descends to what is called the Hades of Tainaron. The episode is constructed as a visit to the undertaker's. Instead of coffins or urns the shop offers only small boxes, some of which would be too small even for the tiniest inhabitants of the city. She is informed that these boxes are used to keep a remembrance of the deceased:

> "Ashes? No, there is no crematorium here," [Longhorn] said. "They are used for a single organ, often an eye or an antenna. But sometimes the family may choose part of a wing, a part with a beautiful pattern." (*Tainaron*, 44)

This explanation provokes another question: "What happens to the rest of the body?" The narrator insists on knowing and is invited to descend to the cellar of the premises with the funeral director who has just appeared out of a back room. The depiction of the director deliberately imitates one of Fabre's descriptions in *Souvenirs entomologiques*:

> Most noticeable about him, however, was not his size but his colours: they were as bright as the complicated patterns of the boxes. His chest ranged from green to lemon, while the knobs of his antennae were as yellow as clementines. He bowed elegantly, and was surrounded by a cloud of scent which I recognised only after a moment: it was undoubtedly musk. (*Tainaron*, 44)

This gentleman with the appearance of a burying beetle leads the narrator to a dark stairway with a foul odour which makes her regret her urge, but she can no longer turn back. However, she forgets the smell of decay and the nausea caused by it when she beholds the strange scene which opens to her in the vaults of the cellar. The sepulchre of Tainaron is a peculiar place:

> I spoke of Hades and a sepulchre, but in reality the space in which I found myself served the opposite purpose: it was a dining room and a nursery. Those who toiled here were not only workers; they were also, above all, mothers. Now I could see that around every larger form flocked a swarm of smaller creatures, its offspring. As they did the work that had to be done for life in this city to be at all possible, these workers were at the same time feeding their heirs; and if the way in which they did it was not to my taste, where would I find more convincing proof of the never-broken alliance between destruction and florescence, birth and death? (*Tainaron*, 46)

The narrator is introduced to the natural processes where death breeds life, the decay of one meaning birth and growth for others. The grotesque drama of death sustaining life is played out here, but the narrator sees the grotesque in a sublime light: the beetles, the allegorical figures representing the processes of decay, "distil pure nectar from filth"; death turns back into life and growth.

The "alchemy" of nature reveals the secret of death seen as a natural process, but it does not provide any final answer to the narrator. She cannot accept that the treasures of the human mind, the soul and conscience, could be extinguished, could just be or become raw matter. To see the look in the eyes of her friend (paradoxically the insect eyes of Longhorn) is to see a mystery to which the scene in the sepulchre does not offer a solution. The narrator remains in a state of doubt, in the middle of the enigma of death, in the shadow of Hades, like all humans.

Tainaron, as a whole, seems to open to the reader the experience of "being toward death", something that Martin Heidegger thought essential to authentic life. Confronting one's own mortality has been seen as a hallmark of existentialist thought. Against the avoidance of death and efforts to hide and forget it, which is the common cultural attitude in modern societies reflecting fear of death, Krohn seems to conjure up a region where death cannot be forgotten. The citizens as well as the narrator try to live in the careless everyday of amnesia, but the thin trembling crust (lithosphere) under the city signals the fragility of human existence, and at least the narrator is constantly confronted with experiences which force her to "be toward death". And the reader is led to the gate of Hades by Krohn's text.

The Place in Your Own Mind

Tainaron is a distant place that reminds us of every place in the world in its plasticity, strangeness, frightfulness. But its properties are the properties of our own heart (Leena Krohn in the interview with Cheney.)

The paratexts, which have already offered us some indications about the worldmaking of *Tainaron*, also give a clue to one further allegorical level present in Krohn's *Tainaron*. The motto of the book is taken from Angelus Silesius: "You are not in a place; the place is in you." This ambiguous saying may have several meanings but in connection with Krohn's novel it actualizes the most persistent genre-creating feature in the history of allegorical narratives; the building of analogy between the events in a fictional world and the inner processes in the mind of the protagonist. In allegories, the ancient analogy of microcosm and macrocosm constantly reappears in various forms. One of Krohn's sources of inspiration is Dante, whose *Divine Comedy* describes a "concrete" journey through otherworldly places but symbolizes an inner process of moral reflection and transformation as well.[20]

Krohn's fantastical city is, in a sense, both an image of society and an image of the human mind, but, moreover, it exemplifies the complex interaction

35

between mind and reality, between perception and varying constructions of the external world. In the episode "The Day of the Great Mogul" the narrator feels that the city has changed, "as if it has been unclothed," but the change would not be visible in a photograph. Nevertheless, what has changed is "the most important thing," the thing that "made me strong and happy". (*Tainaron*, 55.) Portending the "Sand" episode, the description hints at the process of decay and death:

> If the sound of the city were to be muted for a moment, I could hear a secretly crumbling sound as if a trickle of sand were falling from the side of a sandpit. And the vital force, which I believed to be inexhaustible, runs and runs somewhere where no one can use it. (*Tainaron*, 55)

And the narrator understands that she is projecting to the outside world something that exists only inside herself. She questions the idea of a stable reality independent of the observer: "But in that case how can I know anything of what Tainaron is, what it is like?" (*Tainaron*, 55). What has been already alluded to in some images and scenes is brought to the level of explicit reflection at this point. The unreality of the city and its ambivalent ontological status even within the fictional world makes the reader pay attention to the unsolvable paradox of reality and "Being in a world" that we have to accept and in which we must live.

Krohn connects the idea of change with this idea of the entanglement of perception and reality. When the narrator wants a map of Tainaron, Longhorn informs her that there are no maps. He takes her up to a tower to see how enormous Tainaron is and how quickly it is changing. In a scene reminiscent of how Dante and Virgil observe the (immutable) spheres of hell below, the narrator is led to see the infinite forces of mutability and change shaping reality, changing the city/world/mind at a pace that makes mapping futile.

Here, the reader is taken by the hand and led through the interpretation process of the allegorical images and scenes. More often than not, allegories tend to provide their own interpretations of what could be enigmatic.[21] Krohn's narrator is, in a sense, the reader inside the fictional world. While she is finding out about the strange world to where she has come for unknown reasons, her interpretations and her dialogues with Longhorn open its secrets to the reader as well. The reader is involved in the process of deciphering by the narrator, while having, at the same time, the advantage of seeing things from the outside, over the head of the naive narrator who writes her letters without the afterthought possible for normal homodiegetic narrators.

Compared to a modern allegory like Conrad's *Heart of Darkness* where a journey in the outer world is clearly an analogy of a journey into the human mind and where the inner journey seems to be the dominant allegorical level, Krohn's allegory shows itself to be more like a hybrid of a satirical allegory – where the focus is shifted to the moral flaws of individuals or society as a whole – and an individual inner quest, where the progress of understanding is foregrounded. But the allegory of the soul also underlines the existentialist undercurrent of the novel: by choosing insects to people her city, Krohn seems to reveal a tendency to see human relations in the light of utter estrangement, a tendency towards misanthropy or *la nausée*, echoing Jean-Paul Sartre's portrait of a melancholic in his novel of the same name. *Tainaron* can be read as the story of the protagonist's melancholy and estrangement from her fellow humans: the journey to the city of Tainaron can be interpreted as a mental event dramatized by the expansion of this initial metaphor of estrangement into a full-blown travelogue.

Philosophical Images

Literature has been described as a form of "thinking in images" (Camus): with Leena Krohn's fiction it is often a thinking in strange and grotesque images that nevertheless turns out to explore familiar issues of our common world. Krohn has characterized common reality as the "dreams we share" in contrast to more idiosyncratic realities that often clash with these shared views but which are given an important role in Krohn's works. The competing dreams highlight the uncertain and "Tribar-like" character of our reality. Krohn adopted this term from Roger Penrose to refer to the "logically impossible constructions" that characterize our experience of life and "lie at the bottom of our society" (Krohn, interview with Cheney). In her novel *Umbra* she also uses the image of "the archive of paradoxes" to depict the hybrid nature of our reality, both its social and psychic realms. These ubiquitous paradoxes induce the constant questioning and image-creating in Krohn's allegories, and animate her satirical "gaze" when she turns her attention to the paradoxes of our contemporary life and its untenable foundations.

NOTES

1   Todorov 1970.
2   This coincides, at least to a certain extent, with the old rhetorical definition of allegory as a chain of metaphors (and contrasts with the idea of allegory as primarily a matter of personification, which seems to restrict the domain of allegory to certain traditional forms).
3   I am referring to the concept developed by Mark Turner and Gilles Fauconnier. See Turner 1996.
4   I will be able to neither discuss Turner's ideas about parables (in the book *The Literary Mind*) in the space of this article nor relate his ideas to older approaches to allegory which still, more often than not, rely on Quintilian's idea of continued metaphor or the idea of personification.
5   Finding allegory revived in postmodernism should not hide from view the fact that different, often less playful forms of allegory are typical of modernist fiction as well. In interpreting Leena Krohn, this background, including Albert Camus with his seminal modernist allegory *The Plague*, Franz Kafka with his mysteriously allegorical works, and even T. S. Eliot's *Waste Land* with its important references to

Dante, plays an important role. Krohn is one of those authors participating in the transformation of the "divine" comedy into forms of earthly hell and purgatory – without paradise; modernist "paradises" only appear as fragile or illusory glimpses of a better life.

6 Quilligan, however, takes them to be allegories.

7 The depictions by Poe that Krohn quotes here are used in a dramatic way in *Pereat mundus*, but Poe's short story haunts in many ways almost all of Krohn's novels. The interview can be found at http://www.sfsite.com/03b/lk196.htm.

8 See, e.g., <http://www.locusmag.com/2005/Features/01_VanderMeer_BestOf2004. html> *Tainaron* was a candidate for World Fantasy Awards (2005).

9 See, e.g., McHale 2010.

10 Strictly speaking, the letters are peculiar in that they have titles like short stories (and Krohn's episodes in other works) and in that their outward form is not that of a letter. The letterwriter has no name (there is no signature) and the recipient is not given a name either: he – if it is a he – is just "you" like the narrator is just "I", whose gender is not revealed but who appears to be feminine, as can be inferred from the memories she reveals about herself and the recipient (her former lover).

11 "*Si aventure il y a, elle n'est pas là où on croyait la trouver : elle n'est pas dans l'action mais dans l'interprétation que l'on acquerra de certaines données, posées depuis le début."*

12 In many historical or political allegories, however, there might be a double plotline from event to event, while the mimetically present events refer to other events rather than ideas: Northrop Frye (1974), for example, distinguishes between "historical or political allegories, referring to characters or events beyond those purportedly described in the fiction; and moral, philosophical, religious, or scientific allegories, referring to an additional set of ideas."

13 Compare Sara Ahmed's study *Strange Encounters* (2000).

14 *Rapina*, 46.

15 Reminiscent of the melancholic themes in Charles Baudelaire's *Spleen de Paris* as well as the existentialist melancholy of the protagonist in Jean-Paul Sartre's *La nausée*.

16 Articles in Finnish have been written about these issues in Leena Krohn's works: see Rojola 1995 and 1996 and Lyytikäinen 1996.

17 *The Questions of King Milinda*, translated by T. W. Rhys Davids, at www.sacred-texts.com/bud/milinda.htm -

18 There is a discernible existentialist background in *Tainaron*.

19 Krohn uses this death scene from Lampedusa's novel in her essays as well to discuss questions of death and immortality; see *Tribar*, 206–207.

20 The model of "psychomachia", which has inspired writers of allegory since Prudentius wrote his allegory *Psychomachia* describing the battle between virtues and vices, where concrete warfare symbolizes the inner moral battles waged in the minds of Christians, can be seen still lurking in the background, although the tradition of allegorical journeys and encounters has been much more productive than the battle model (which still can be used but has usually been integrated into the journey and shunned by the battle of words in dialogues) and much more refined and ambiguous inner processes are involved.

21 Maureen Quilligan emphasizes this aspect of allegories, and it fits well with the idea of blended spaces as a constituent element of allegories.

References

Krohn, Leena 1983: *Donna Quijote ja muita kaupunkilaisia: muotokuvia.* [Doña Quijote and Other Citizens: Portraits.] Helsinki: WSOY.

Krohn, Leena 1985: *Tainaron: postia toisesta kaupungista.* [Tainaron: Mail from Another City.] Helsinki: WSOY.

Krohn, Leena 1987: *Oofirin kultaa.* [Gold of Ophir.] Helsinki: WSOY.

Krohn, Leena 1989: *Rapina ja muita papereita.* [Rustle and Other Papers.] Helsinki: WSOY.

Krohn, Leena 1990: *Umbra: silmäys paradoksien arkistoon.* [Umbra: Glance at an Archive of Paradoxes.] Helsinki: WSOY.

Krohn, Leena 1991: The paradox archive. Transl. Herbert Lomas. *Books from Finland* 3/1991, 138–147.

Krohn, Leena 1992: Invisible cities. *Books from Finland* 4/1992, 214–218.

Krohn, Leena 1992: *Matemaattisia olioita tai jaettuja unia.* [Mathematical Beings or Shared Dreams.] Helsinki: WSOY.

Krohn, Leena 1993: Gorgonoids. Transl. Hildi Hawkins. *Books from Finland* 1/1993, 3–7.

Krohn, Leena 1993: *Tribar.* Helsinki: WSOY.

Krohn, Leena 1995: *Doña Quixote and Gold of Ophir.* Transl. Hildi Hawkings. Manchester: Carcanet.

Krohn, Leena 1998: *Pereat mundus.* Helsinki: WSOY.

Krohn, Leena 2004: *Tainaron: Mail from Another City.* Transl. Hildi Hawkings. Prime Books. Rockville, Maryland: Wildside Press.

Krohn, Leena 2004: *Unelmakuolema.* [Death Dreamed.] Helsinki: Teos.

Krohn, Leena 2006: *Mehiläispaviljonki.* [Pavilion for Bees.] Helsinki: Teos.

Ahmed, Sara 2000: *Strange Encounters: Embodied Others in Post-Coloniality.* London: Routledge.

Cheney, Matthew 2009: A Conversation With Leena Krohn. An Interview With Matthew Cheney. February 2005. <http://www.sfsite.com/03b/lk196.htm> (15.1.2009).

Fletcher, Angus 1964: *Allegory. The Theory of a Symbolic Mode.* Ithaca, New York: Cornell UP.

Frye, Northrop 1974: Allegory. In: Alex Preminger (ed.), *Princeton Encyclopedia of Poetry and Poetics.* Princeton, New Jersey: Princeton UP.

Lyytikäinen, Pirjo 2000: Äärettömiä olioita: subliimi ja groteski Leena Krohnin tuotannossa. [Infinite Beings: The Sublime and the Grotesque in Leena Krohn's Works.] In: Outi Alanko & Kuisma Korhonen (eds.), *Subliimi, groteski, ironia. Kirjallisuudentutkijain seuran vuosikirja 52.* [The Sublime, the Grotesque, and Irony. Yearbook of Finnish Literary Research Society 52.] Helsinki: SKS, 11–34.

Lyytikäinen, Pirjo 1997: Toinen tapa nähdä: Leena Krohnin todellisuudet. [Another Way of Seeing: Leena Krohn's Worlds.] In: Mervi Kantokorpi (ed.), *Muodotonta menoa: kirjoituksia nykykulttuurista* . [Formless Forms: Writings on Contemporary Culture.] Helsinki: SKS, 180–198.

Lyytikäinen, Pirjo 1996: Muodonmuutoksia eli maailmanpyörä ja Orfeus. [Metamorphoses or Ferris Wheel and Orpheus.] In: Tuula Hökkä (ed.), *Naiskirja: kirjallisuudesta, naistutkimuksesta ja kulttuurista.* [Women's Book: On Literature, Feminism and Culture.] Helsinki: Helsingin yliopisto, 168–183.

McHale, Brian 1987: *Postmodernist Fiction.* London and New York: Routledge.

McHale, Brian 2010: Science Fiction, or, the Most Typical Genre in World Literature. In: Pirjo Lyytikäinen, Tintti Klapuri and Minna Maijala (eds.), *Genre and Interpretation.* Helsinki: Department of Finnish, Finno-Ugrian and Scandinavian Studies & the Finnish Graduate School for Literary Studies, 11–17.

Rojola, Lea 1995: Kotelokehto ja uusi identiteetti. [Pupal Cells and New Identities.] In: Kaisa Kurikka (ed.), *Identiteettiongelmia suomalaisessa kirjallisuudessa.* [Problematic Identities in Finnish Literature.] Turku: Turun yliopisto, 13–34.

Rojola, Lea 1996: Me kumpikin olemme minä: Leena Krohnin vastavuoroisuuden etiikasta. [We both are I: The Ethics of Reciprocity in Leena Krohn.] In: Päivi Kosonen (ed.), *Naissubjekti ja postmoderni.* [Female Subjects and Postmodernity.] Helsinki: Gaudeamus, 23–43.

Quilligan, Maureen 1979: *The Language of Allegory. Defining the Genre.* Ithaca and London: Cornell UP.

Todorov, Tzvetan 1970: *Introduction à la literature fantastique.* Paris: Seuil.

Todorov, Tzvetan 1978: Connaissance du vide: *Cœur de ténèbres.* In: *Poétique de la prose; choix, suivi de Nouvelles recherches sur le récit.* Paris: Seuil.

Turner, Mark 1996: *The Literary Mind.* New York: Oxford UP.

MIKA HALLILA

The Unbearable Darkness of Being

Subject in Asko Sahlberg's Fiction

Introduction

This article examines the representations of human subjects in the novels
of Asko Sahlberg. The aim is both to analyze which features in particular
define the subjects represented in Sahlberg's fiction and to contextualize
these representations into the field of the contemporary Finnish novel.
The analysis will show that the concept of 'subject' in Sahlberg's fiction
can be considered quite innovative when compared to other present-day
Finnish fiction. Thus, Sahlberg's fiction will also appear as an interesting
turning point in Finnish literary history. The analysis is preceded by a
brief discussion of the relevance of considering subject representations in
contemporary literature studies, and the problems of examining fictitious
subjects and the context of the contemporary Finnish novel in terms of
subject representations.

A human subject or an individual and the problems of his/her identity
and self-construction are all significant themes for research in contemporary
literary studies. The question of identity has been one of the main topics of
the study since the early 1990s, due to the increasing interest in different
aspects of 'the subject' (Kaarto & Kekki 2000, 7). The question of subject
is, of course, fundamentally philosophic. Consideration of the problems of
the subject, the individual, identity, and the self belong to broader ongoing
scholarly and philosophical debates. One paradigmatic and topical work
in this research field is Charles Taylor's *Sources of the Self. The Making of
the Modern Identity* (1989), in which he traces the sources of the modern
selfhood by reading European philosophy from Antiquity to the present. In
his ambitious work, Taylor aims at exploring in particular how the moral
foundations of the modern identity have been constructed throughout
history.

While Taylor and other philosophers examine the formation of the
subject diachronically and universally, the greater part of today's discussions
on the topic concern the current themes of modernity, postmodernity, and
globalization. A good exposition of these discussions is Erkki Sevänen's
extensive introduction in the anthology *Cultural Identity in Transition*

(2004), in which he describes the debates of modernity and postmodernity from sociological and cultural-theoretic viewpoints. According to Sevänen (ibid. 5) the contemporary interest in identity arose from the philosophical challenges of French post-structuralist thought in the 1970s and 1980s. Since then theorists and scholars from different disciplines have been handling the problems of identity within the context of the modern and postmodern, and most recently globalization.

These themes bring out the intractable problem of the change in sub-jectivity. Has the modern subject turned postmodern? If this is the case, the solid, independent, and personal Enlightenment-born modern subject has turned into the ever-changing and fragmented subject of postmodernity and globalization. The relevance of this topic to contemporary literary stud-ies also originates in these debates, but only in part. Furthermore, studies of the human subject in literature are examined from feminist, postcolonial, ethnic, and cultural approaches (see e.g. Kaarto & Kekki 2000).

Studying Fictitious Subjects

In literary studies the concepts of 'the subject' and 'the individual' as well as those of 'identity' and 'the self' all refer to the human agent being, but more often the focus is on the subjectivity of a fictitious character or a narrator than an actual person. As the main objects of research are fictional works – excluding empirical and sociological research – the focus should be on the representations of fictitious subjects.

Nevertheless, merely speaking of *representation* causes problems which confuse the issue: in what terms can we speak about the representation of the subject and the like in fiction? Are we speaking about production of reality or the reference to reality? Or do we speak of both? The answer depends on whom you ask. For instance, social constructionism and emancipatory research such as feminist or postcolonial studies tend to support the first argument, whereas (naïve) philosophical realism tends to support the second.

In this article, the concept of representation will be used quite unprob-lematically and practically in order to discuss what it is that defines the number of different fictional characters in the novels of one particular au-thor, Asko Sahlberg. Hence, herein the term 'representation' is broadly de-fined to mean the manner by which fictional characters are depicted. For its part, 'the subject' is used as a discursive abstraction which refers to generic features of the self, identity or the individual represented in the novels.

In addition, it should be noted that the representations of subjects will be analyzed within the context of the art of the novel. Since the beginning of its history, the modern novel has represented the self of the modern individual (i.e. *the modern subject*). The novel is an individualistic genre particularly because it offers the individual's personal and subjective point of view on reality (Saariluoma 1989, 22–29). Contrary to the ideal hero of the classical epic, the problematic hero of the modern novel is always somehow in conflict with the outside world. In her studies of the modern novel, Liisa Saariluoma has emphasized that the novel represents individuals whose experiences are bound to the epistemic confines of their own historical contexts (Saariluoma 1989; 1992; 1999).

Furthermore, individualism of the novel means that every remarkable novel has the potential to redefine what the novel is, as the novel is fundamentally defined by its continuous transformation and not by any fixed quality (Saariluoma 1989, 11). As a result of these claims, the novel can be understood as an individualistic genre which reflects its own time. Nevertheless, it is important to consider Raymond Williams' argument that simultaneously and within the same historical context, there always exist residual, dominant, and emergent cultural traditions (Williams 1977; see also Saariluoma 1992, 10). Therefore it can be argued that in the real life situation, the novel is extremely heterogeneous and that the representations of subjects in novels are diverse by nature.

The Subject and the Contemporary Finnish Novel

The contemporary Finnish novel is also palpably heterogeneous in terms of subject representations. Various representations of the construction of identity or the subject's self-formation in Finnish novels are not composed of shared assumptions about the subject's essence, existence, or position in modern society or in history. Recent Finnish literature altogether disengages from the tradition of representing a subject's identity as a solid entity which is determined by society and history, and particularly the contemporary Finnish novel represents identity more as a problem than a solution.

This is, as Pertti Karkama (1994, 18–19) notes, specific to modern literature. According to Karkama, modern and especially modernist literature thematizes the estrangement and represents the identity as multidimensional and ambiguous. A modern literary work of art engages in a dialogue with culture and society and sketches new identities for human beings in the modern situation. The logic of modern literature is the logic of questioning rather than the common logic of everyday life or philosophy – therefore the works' sketches of identity are divergent and heterogeneous. (Ibid. 15, 19, 21.) The modern logic of questioning relates to the representations of subjects in the contemporary Finnish novel, too. Regardless of their attitude towards the modern and the postmodern, or modernism and postmodernism, Finnish novels represent subjects whose selfhoods and identities are controversial and problematic. Though presenting the constant change of the incoherent identity is more important in postmodernism than questioning it (ibid. 316), it does not affect the fact that identity is still perceived as a problem.

The two topics most often considered in Finnish contemporary novels are present-day Finnish society and Finnish history, above all the wars in the twentieth century (see e.g. Kirstinä 2007; Hallila & Hägg 2007). The authors either write about social themes or rewrite Finnish history from the current point of view. In terms of the idea of the human subject, the focus can be on a subject's position in late capitalist society or on new ways of thinking about the subject's place in history (see e.g. Hallila & Hägg 2007; Ojajärvi 2006). In this broad sense, contemporary Finnish novels have something in common regarding their subject representations, but, nevertheless, it can be claimed that significant and fundamental discrepancies between them occur in their presentations of the selfhoods and identities.

The most blatant is certainly the difference between constructivism and realism. Finnish postmodernists – such authors as Rosa Liksom, Lars Sund, and Antero Viinikainen – often point out that the subject represented in fiction is a fictive construction. At the same time, more realistic fiction by such authors as Kjell Westö, Juha Seppälä, or Sofi Oksanen endeavour to sustain the referential status of a fictive subject whose selfhood and identity their fiction represents. Depending on their philosophical influences or relationship to Finnish literary tradition, the novels may draw identity sketches that differ from each other. In addition, different authors emphasize the meaning of different features of the human subject in their works. For instance, gender or queer themes in the fiction of Johanna Sinisalo, Pirkko Saisio, and Helena Sinervo (see Karkulehto 2007), the representations of subject formations controlled by the economic laws of capitalism in the fiction of Mari Mörö and Juha Seppälä (see Ojajärvi 2006), or identity presented as a textual construction in the fiction of Juha K. Tapio (see Hallila 2008a) demonstrate how the representations of the subject in terms of features vary in the contemporary Finnish novel.

The Novels of Asko Sahlberg

The point of departure for this article is the *oeuvre* of Asko Sahlberg, the Finnish-born emigrant writer who resides in Sweden. Sahlberg's works are written in Finnish and published in Finland, and during this decade he has become an established Finnish author. Thus far, Sahlberg has published ten novels: *Pimeän ääni* (The Sound of Darkness, 2000), *Eksyneet* (The Lost Ones, 2001), *Hämärän jäljet* (The Traces of Twilight, 2002), *Höyhen* (The Feather, 2002), *Tammilehto* (The Oak Grove, 2004), *Takaisin pimeään* (Back to Darkness, 2004), *Yhdyntä (Reunahuomautus sotahistoriaan)* (The Intercourse. [Marginal Note to War History], 2005), *Siunaus* (The Blessing, 2007), *He* (They, 2010) and *Häväistyt* (The Dishonoured, 2011). The novels *Pimeän ääni, Hämärän jäljet*, and *Takaisin pimeään* comprise the 'Göteborg trilogy', named after the Swedish city in which the narrated events take place.

All of the novels deal with the same ethical and existentialist topics, namely death, violence, crime, failure, victimization, sexuality, and the fundamental loneliness of man. The dark tone of the language, the ruminative narrator's voice and pessimistic world view characterize Sahlberg's prose. The most obvious literary influences come from existentialist philosophy and prose. Albert Camus' novel *L'Étranger* (1942) is an especially important subtext in Sahlberg's early works. Furthermore, psychological realism and Fyodor Dostoyevsky's fiction in particular have evidently influenced the novels' themes and style. These elements form the basics of Sahlberg's style and the Sahlbergian fictional universe, which can be considered a deviation from contemporary Finnish literature, as neither existentialism nor psychological realism has been in fashion in recent years. Sahlberg recontextualizes them into the field of the contemporary Finnish novel in a unique way, and in this sense, Sahlberg's *oeuvre* can be considered one of the turning points in Finnish literary history. Time will tell if any successors appear and if there is a reason to speak of Salhbergian influences in Finnish literature. For the present purpose, we are left to analyze Sahlberg's fiction and its place in contemporary Finnish literature.

This analysis considers the representations of the subjects in his first eight novels in order to determine what defines the identities and selfhoods of the characters in the fiction of Asko Sahlberg. I will herein examine the subjectivity of the characters in Sahlberg's fiction from two important thematic aspects: outsiderness and time. These will open up views to the subject and its place in history and society presented in Sahlberg's fiction, though many relevant and important thematic topics of the novels – such as ethics chance and faith, and free will – have to be excluded from the analysis. In addition, the purpose of the examination is to outline how these subject representations can be contextualized into the field of the contemporary Finnish novel by asking such questions as: Do they depart from the ideas of the subject presented in fiction by other Finnish contemporary authors and if so, how? What importance do they have if considered from the viewpoint of Finnish literary history? And what would be their contribution to the question of modernity or postmodernity of the subject?

The Outsiders in Escape

A typical character for Sahlberg is an estranged individual – an outsider – whose life is in crisis. Due to certain circumstances the characters suffer overmuch from their living conditions and are reduced to questioning the meaningfulness of existence. In particular the milieu of the modern urban city, institutions for the intellectually disabled, or the war are presented as the states of affairs in which an individual loses the ability to lead a human life, and, ultimately, human dignity. The characters can act pathologically as a result of alcoholism, cognitive disabilities, perversion, or overactive sex drive.

Furthermore, the estrangement of the characters becomes evident especially in one of the subthemes that interrelates all of the novels: escape. The characters are almost without exception trying to run away either from actual places or an unpleasant state of mind, in one way or another.

In the following I examine how being an outsider is thematized in the novels of Sahlberg. In the same context, it is also necessary to analyze the escape as an important aspect that determines the identities of the characters. Thus, the conception of 'the outsiders in escape' refers to the modern world experience in which the estrangement is an essential component of the subject's identity (see Karkama 1994, 21).

Outsiderness is a common theme in modern literature (see Wilson 1978) and it can be argued that in this sense Sahlberg's fiction is not exceptional in the representation of subjects. Nevertheless, it is striking how being an outsider stigmatizes, almost without exception, the selfhoods of the subjects in his works. Almost all of the subjects are outsiders – albeit there are still many differences between them depending on what is meant by 'outsiderness'.

A simple definition of the term 'outsider' could refer to a person who does not belong to the place where he/she is, or who does not share the same information as others. According to the *Oxford English Dictionary*, the word 'outsider' is defined as

> [a] person who does not belong to a particular circle, community, profession, etc.; a person originating from elsewhere. Also: a person unconnected with a matter; a person lacking special knowledge of a subject.

The dictionary definition gives important – though inadequate – clues to the outsiderness represented in the novels of Sahlberg. In addition to these things, being an outsider can refer to an experience of outsiderness, the feeling that the subject is not internally bonded to the ideologies, contexts or discourses within which he/she acts. Furthermore, the characters can also be outsiders because they are alienated from themselves or because they lack particular abilities held by the majority, as is the case of the intellectually disabled persons depicted in the novels.

Thus, at least three distinctive types of outsiders can be found in Sahlberg's novels. First, many of the characters are estranged from society and are therefore outsiders in the truest sense of the word. The escapees, the handicapped, the unemployed, the criminals, the alcoholics, and the drug addicts belong to this category. Second, the contradiction between the character's inner life and external values leads to the experience of being an outsider. In this case, the selfhood and identity of the character is constructed based upon the conflict between external acts based on a certain ideology or discourse and inner skepticism toward these. Third, some characters are alienated from themselves. They do not recognize their own emotional or physical needs. This leads to perverse and odd behaviour in which the person is an outsider to his/her own inner motives. Sahlberg's description of sexuality, in particular, is often based on such a situation.

The estrangement from society is clear in looking at the identities of the protagonists of the Göteborg trilogy and *Eksyneet*. The protagonist of the Göteborg trilogy has left his former life in Finland and emigrated to Sweden. His earlier life in an idyllic Finnish small town was surrounded by the symbols of middle-class life such as the wife, car, house, and the ownership and the editorship of a local newspaper. Now these have changed to loneliness and unemployment in the city of Göteborg. Hatred and despair alternate with hope and empathy when he, in the role of the first-person narrator, attempts to make contact with the addressed reader – 'you' – whom he suspects is not reading his words at all. Even though the protagonist every now and then goes to work and dates women, he feels lonely and isolated most of the time. Furthermore, he is involved in the shady transactions of his friend, a Swedish-Finnish villain named Jakobson.

Being an outsider is thematized in the position of the narrator-protagonist of the Göteborg trilogy. The voice of the immigrant is not heard, and thus the narrator feels a sense of detachment from the outside world. Loneliness and criminality determine his identity. As an immigrant he is not integrated into society but rather kept apart from its demands. Immigration is presented as an escape from a solid identity. This fact is made explicit at the end of the trilogy, when 'the moon-faced man', a mysterious figure who seems to know the life of the protagonist completely, reproaches him for selfishness. He delivers the key line with these words: "You don't yet seem to understand that the question is about *immigration*." (*Paluu Pimeään*, 204; transl. and ital. M.H)

In *Eksyneet* the main characters, Joel and Laura, likewise are the outsiders who are alienated from society. They are both unemployed and try to keep out of the reach of communal life. Both of them avoid contacts with authorities and would sooner escape and hide than give in to the social system of society. Joel and Laura remain outsiders throughout the narrative, except for the end of the novel when Joel surrenders to the police. Each of them is also escaping from something in particular. Laura tries to escape from the emptiness of her family life with her mother and religious stepfather, and Joel tries to escape from his accidental murder of a man. Much like the protagonist of the Göteborg trilogy, they have been drawn to criminal activities, which at least confirms their estrangement from society. The only workplace featured in the story is an outlying refugee centre, further emphasizing the theme of outsiderness and the subtheme of escape. Laura and Joel both represent the selfhood of the estranged subject but, in this case, contrary to the position of the narrator-protagonist of the Göteborg trilogy, the outsiderness is thematized by refusal to succumb to societal control rather than otherness due to being an immigrant.

From all of Sahlberg's novels one can find a number of characters like those described above who either belong to 'the Others' that are out of touch with the society in which they live or to the misfits who have dropped out from the ordered society. Jakobson in the Göteborg trilogy, Laura's alcohol-addicted father in *Eksyneet* and the prostitute Emma in *Tammilehto* are all good examples of this. Indeed, most of the characters that at first glance seem to represent socially acceptable people turn out to be either criminal, perverse, or at least asocial. In this category are, for example, the careless nurses in *Höyhen* and Joel's bourgeois sister in *Eksyneet*.

Furthermore, the estrangement from society is thematized by the characters with diminished responsibility: the drug addicts, the sick, the intellectually or developmentally disabled persons, who are either irresponsible subjects or powerless objects of society's clinical operations, number among this group. For instance, the unnamed 'he' in *Tammilehto* and Aulis in *Eksyneet* are persons with cognitive disabilities whose irresponsible actions emphasize their position as outsiders. However for Ville, who is the handicapped protagonist of *Höyhen*, the outsiderness is passivity in hospital care. Ville is an inmate of an institution, who had had a sexual relationship with his sister before institutionalization. Ville, as well as Aulis in *Eksyneet*, is sexually repressed, which causes problems that impede living in the society. Ville commits sexual harassment, and Aulis tries, with help of his mother Selma, to rape Laura, who visits their backwater home. All these characters can be considered outsiders who are alienated from society due to their lack of normal social skills, and thus do not have the responsibility required in societal life.

In all of these categories of the society-estranged individuals, one can, of course, hear echoes of the Foucauldian thought of power. The criminals, the misfits, the intellectually and developmentally disabled persons, or the immigrants are all subjects against whom the authorities use the power of determination. But the estrangement from society in this sense is still possible because the power is not directed towards individuals from top to bottom, but is instead practised by panoptic control and disciplinary operations. In the Foucauldian sense, either the subject is objectified for clinical operations as in the case of Ville, or the power is infiltrated into individuals regardless of their endeavours to avoid contact with society and the authorities as in the cases of Laura and Joel. It can be argued that identities of the characters are still construed based upon social determination (cf. Foucault 1976; 1989; 1993).

As stated above, existentialist philosophy has clearly influenced the Sahlbergian representations of the subject's position in history and society. This fact is relevant when considering the second category of the themes of being an outsider. The characters of the novels come across as if they have been "thrown into the world" – as Heidegger's famous expression goes (see Heidegger 1962). Thus, the theme of being an outsider is in addition connected to the subject's own experience of his/her outsiderness. The subjects are, in principle, free to choose their identity, but the historical and ideological contexts in which they live restrict their choices. In this sense, the subjects are represented partly as slaves of circumstances without any real opportunity to choose the life path on which they are travelling. This leads to the situation in which the subject can externally act according to some ideology but still has an inner skepticism toward it. Particularly Sahlberg's war novels, *Tammilehto* and *Yhdyntä*, represent outsiderness in that manner.

A good example is Aarne in *Tammilehto*, whose action as a socialist revolutionary leader in the Finnish civil war is contrasted with his disbelief in the proletariat and socialism. Due to questioning the significance of the class struggle in which he still takes an active part, Aarne's character represents the experience of outsiderness. A few other characters also have the very same contradiction between their inner thoughts and external acts. For example, Martin in *Tammilehto* also represents this outsiderness because he is a degenerate aristocrat who cannot find any justification for the victory of his own class. Axel and Valma, the protagonists of *Yhdyntä*, both experience being an outsider during the Second World War because of their overwhelming solitude in the middle of collective historical events.

The subjects who are alienated from themselves comprise the third type of outsiders in Sahlberg's fiction: characters whose subjectivity is problematic because they act inappropriately in terms of their position in society. This chiefly concerns the subject's inability to control his/her subconscious sexual instincts, but other representations of this kind of lack of self-control and self-knowledge can be found in the novels. Though Ville and Aulis can both be regarded as the representatives of this type, their outsiderness is defined more by their irresponsibility resulting from their disability than by their proclivity to act perversely. Major examples of outsiders in this sense are Gustav, the pedophilic protagonist of *Siunaus*, and Edith, the chatelaine in *Tammilehto*. They both behave in sexually perverted manners due to not understanding their own emotional and physical needs and motives. Edith, when disappointed by her empty upper-class life and sexually unsatisfying marriage to her alcoholic husband Martin, seduces the land steward's young son Aarne and forces him to watch her masochistic masturbation:

> Horrified and enchanted he [Aarne] watched the knife which, with the support of the stable hand, was pressed to the inside of motionless, seized up thigh and slashed the fragile skin. The cut bleed just slightly [...] but when madam Edith moved the knife to her crotch and let out a long whispering and suffering sound, the exhausted last squeak of the worn-out bird, he predicted that he would get caught to witnessing the act which transgresses even the most terrible limits of sorrow, which reached past he limits of the most filthy unchastity and immorality and beyond the unnaturalness of the human ruin who lashed her own flesh. (*Tammilehto*, 283; transl. M.H.)

The secret and desperate masochism of Edith represents both the subject's inability to recognize her emotional and physical needs and inner motives for action and an attempt to escape from an unfavorable mental and physical states of affairs. Thus it thematizes the subject's estrangement from him- or herself in general terms. The same is true with Gustav in *Siunaus*, who has an uncontrollable desire for sexual intercourse with children. As opposed to Edith's determined behaviour, Gustav feels powerlessness and a moral indignation toward his own instincts. As a result of pedophilic desire, his mental health collapses and he commits suicide. Considered from a psychoanalytic point of view, both of these situations can be interpreted as representations of either the break of Freudian prevention, a semiotic fracture in symbolic order or the coming up of the abject (cf. Kristeva 1982; 1984). But more important herein is to notice that these characters as well as others in Sahlberg's fiction represent subjects who are, for one reason or another, tumbled into outsiderness.

Lost in Time

The question of time or temporal existence is prevalent throughout all of Sahlberg's novels. Almost all of the narrators in his novels explicitly deal with the question of time. In addition, the theme of time is often taken up more implicitly. Either the character's thoughts about time are presented in focalization and in free indirect discourse, or the issues concerning temporality are otherwise considered thematically. Obviously, the theme of time in Sahlberg's fiction has great importance. It is one of the most significant themes, if not the main theme, of the whole *oeuvre*. It is most evident in the novel *Siunaus*, in which the narrative's historical time goes backwards.

When considering the representations of subjects of the novels this next point must be emphasized, as temporality is a primary factor of the construction of identity. According to Paul Ricoeur, the construction of identity is substantially involved in the temporality of existence and the subject's experience of time. A narrative – a novel or any narrative – is a mimetic process within which the temporal relations are emplotted such that the narrativization can give significance to the experience of being. Through narratives, individuals structure their experience of time and try to puzzle out the problems of temporality. Ricoeur argues that a human being has 'a narrative identity' due to his/her propensity for narrativizing. (See Ricoeur 1988, 241–274; see also Hallila 2008b.) It can be argued that the problems of time are similarly the problems of identity.

In Sahlberg's fiction this association between time and identity is obvious, and in order to show how time and temporality define the represented subjects, they will be analyzed by considering two senses of the theme of time. The analysis will, on the one hand, focus on the ideas of time presented in the novels and, on the other, on the representations of the subjects' experiences of time.

First, the ideas of time are often explicated by the narrators of the novels as they ruminate on questions of time and temporality. It is typical in Sahlberg that despite the narrator's status or position in the story, he/she/it regularly gives thought to time and temporality. These overt reflections on the essence of time arise here and there in the narration of the novels, and the concept of time gets several different definitions within them. For example, time can be presented as parallel to some other quite surprising entities such as earth or woman, or place as in this excerpt from *Yhdyntä*:

> Time is place. The years are passing and everything is changing, the trees are growing, the houses are deteriorating, the furniture is smothered by the dust. The moments swallow each other, and when a man moves in time, not even one moment recalls another or a place thus is not the same place all the time. [...] Yes, time is place is state of mind [...] (*Yhdyntä*, 59; transl. M.H.)

Time can be personified and act as a living agent. It waits, it nods (*Siunaus*, 68), or it "weaken[s] the feelings, flatten[s] out the passion" (*Eksyneet*, 89; transl. M.H.). The subject's position in history is determined by time; in *Tammilehto* this fact is thematized in the description of the red revolutionaries Aarne's and Hevonen's inability to choose their roles in the civil war:

> Time was such. Time didn't ask for man's innermost thoughts, it surprised him from his position and sent him flying [...] (*Tammilehto*, 245; transl. M.H.)

Furthermore, the problems of time and temporality of being are topics which relate to the life history of the subject. From cover to cover, each novel deals with such issues as the past, the present, the future, the different periods of life – especially death – in a manner which emphasizes their thematic importance in terms of the problems of time. The same is true with the descriptions of such temporal modifiers as time of day or season. Furthermore, the memories of the characters are often presented in a manner that does not accentuate so much the meaning of the character's past as the theme of time. A fine example of a multidimensional description of temporality is the episode from *Yhdyntä* in which the presentation of Valma's memories functions as a stepping-stone for thematizing the problems of time:

> Flinching, her face burning, she remembered her childish admiration and longing, the dreams of a girl who understood almost nothing about sexuality. How could time disappear like that? How could it unexpectedly return? Over twenty years had passed, and now it was here. Then she had been a young shy girl who dreamed about a kiss, too uncourageous to even scribble down a love letter. Now she was a woman [...]. (*Yhdyntä*, 30–31; transl. M.H.)

Valma's memory represents temporality of the subject. Her subjectivity is described as an intersection of girlhood and womanhood in which time can, concomitantly, disappear and return, have passed and be right now. Similar 'aporias of time' (Ricoeur 1984; 1985; 1988) are repeated in different forms in Sahlberg's fiction, such as Axel's experience during intercourse with Valma in *Yhdyntä*: "Now I am a man and a child and a boy and an old man and I want this woman and I am inside this woman and won't let her go [...]"(*Yhdyntä*, 121; transl. M.H.). In this episode, the instant experience of desire is simultaneous with Axel's whole life history, including his future, and thus temporality appears as an aspect of the subject formation or construction of identity.

In every novel, there occur numerous such presentations of the character's speech and thoughts in which the problems of time and temporality are under consideration and in which the characters, for one reason or another, end up musing about time. Often this is caused by the sense of crisis. Or, to be more precise, it can be a cause of such emotional problems as feelings of loneliness and suicidal thoughts. Examples of this include the culmination point of crisis for both the narrator of the Göteborg trilogy and Gustav in *Siunaus*. They each experience time's multidimensionality, leading them to think of time's effects on their selfhood and identity. In the Göteborg trilogy this concerns the narrator's suspicions of his existence and selfhood:

> What do you think? Do I ultimately have only one past? Could all of my mysterious emotions be interpreted so that I am bearing numerous pasts, futures, destinies? Or at least possibilities, unravelled motifs. Or am I just raving, have I fallen into a chaotic double bind of self-examination? At twilight, when I wander the silent streets, stand on the empty squares of the city, I could be anyone. (*Hämärän jäljet*, 34; transl. M.H.)

Further, in *Siunaus*, after getting caught sexual abusing a girl, Gustav is told to "accept [...] time". And in his stream of consciousness Gustav "listens to time", and thinks that "I was in time because man is doomed to be [...]" and that "after my time ends the second time begins for me; not new, but the transition and concentration of one time instead of two". (*Siunaus*, 183–185; transl. M.H.) These descriptions of characters' time experiences refer to the problems of subjectivity. The unavoidable temporality of a subject's life and the influence of time on his/her selfhood and identity is a focal point in the representations of the experiences of time.

It can be argued that in Sahlberg's novels the theme of time is, on the one hand, linked to the question of the subject's possibilities (or impossibilities) of influencing his/her life and being, and on the other, involved in the weak points of life, the crises such as feelings of loneliness and suicidal thoughts. When considering the theme of time, it is important to note that all of the narrators – as well as many of the main characters – are exceptionally aware of time and the temporality of being. The subjects represented in Sahlberg's fiction are how they are in large part due to their deep awareness that they are temporal.

Conclusion

It can now be stated that both the status of an outsider and an awareness of temporality define the selfhoods and identities of the subjects represented in the novels of Asko Sahlberg. The idea of subject is thus, at least partially, presented in a manner that emphasizes the significance of estrangement in the subject formation. This idea is, of course, rather more modern than postmodern. In this sense, the Sahlbergian representations of subjects can be considered as representations of the modern estranged individual.

Nevertheless, there are also allusions to postmodern subjectivity. For instance, in the Göteborg trilogy the narrator-protagonist constructs his identity by writing the story for the addressed 'you' and hence the question of the linguistic and constructed nature of identity is posed in the narrative. Furthermore, in the story of *Siunaus* – in which the progression of time and historical events are reversed, with Gustav's position as an ageing subject – ironically lays bare his status as a fictitious character, and thus also reveals his identity to be a fictive construction. These are, however, rare exceptions among the Sahlbergian subject representations.

Yet, it is important to note that even if the identities of the represented subjects are reminiscent of the modern estranged individual, the subject's position in history and society seems quite postmodern. This particularly concerns the subject's relation to belief systems and ideologies, or to the so-called 'metanarratives'.

The analysis shows that the postmodernist Lyotardian idea of the death of metanarratives (see Lyotard 1984) is in Sahlberg's fiction thematized by emphasizing the significance of time and temporality of being. In time or in the experience of time there are no such things as (meta)narratives before the subject's act of narrativizing them. When laying bare the subject's position in time, the novels suggest that the subject cannot find a causal or rational explanation for his/her existence. Thus, an abstract idea of time and the subjects' experiences of time's multidimensionality come to replace the metanarratives. Obviously, no metanarrative such as enlightenment, modernization, Christian ethics and so on exists for the subjects of Sahlberg's fiction.

Asko Sahlberg is not a postmodernist author. Yet, surprisingly, his novel art is not continuing the traditions of realist and modernist fiction, either. It can rather be argued that Sahlberg's fiction uses the conventions of realism, modernism, and postmodernism, as well as the ideas of modern psychology and (existentialist) philosophy, but does not repeat them. The novels outline the recent state of the modern subject through them. In this respect Sahlberg's *oeuvre* makes a remarkable departure from Finnish literature.

From the basis of our analysis it can be argued that Sahlberg's fiction represents the modern subject in the postmodern condition. Thus, it might also be argued that, in the age of globalization, it represents the change of subjectivity without committing itself to realism, modernism or postmodernism. This argument comes close to Jussi Ojajärvi's claim in considering Lars Sund's postmodernist novel *Lanthandlerskans son* (Shopkeeper's Son, 1997). According to Ojajärvi the synthesis of a postmodernist play and a new kind of seriousness towards the thematic associated with "the dialectics of [life's] limitedness and experience" is observable in Sund's novel (Ojajärvi 2005, 46; transl. M.H.). Sahlberg's fiction evidently pursues the same synthesis. But contrary to Sund – and to any other contemporary Finnish author as well – Asko Sahlberg welcomes us to *the unbearable darkness of being*.

References

Sahlberg, Asko 2000: *Pimeän ääni*. [The Sound of Darkness.] Helsinki: WSOY.
Sahlberg, Asko 2001: *Eksyneet*. [The Lost Ones.] Helsinki: WSOY.
Sahlberg, Asko 2002: *Hämärän jäljet*. [The Traces of Twilight.] Helsinki: WSOY.
Sahlberg, Asko 2004: *Tammilehto*. [The Oak Grove.] Helsinki: WSOY.
Sahlberg, Asko 2004: *Paluu pimeään*. [Back to Darkness.] Helsinki: WSOY.
Sahlberg, Asko 2005: *Yhdyntä*. (*Reunahuomautus sotahistoriaan*). [The Intercourse. (Marginal Note to War History).] Helsinki: WSOY.
Sahlberg, Asko 2007: *Siunaus*. [The Blessing.] Helsinki: WSOY.
Sahlberg, Asko 2010. *He*. [They.] Helsinki: WSOY.
Sahlberg, Asko 2011. *Häväistyt*. [The Dishonoured.] Helsinki: WSOY.

Camus, Albert 1942: *L'Étranger*. *Roman*. Paris: Gallimard.
Foucault, Michel 1976: *The Birth of the Clinic*. London: Tavistock.
Foucault, Michel 1989: *Madness and Civiliztion: A History of Insanity in the Age of Reason*. Transl. Richard Howard. London & New York: Routledge.
Foucault, Michel 1993: *Surveiller et punir: naissance de la prison*. Paris: Gallimard.
Hallila, Mika & Hägg, Samuli 2007: History and Historiography in Contemporary Finnish Novel. *Avain* 4/2007, 74–80.
Hallila, Mika 2008a: The Novel is a Cultivated Monster. Metafictionality in Juha K. Tapio's Novel *Frankensteinin muistikirja*. In: Samuli Hägg, Erkki Sevänen & Risto Turunen (eds.), *Metaliterary Layers in Finnish Literature*. Helsinki: SKS, 125–134.
Hallila, Mika 2008b: Kertomus, aika ja ihminen. Paul Ricoeurin *Temps et Recit* ja

jälkiklassinen narratologia. [Narrative, Time, and Man. Paul Ricoeur's *Temps et Recit* and Post-Classical Narratology.] *Avain* 3/2008, 22–37.

Heidegger, Martin 1962: *Being and Time*. New York: Harper & Row.

Karkama, Pertti 1994: *Kirjallisuus ja nykyaika. Suomalaisen sanataiteen teemoja ja tendensseja*. [Literature and the Present Day. Themes and Tendencies of Finnish Literary Art.] Helsinki: SKS.

Karkulehto, Sanna 2007: *Kaapista kaanoniin ja takaisin. Johanna Sinisalon, Pirkko Saision ja Helena Sinervon teosten queer-poliittisia luentoja*. [From Closet to Canon and Back. Queer Political Reading and the Novels of Johanna Sinisalo, Pirkko Saisio and Helena Sinervo.] Oulu: Oulun yliopisto.

Kirstinä, Leena 2007: *Kansallisia kertomuksia: Suomalaisuus 1990-luvun proosassa*. [Narrating Nation: Finnishness in the Prose of the 1990s.] Helsinki: SKS.

Kristeva, Julia 1982: *Powers of Horror. An Essay on Abjection*. Transl. Leon S. Roudiez. New York: Columbia University Press.

Kristeva, Julia 1984: *Revolution in Poetic Language*. Transl. Margaret Waller. New York: Columbia University Press.

Lyotard, Jean François 1984: *Postmodern Condition. A Report on Knowledge*. Minneapolis: University of Minnesota Press.

Ojajärvi, Jussi 2005: Leikki, historia ja kuolema – Lars Sundin *Lanthandlerskans sonin* postmodernismi. [Play, History, and Death – Postmodernism in Lars Sund's *Lanthandlerskans son*.] In: Anna Helle & Katriina Kajannes (eds.), *PoMon tila. Kirjoituksia kirjallisuuden postmodernismista*. [The Space of PoMo. Writings on Literary Postmodernism.] Jyväskylä: Kampus kustannus, 17–55.

Ojajärvi, Jussi 2006: *Supermarketin valossa. Kapitalismi, subjekti ja minuus Mari Mörön romaanissa* Kiltin yön lahjat *ja Juha Seppälän novellissa "Supermarket"*. [In the Light of the Supermarket. Capitalism, the Subject and the Self in Mari Mörö's *Good-Night Gifts* and Juha Seppälä's "Supermarket".] Helsinki: SKS.

Ricoeur, Paul 1984: *Time and Narrative* Vol. 1. (*Temps et Récit*, 1983.) Transl. Kathleen McLaughlin & David Pellauer. Chicago & London: The University of Chicago Press.

Ricoeur, Paul 1985: *Time and Narrative* Vol. 2. (*Temps et Récit*, vol. 2, 1984.) Transl. Kathleen McLaughlin & David Pellauer. Chicago & London: The University of Chicago Press.

Ricoeur, Paul 1988: *Time and Narrative* Vol. 3. (*Temps et Récit*, vol 3, 1987.) Transl. Kathleen McLaughlin & David Pellauer. Chicago & London: The University of Chicago Press.

Saariluoma, Liisa 1989: *Muuttuva romaani. Johdatus individualistisen lajin historiaan*. [The Changing Novel. Introduction to the History of Individualist Genre.] Hämeenlinna: Karisto.

Saariluoma, Liisa 1992: *Postindividualistinen romaani*. [The Postindividualistic Novel.] Helsinki: SKS.

Saariluoma, Liisa 1999: *Modernin minän synty 1700-luvun romaanissa: Valistuksesta Wilhelm Meisteriin*. [The Birth of the Modern Self in the Novel of 18th Century. From Enlightenment to Wilhelm Meister.] Helsinki: SKS.

Sevänen, Erkki 2004: Introduction: From Modernity and Postmodernity to Globalization. In: Jari Kupiainen, Erkki Sevänen & John A. Stotesbury (eds.), *Cultural Identity in Transition. Contemporary Conditions, Practices and Politics of a Global Phenomenon*. New Delhi: Atlantic Publishers and Distributors, 1–30.

Subjektia rakentamassa 2000: [Constructing Subject.] Eds. Tomi Kaarto & Lasse Kekki. Turku: Turun yliopisto.

Taylor, Charles 1989: *Sources of the Self. The Making of the Modern Identity*. Cambridge: Cambridge University Press.

Wilson, Colin 1978: *The Outsider*. London: Pan Books.

Päivi Koivisto

The Author as Protagonist: Autobiographical Narrative in Finland

The popularity of autobiographical literature in Finland skyrocketed in the 1990s, so much so that it became a recognized literary trend in its own right. During this time, increased numbers of Finnish authors wrote novels about adventures of protagonists with their name, and researchers began to focus on the different forms of autobiography found in Finnish literature and other retrospective texts. Mass collection of memoirs and associated material also took place at this time: The Life Story Society of Finland[1] was founded, and local community education centres set up writer's circles for those keen to impart their personal stories.

Starting in the mid-1990s and continuing until today, the country's literary intelligentsia were complicit to the trend – proven in part by the number of autobiographical novels winning or named as top contenders for the most prestigious literary award in Finland, the Finlandia Prize. Autofiction, a metafictional blending of fiction and autobiography, became established as a particular favourite of the Finlandia Prize jurors. The peak year was 1998, when veteran author Pentti Holappa, whose literary debut appeared in 1950, was granted the award. His novel, *Ystävän muotokuva* (Portrait of a friend) tells the story of "Pentti Holappa", utilizing quotation marks to differentiate the main character from the narrator, or the author, as it were. Other nominees that year included the first instalment of a memoir trilogy from Pirkko Saisio entitled *Pienin yhteinen jaettava* (The smallest common multiple) featuring Pirkko Saisio as the protagonist, and Harri Tapper's 1998 novel *Missä kurkien aura on* (Where cranes plough the sky) about the author's childhood family. Autobiographical works that have subsequently won the Finlandia Prize include the final instalment of Pirkko Saisio's trilogy, titled *Punainen erokirja* (Red book of separation) in 2003 and Hannu Väisänen's 2007 novel *Toiset kengät* (Other shoes).

In addition to their work as writers, Saisio, Tapper and Väisänen are all significant figures in the Finnish cultural discourse. Saisio is an accomplished dramaturgist, actor and director, whose 1976 author debut on the working class, *Elämänmeno* (Course of life), succinctly captured the experiences of many blue-collar urban families. Harri Tapper, for his part, is one of four talented Tapper brothers, all artists. His rendition of the Tapper family history sheds light on numerous iconic cultural figures in Finland. Before his three-book memoir was published, Hannu Väisänen was best known in Finland for his work as an artist. It is clear that the popularity of autobiographical literature is tied to people's interest in the "unique individuals" that are celebrities. This interest can be traced in part to the late twentieth-century push to mould authors into market-boosting media personalities, but its roots are grounded farther back in time – in simple curiosity. The evolution of budding artists and the secrets to unravelling the mystery of their artistic creativity has never ceased to intrigue.

Be that as it may, mere inquisitiveness into the enigmatic life of artists is not enough to explain why Finland experienced a renaissance in the writing, reading and discussion of autobiography in the 1990s. Professor Lea Rojola has proposed a link between the Finnish autobiography boom of the 1990s and a variety of foundations and underlying ideologies. Studying both writers' memoirs and factual prose from the era like the autobiographical works of politicians and other public figures,[2] Rojola concluded that autobiographical literature in Finland in the 1990s was a response to not only the sense of fragmented identity that was tormenting modern man at the time, but also the rise of the therapy culture in which self-analysis was seen as a necessity. Reflectivity was a buzzword in the fields of sociology and education in the 1990s. Although Rojola takes care to point out several positive aspects of the autobiography frenzy, including the emergence of marginalized voices and the discussion of many concealed and hurtful experiences, her take on the rampant confessional culture of the 1990s is for the most part critical. At the conclusion of her article, Rojola sums up the autobiographical literature trend as a part of Michel Foucault's (1998) theorized contemporary need for exposure, or confessionary compulsion – independent of the will of the individual. The phenomenon is fundamentally entwined with the commercialism represented by the media. Rojola even goes so far as to propose that the media has displaced priests and judges as the contemporary confessional authority. That which sells and interests the media is the true content of any published autobiography.[3]

The significance of self-reflection is linked to one's understanding of the dismantling of absolute truths, whether individual or universal. Rojola observed that self-reflection is by no means obligatory in Finnish autobiographies: only a portion of the autobiographical texts she examined consider the inherent suspicion attached to the task of describing one's self, while for others the question wasn't even broached. Professional writers in particular were critical of the self's ability to relate the truth faithfully. (Rojola 2002, 75–78.) Upon more careful inspection of the autobiographical novels, however, it becomes apparent that several follow a typical coming-of-age story trajectory, with no associated self-authorship problemization. Nevertheless, it can be said that the large majority of works utilizing the author as protagonist or author's life events as content note the problematic nature of the author's egocentric role.

This division between novels that recognize the questionability of their personal narrative and those that avoid the issue altogether provide yet another perspective on the field of autobiography in contemporary novels. In any event, the book's relation to real events and the author's life is used for varying purposes, in accordance with each book's specific thematic and agenda.

Depictions of Reality

Extending as it did into the 2000s, the success of the traditional autobiographical *Bildungsroman* in Finland is exemplified by the popularity of Hannu Väisänen's three-part memoir. Väisänen's second instalment *Toiset kengät* (Other Shoes) won the Finlandia Prize in 2007. The trilogy is rounded out by the first book, *Vanikan palat* (Pieces of Hard Bread) from 2004, and the last, *Kuperat ja koverat* (Convex and Concave) from 2010. The series tells the story of young Antero's journey into an artist. Väisänen calls his protagonist Antero in an apparent effort to separate the author and his main subject, but savvy readers are aware that Antero is indeed Väisänen's middle name. The autobiographical connection is hidden as it were, although the books make no mistake about describing the development of an artist, which naturally leads the reader to associate the experiences of the book's protagonist with the author.

Characteristic of the crises often found in autobiographies, Antero's mother dies early and the boy is left alone to be raised by his rather peculiar father. Although the work is written as a novel, the childhood tribulations it contains are just as easily recognized as the building blocks of the *Bildungsroman*. Indeed, one can ask if Väisänen's life is tranformed into fiction in part because of the suffering, feelings of being different, and detachment that was no doubt brought on by his mother's death – thus caused his evolution into a mythic artist. Teasing at school, setting out for the city and then into world to find himself, and of course, yearning for love, are all familiar arcs of typical *Bildungroman* storylines. It is archetypal that a work that has been written as a novel but touches closely on the author's own life, with its resulting synthesis of the fictitious first-person narrative and the prototypical storyline continuum, declare the relativity of individuality. Novels specializing in the description of individual experiences have endured in part because the individuality of the subject matter is often revealed as communal by nature. It is not difficult for many of us to identify with and even share in the experiences of other individuals.

The trilogy describing the evolution of writer Hannu Niklander is a similarly structured body of work. His first novel in the series *Aurinko katsoo taakseen* (The Sun Looks Back) from 1999 won Niklander the State Prize. The later instalments, 2003's *Radan varrella varjo* (A Shadow on the Side of the Tracks) and 2006's *Kuu jättää jäljen* (The Moon Leaves a Trace) follow the young Niklander's journey towards becoming an author. Väisänen and Niklander had many things in common beyond their development into artists. Wherein Väisänen's series of novels, the young boy's mother dies, Niklander in turn loses his father, who bequeaths to his son a love of art.

Hence each author writes our familiar artist-myth from a half-orphaned perspective. The principle of communal individuality is nearly parodied when one considers that both authors are named Hannu and are virtually the same age. While Väisänen writes about Antero, Niklander uses the name Hannu directly as the name of his protagonist.

Reading Niklander's work as part of the larger Finnish autobiography canon of the 1990s demonstrates that giving the protagonist the author's first name does not inevitably make the book a personal narrative. Among certain age groups, Hannu is one of the most popular names in Finland. Hannu Mäkelä and Hannu Raittila are two other successful Finnish writers who have written self-reflective works after the 1990s, relaying the events of their lives in their own name. By employing a common name such as this in these novels, the authors were able to simultaneously provide clues to both their personal development and that of anyone else with the same name. In addition to describing the conditions under which their growth as artists took place, Niklander and Väisänen's titles do much to describe a post-1950s Finland that many readers recognize.

A second cluster of work, in which the description of reality is not called into question, is known as *tilitysteokset* in Finnish, or "account-settling books". In these novels, the author attempts to describe and process a painful experience they have gone through in a documentary style. Where novels aspiring to *Bildungsroman* status tend to try not to distract the reader's identification with the fate of their hero by adding metafictional comments, in these account-settling stories of crisis the voice of the narrator rings strong and clear – and sometimes preachy. Anja Kauranen's 1993 work *Ihon aika* (The time of skin) can be examined as a poetic depiction of the mother/daughter relationship, but it also included diatribes that went on to engender an animated discussion on elderly care in Finland. In this sense, the book is a candid argumentation of the role women assume as unpaid care resources in the care of the elderly. The book follows the narrator as she tends to her dying mother in the Koskela Hospital, where she becomes in effect a hospice caregiver. Kauranen argues that these kinds of dirty jobs are inevitably the responsibility of women, while men choose to do other things like run the hospital. No matter that men know that it is wrong for "women to first care for their children and husbands, and then care for their parents", because "in the western welfare state, men disappear from view as fast as lightning when someone is needed to change a diaper, tip a cup or fluff up a pillow."[4] Here Kauranen's writing style is almost better suited to a political pamphlet than a novel.

Two novels that can be regarded as in their entirety as crisis books are Anna-Leena Härkönen's works *Heikosti positiivinen* (Slightly positive) from 2001 and 2004's *Loppuunkäsitelty* (Concluded). The former discusses post-partum depression and the good mother myth allied with the affliction, while the latter ponders the suicide of Härkönen's sister and the deficiencies of mental health care. The books have both been released as novels, although their connection to factual events is indisputable. As such, they aspire to universal applicability, even though the point of departure is essentially singular. This perhaps can be defended as a contribution to the history of the feminist struggle: "Before we had to defend our right to not have a child. Now we have to defend our right not to have a second child. If I were to have myself sterilized, I probably wouldn't dare to tell many people about it – except you."[5]

In the previous example, Härkönen touches on the contradiction of autobiographical literature: how the most shameful "sin" becomes a potential literary revelation. On the following page, the narrator explains how she was approached to write a film manuscript about her subject. She contemplates her inability to go through with it because she "promised the childless couples I visited with" (cf. note 5) to keep their experiences to herself. Hence the reader duly discovers that he or she is in the midst of reading a treatise on a subject that was supposed to remain untold. Those in search of facts, moreover, will note that Härkönen did indeed write that movie script eventually.[6]

Among the more recent works from Finland, Anniina Holmberg's 2009 novel *Kaiku* (Echo) is linked to this same literary subset. The novel tells the story of a girl named Anniina and her father's influence on her childhood. Holmberg's father Kalle Holmberg is a Finnish theatre director who was very famous in Finland in the 1960s and 70s. He was also a part of a radical leftist movement that flowered among artists during that time. Anniina Holmberg underwrites her childhood memoirs with the story of her adult life, in which the author explains her motherhood complex. Among other things, she uses her text as a springboard to declare her "party platform" with a list of mother's rights. Holmberg paints a contrast in her book between her political crusading father of the 1970s and her self-proclaimed "apolitical" self. And yet when her children's school is in danger of being closed, the protagonist suddenly finds herself in the front rows of a parent protest. Holmberg's novel concurs with Lea Rojola's suggestion that one factor contributing to the popularity of autobiographies is the focus on self-centeredness in modern society, accordingly reflected in our private lives as eroded participation in political and social activity, as Richard Sennett (1977) has theorized. In Holmberg's text, her political self is activated only when events affect her immediate family: perhaps it is true that altruism is a vanishing natural resource.[7]

Finnish Writers of Autofiction

In the 1990s, three recognized and esteemed Finnish authors, Pentti Holappa, Kari Hotakainen and Pirkko Saisio, wrote novels in which the conventions of autobiography were written as a component of a novel. Central to the books is a main character with the name of the author and events that resemble, at least in part, moments from the author's life. The coincidence is strongest with Saisio, less so with Holappa and Hotakainen.

Saisio, Hotakainen and Holappa each wrote about different subjects, reflecting on the methods of autobiographical rendering in the process. The phenomenon is most closely mirrored in the history of literary genre by the autofiction movement in 1970s France, spearheaded by the essays of autobiographical researcher Philippe Lejeune.[8] Lejeune formulated categories of autobiography and its attendant autobiographical pact. According to Lejeune, an autobiography is defined above all by the fact that the work tells the life story of someone with the same name appearing on the cover of the book as author. Interestingly, literature researcher and author Serge Doubrovsky saw a challenge in Lejeune's claim and wrote a novel containing events that he claimed were entirely factual, giving his protagonist his own name. He defined the category of his creation as autofiction. In a later theoretical essay, he expanded upon this definition, saying that in autofiction, the psychoanalytical perspective of the subconscious is vital, whether in the form of psychic rejection or ideologies that have been adopted unwittingly. As a result, the works include various depictions of the self that are dissected in many ways. Literature and its contribution to collective myths are a part of the unknown: the tracks of what came before lead from individuality to the communal. A post-structural understanding of language is evident when it is believed that the language is the source of self-imposed law.[9]

According to the committed definition of autobiographical theory, it is important that the events in an autofiction are mostly true. Of course an outsider has no way of knowing anything for certain about the truth of writers' output, but comparisons of public information about the writers and the content of their works can be made. In Pirkko Saisio's trilogy, *Pienin yhteinen jaettava* (1998), *Vastavalo* (2000) and *Punainen erokirja* (2003), the protagonist Pirkko's life is very reminiscent of the life we know Pirkko Saisio to have led, and the themes of the trilogy are also familiar from interviews Saisio has given over the years. In Pentti Holappa's *Ystävän muotokuva*, however, the closet "Pentti" is not recognizable as the same Pentti Holappa that socialized openly with his male partner already back in the 1960s. Yet, of the three, Kari Hotakainen's *Klassikko* takes the most obvious flights of fancy. Anyone following current events in the 1990s knows that the author Kari Hotakainen had nothing to do with a drunken driving accident that was widely reported on at the time. Both Hotakainen's and Holappa's books are closer to the juxtaposed definition of autofiction, in which characters with the author's name are exposed to events that never really happened to the author in real life.[10]

In many ways, Saisio's trilogy best emulates the ideal concept of autobiographical autofiction. She has made it clear that her books are novels, even if the main character strongly resembles the author.[11] Devotees of literature have had the opportunity to follow Saisio's public life as an author, actor, director and professor of dramaturgy at the nation's premiere theatre academy. In the early 1990s, she campaigned for the right of homosexual couples to declare their partnerships legal, when a proposition to that effect was in danger of defeat in parliament after resistance from conservative politicians.

In her trilogy, Saisio writes a coming-of age story that fulfils the basic tenants of autobiography about a girl who grows to accept her homosexuality and discover her vocational calling. Despite these typical autobiographical elements, the trilogy still holds its own as a novel, if only for the fact that it clearly displays all of the conventions of the *Bildungsroman*. As a whole, various intertextual references abound in Saisio's texts: some seem consciously written while others seem activated by the author's intuitive knowledge of the tradition. Doubrovsky's divisible self is easily apparent in Saisio's work, with the protagonist referred to as "I" in some instances and at other times as "she". The poeticism unique to autofiction is also clearly on view in Saisio's novels, where the text on the page often looks more like poetry. Sentences are split haphazardly to emphasize meaning, not necessarily in line with the margins, and blank space can be left in the middle of a thought on the page.

Beyond the poetic elements, Saisio's trilogy can also be read as an enticing and nostalgic description of life in Finland after the 1950s. In *Punainen erokirja*, the individual landscapes of childhood and youth are traded for an adult life in the public eye. Her memories of performing with and directing the university theatre company and studying at the Theatre Academy with the other rising stars of the art elite now show more congruence with her actual past than the stories in the first trilogy instalment – at least as corroborated by people who were active in the artistic circles at the time.

An important component of *Punainen erokirja* is the depiction of the leftist radicalism that surged through the protagonist's university and theatre community in Finland in the 1970s. One of the key figures of the times was the aforementioned Kalle Holmberg, although Saisio reserves no role for him in her book. The fascination with communism that consumed the artistic community in Finland in the 1970s is a tender spot among the cultural elite of the country, something Saisio analyzes in both this book and in her 2004 play *Baikalin lapset* (Children of Baikal). In Saisio's trilogy, her communist awakening was tied to the religious development of the main character, with leftist leanings the conduit between her ongoing search for Christian faith and her journey towards a personal spirituality largely represented by cultural experiences she finds in the art world.[12]

An interesting parallel to *Punainen erokirja*, and the whole trilogy at that, is Henrik Jansson's autobiographical work from 2007 *Protokollsutdrag från subversiva möten* (Excerpts from minutes of subversive meetings)[13], which makes reference to *Punainen erokirja* by name. The principal character, named Jansson, declares to have received the inspiration to write a memoir about his political past after reading Saisio's depiction of the 1970s. The parallel works highlight the differences between Jansson's and Saisio's portrayal of the time: if student radicalism in Helsinki is equated with wide-ranging leftist student radicalism in Saisio's work, Jansson's story moves the phenomenon to the Swedish-speaking community of Turku, away from the capital city region. Where the homosexual identity of Saisio's protagonist grates against the levelling playing field of collectivism found in the Finnish pro-Soviet movement, Jansson's protagonist struggles to harmonize his leftist-leaning allegiances with his cultural identity as a Swedish-speaking Finn.

Anja Snellman's work can also be assessed from the autofiction perspective. Both 1989's *Kiinalainen kesä* (Chinese summer) and 1998's *Side* (Bond) contains strong autofiction elements. In the latter work, pictures of the author in her youth adorn the cover and illustrate the book, suggesting a personal narrative recognizable from her earlier works when she was still writing under her maiden name of Kauranen. The division of self is evident, as the author's name had since changed to Snellman. Snellman does not leave this aspect unexploited in her book: the definition of the Finnish word *side* is established by referring to an article from The Dictionary of Contemporary Finnish (*Nykysuomen sanakirja*) that contains a sentence from one of her earlier works as Anja Kauranen. In her decision to share authorship with the artist Ulla Jokisalo, Snellman splite the ego of the author in *Side* even further. Other titles from Snellman combine with the two mentioned to form a broader "autobiographical space"[14], namely 1993's *Ihon aika* and 1995's *Syysprinssi* (Autumnal Prince). All of these novels are connected to the same subject matter, mother/daughter relationship, and in part narrate the same events. The connection between them all is confirmed by the author's prologue to *Side*, in which the earlier books are associated with the *Side* thematic.

I wrote earlier about author Härkönen's literary topos of revealing the private secrets of her confidants. In Anja Kauranen's 1996 novel *Syysprinssi*, one of the books in her "mother series", the author similarly betrayed a source. This led to a minor scandal of the sort hungry patrons of contemporary literature today thrive on. After publication of the novel, the tabloids hotly contested the morality of the author in her decision to candidly discuss the clinical depression of her ex-partner, the writer Harri Sirola. This despite assurances in the text from the narrator – whom the readers clearly interpret to be the author herself – that she would not write about her former lover. It was highly ironic that the connection between Harri Sirola and the book's protagonist, the "autumnal prince" was actually revealed in the work with mention that Sirola had read and approved of the draft. The last page contained a dedication: "To Harri – thank goodness you enjoyed reading the draft."

The conventional devices of the autobiography contained in *Syysprinssi* are further anchored in the work's intertextual link to Marguerite Duras' 1992 novel *L'Amant de la Chine du Nord (The North China Lover)*, which uses the same topos of betrayal and is also similar in many other respects. This is supported by the fact that other works in Kauranen's mother series are also linked to Duras' *L'Amant (The Lover)* and *L'Amant de la Chine du Nord*.[15]

After the first work of autofiction received the Finlandia Prize, the genre picked up speed in Finland. Established writer Anu Kaipainen even categorized what was to remain her last novel, the memoir *Vihreiksi poltetut puut* (Wood burnt green) as autofiction. Hence autofiction had come to stay, assuming a part in the Finnish literary tradition. The tone of Kaipainen's work is very much one of a traditional memoir, but familiar autofiction elements like using interchangeable pronouns for the protagonist and the seamless incorporation of quotations from Kaipainen's earlier works appear throughout.

Champions of the Fictitious Autobiography

At the turn of the 21st century, many writers presented themselves as main characters in a work of fiction, but interest soon turned from self-reflection and autobiographical writing to exterior themes. Kari Hotakainen's *Klassikko* (Classic) is a good example of using the author's figure as an instrument for examining the novel and the prerequisites of literature in general. The cover features Hotakainen staring at the reader through his thick glasses and assuming a contrived pose, in line with the author-photo cliché. Although the inner pages have some connection to the writer's own life, Hotakainen's novel does not paint a pretty picture of autobiographies written in earnest. Any serious attempt to describe one's true self is self-deception, for Hotakainen's protagonist believes the ego to be varied and unpredictable, not limited to the self as captured in a book. This human variance is a key reason why there are writers of prose in the first place. It is just this reason that allows Hotakainen to intersperse his first-person story with extensive footage about an unemployed man named Pera and a lonely used car salesman named Kartio, written from their perspective. This despite the fact that the poet-cum-writer's life has nothing in common with the men he describes.

Hotakainen's *Klassikko* has been mentioned by both Lea Rojola[16] and Mikko Lehtonen[17] as an example of a work whose thematic parodies the influence of the contemporary commercial writer/celebrity and commodification of authors. It is shocking to note that *Klassikko* went on to become Hotakainen's breakthrough work, generating many interviews and public engagements. The success of *Klassikko* demonstrates that penning a personal narrative is a major boon on the path to literary success.

In the interest of truthfulness it has to be said that in addition its autobiographical flirtations, *Klassikko* is an immensely entertaining book. But Hotakainen has written humorous books before, for example his 1991 postmodern parody of the biography/portrait of an artist tradition *Buster Keaton*. Proceeding in fragments, this small book was not as successful as attracting readers as the mocking *Klassikko,* his version of the confessional novel the media and the public was thirsty for.

In *Klassikko*, Hotakaisen's hero fights against the media's controlling power in a desperate bid for notoriety. He determinedly seeks exposure in the newspapers and the evening news, if only for his drunken driving. Here the writer is a victim of the fickle media: his livelihood is defined by how much has been written about him. A Hotakainen successor, the Finnish author Tuomas Vimma published his debut *Helsinki 12* in 2004. Together with his other works, 2005's *Toinen* (The Second) and 2008's *Gourmet,*

Helsinki 12 brings to life the writer Tuomas Vimma, who is also the novel series' protagonist. The first novel presents a young advertising executive living the high life in the 1990s heyday of the hip advertising world. Vimma's main character works very little and rakes in an enormous salary for sitting in pubs. His behaviour includes immoral lechery and spineless deceit of people he is fond of. At the end of the novel, our hero runs into misfortune and assumes the name Tuomas Vimma.

The *Helsinki 12* novel mirrors Brett Easton Ellis's *American Psycho* in many ways – a feature many reviewers were quick to pick up on. Although the violence is not as gratuitous, Vimma's nonchalant nature and pursuit of carnal pleasures is identical. The requisite list of brand name clothing, foods and luxuries of interior design is also present. Vimma's writing style is entertaining, and for this reason many don't consider his work of high enough merit to be considered fine literature. Along with *Toinen*, however, *Helsinki 12* certainly contributes to the discussion spearheaded by Hotakainen on the role of the author.

Toinen continues the hero's story by revealing that the *Helsinki 12* book was in actuality written by his girlfriend, another ex-advertiser, who used Tuomas Vimma as a pseudonym. The girlfriend is well aware of the power of the media and is eager to shield herself from it. The media wins out eventually when the pen name scam and real author are published in the papers along with pictures. Despite their entreaties to the contrary, a skilled reporter manipulates the interviewees at his whim. A similar situation is pictured from the tabloid perspective in Taina Latvala's 2009 novel entitled *Paljastuskirja* (Book of Revelation), another work that dabs in autofiction, as Latvala worked previously as an entertainment reporter for the tabloids and the main character is mentioned as having written Latvala's debut novel.

Vimma's next book *Gourmet* (2008) thrusts us into the world of restaurants. Vimma is once again someone else entirely: a Frenchman from a culinary family who has cooking in his blood but whose haughtiness prohibits the advancement of his professional career. The book's theme follows that of the previous works; just as the writer unwillingly falls prey to media modification, the protagonist of *Gourmet* is not aware of his supposedly supportive father's conspiracy against him that forces him along an inescapable course. In line with the genre, the father represents any kind of far-reaching power the young man is powerless against. This same thematic is present in the narrative on down-on-his-luck Pera in Hotakainen's *Klassikko*, showcasing a depiction of social service professionals who control, assess and define people, leaving individuals seeking assistance with no say in the matter. Fictitious autobiography often hides a hefty dose of social criticism just under its seemingly shallow surface.

Another earlier novel that can be included in the category of socially critical autofiction is theatre director Jouko Turkka's *Häpeä* (Shame) from 1994, in which a man resembling Turkka reveals things about himself that readers are able to connect with news they have read about the author in the papers. The events of the novel are not realistic, however, as in the beginning of the book when Turkka sets off on horseback to lecture to a group of secretaries. On his journey he meets many strange fates as he ponders his life and identity. In her analysis of the novel, Sari Salin links the novel to the confessional tradition and its attendant self-sacrifice. The unrealistic events work to protect Turkka, one of the many devices he utilizes to demote himself in the text. Not only does he reveal shameful things about himself, but he also shares opinions about his invented characters that most would find despicable. An example is his inclusion of Jammu Siltavuori, who horrified Finns in the 1980s with his murder of children. Salin believes that by admitting to understanding at some level the motives of a man who had been reduced to a monster in the public conscience, Turkka chose to take upon himself all of the sins of his countrymen. The actual events themselves are not the point in Turkka's book, instead his intention as a writer is to attribute forbidden actions and desires to the narrator.[18]

Hotakainen and Vimma can be interpreted in this same light. In the case of Hotakainen, it is a horrendous vision of just how far a desperate contemporary writer like himself is willing to bend. Vimma gives readers the opportunity to identify first with an unscrupulous hedonist and misogynist, and then as a man in servitude to his girlfriend. Holappa's *Ystävän muotokuva* also conforms to this same ethos, as "Pentti" dons the cloak of a cowardly closet homosexual.

Of the Swedish-speaking Finnish writers, Peter Sandström seems bewilderingly bent on incurring the disdain of his readers. In his 2004 novel *Manuskript för pornografiska filmer* (Manuscripts for pornographic films), Sandström writes about a so-named protagonist that has failed as a writer and a father and is forced to earn a living by writing scripts for porn films. He has been ordered a restraining order forbidding contact with his wife and two children, all of whom he has struck in anger. He shares an incestually-tinged and similarly violent relationship with his sister.

Of all the previous examples, Sandström's novel is the hardest to digest: the style is neither parody nor humour; the events are not overblown – they are tragically realistic. The novel is like any relation of a young man's transformation into a violent adult. The protagonist with the author's name does things that most of us would never want to own up to. At times, the narrative tries to explain the motives behind his actions, but the explanations just aren't convincing: like when he explains to the reader that he will stop hitting his children when they become old enough to remember what happens. The novel contains no direct explanation for the main character's behaviour. His relationship with his father, "a master bringing darkness to every room he enters", remains a mystery, with no attempt to explain it. It is in any case clear that the two men are not close and the boy feels less a man than his father.

A common denominator of the works examined here is that these authors, by giving their unsavoury protagonists their name, in effect refuse to make evil and banality the burden of alternate characters, or "the others". As if to say that no one is without fault, even me. This construction can be equated with that of Michel in the novels of Michel Houellebecq. In the novel *Plateforme* (*Platform*), for example, Michel is depicted as a realistic person one can relate with, even if his opinions represent mercantile capitalism and colonial sentiments. There has been animated discussion of Houellebecq in Finland of late in literary circles,[19] and I wouldn't be surprised to find more of his methods appearing in Finnish literature in the near future.

The Emperor's New Clothes?

Many feel that the autobiography boom in Finland that began in the 1990s is archetypal for our times. Anna Makkonen (now Kuismin) reminds us however in her 1996 article "Paljastuksia kaikilta vuosilta" (Revelations throughout time) that autobiography is certainly nothing new in the field of literature. The roots of the latest interest in the personal narrative in the Finnish literature community can indeed be traced back to a previous autobiographical literature boom that took place in Finland in the 1970s.[20] The boom of the 1970s set in motion a continuum, whose existence encouraged the predilection of important authors towards serial writing, as many autobiographical works begun in the 1970s were expanded into series completed in the 1980s or 1990s. Christer Kihlman's famous confessional *Människan som skalv* (The Quaking Man) was written in 1971, for example, but the author continued on the same theme in later works, like 1986's *På drift i förlustens lanskap (Adrift in a Landscape of Loss)*. In the same matter, the writer Henrik Tikkanen began his famous "address series" with the book *Brändövägen 8* in 1975, continuing through until 1982. In the same vein, the first instalment of the wartime memoirs of the great Eeva Kilpi, *Talvisodan aika* (During the Winter War), appeared in 1989 and the last book in the series was published in 1993. The popularity of the traditional memoir series in Finland is made manifest by the fact that a new edition of Kilpi's series was released under one cover in 1998, with Kilpi adding yet another piece to her childhood memory collection in a new novel published in 2001: *Rajattomuuden aika* (The Era of Infinity).[21]

Literature professor Juhani Niemi has written about the requirements and collectivism associated with participation in the 1960s and 70s literary community. Concurrent with this movement, the significance of authorship paradoxically rose, affecting the new media's interest in elevating writers to celebrity status.[22] This same contradictory parallelism is identified in Anna Makkonen's analysis of Christer Kihlman's *Mannen som skalv*, in which collectivist spirit and politics combines with the exaltation of individualism.[23] Tarja Hypén has proposed that the 1990s author-celebrity phenomenon in Finland caused the perception of the author's work to be formed in large part by different kinds of media exposure. She speaks of the media author as a contemporary literary figure whose face is typically visible in the media as much as their printed output.[24] This "mediazation" of literature began back in the 1960s, however, during the first autobiography craze. The legendary Finnish poet and translator Pentti Saarikoski became a media favourite during this time, amusing the press greatly with his exploits.

Already in these works from the 1970s, the author's search for identity is clear. Kihlman uses the opportunity to vehemently deny repenting his homosexuality and alcoholism, while Henrik Tikkanen grumbles about women's rights in his book *Ihmisen ääni* (The Human Voice)[25] in much the same way that Hotakainen does thirty years later in *Klassikko*, in his efforts to give voice to the men's movement. Tender spots in the generation are particularly lucid in the confessions of the Swedish-speaking Finnish authors of the 1970s, with Saisio and Kauranen most vocal in the 1990s and 2000s and Hotakainen and Holappa remaining more impervious.

As the first decade of the 21st century drew to a close, the interest in autobiography in Finland has begun to fade. Multifaceted parodies of autobiography like those from Hotakainen and Tuomas Vimma, on the other hand, have multiplied. Books released in 2010 like Juha Itkonen's *Seitsemäntoista* (Seventeen) and Jussi Siirilä's *Historia on minut vapauttava* (History shall vindicate me) features caricatures of the authors for all to read. Siirilä joins Hotakainen and Vimma as a fierce critic of author mediazation, while Itkonen mimics Hotakainen's 2009 novel *Ihmisen osa* (The Human Condition) in his analysis of the right of writers to exploit other people in their work. Itkonen plays with the conventions of roman à clef in his book by writing under the pseudonym Julius Ilonen.

The behaviour of the author figure as fiction follows a certain development arc over different periods in time. The traditional autobiographical novel has maintained its popularity in Finland into the early 21st century, as the esteem for Hannu Väisänen's series of novels shows. And yet over the last two decades, we have learned to appreciate the proliferating amount of work with metafictional elements. People are buying and reading Pirkko Saisio's trilogy, even though, at first glance, its diction could be considered challenging. The majority of the new Finnish novels with personal narrative, including autofiction novels, have not managed to break the charm of a well-cast tale. It is not, after all, so artistically writ large that it would frighten unseasoned readers away. Many of the texts in question ponder universal questions of identity underneath their seemingly airy surface; others bemoan the state of society – equally the worry of a great number of Finns. Other works simply strive to express their longing for a world gone by that cannot be reclaimed, whether Karelia in the early 1900s or the courtyards of the 1950s apartment blocks.

On the one hand, the parodies of the writer persona found in the latest contemporary literature can be so strongly caricature-like that reader identification is impeded. On the other hand, this may not bother the majority of readers who have never identified with an artist and are more interested in reading about exotic fantasy than the lives of the artists themselves. In our multimedia era, it is clear that these kinds of idiosyncratic spectacles are what people want to see on the pages of their books, on their television sets and in the columns of their favourite newspaper.

NOTES

1   The Life Story Society of Finland (Suomen Elämäntarinayhdistys) was founded in 1999 with the goal of promoting the appreciation of personal history and creative expression by means of autobiography. Each year the Society organizes a seminar on the personal narrative, with invited speakers such as Philippe Lejeune. The Society's newspaper publishes personal and autobiographical texts and research articles on the subject and arranges instruction on writing autobiographies (www. elamantarina.fi).

2   In general, it can be said that the demarcation between a novel and a published work became more permeable in the 1990s in Finland. In general, the books contained no definition of the genre in question on the cover or the introductory pages of the text. Library classification codes for literary prose, 84 and 84.2, became elastic in practice and the Finnish concept of "narrative literature" apt for novels and factual memoirs alike. Personal history has its own classification, 89, which is clearly devoted to works with an historical emphasis. The classification of a book is often also subject to extraneous factors, like whether the author is a writer or a politician. Library classifications can also indicate variance in quality: artistically ambitious publications are invariably classified as narrative literature. (See Gasparini 2004, 69–70.)

3   Rojola 2002.

4   Kauranen 1993, 73–74.

5   Härkönen 2001, 130.

6   The movie in question is 2005's *Onnen varjot (Shades of Happiness)* from the director Claes Olsson. Härkönen is one of many Finnish actors doubling as a novelist writing largely autobiographical works. Professors at Finland's Theatre Academy in Helsinki, Pirkko Saisio and Jouko Turkka are both authors that appear later in this article. Jouko Turkka has gained a reputation in Finland for his humiliating teaching methods, but also for encouraging his students to seek out diverse forms of artistry. Several of his students have written a novel or a literary memoir on the suffering they endured under Turkka's tutelage. The autobiographical works of Turkka-protégées and theatre directors Reko Lundán and Juha Hurme were starkly different, however. Lundán and his wife wrote a dialogue novel about their experience after his diagnosis with a deadly brain tumour, while Hurme wrote a novel describing the chaotic exploits of a person named Juha Hurme in the interface between the theatre world and reality. The influential teaching of Turkka were perhaps partly responsible for the creation of these books, but seeing as how the theatre uses the body and persona as the material for its art, expressional autofiction literature may seem a natural choice for the theatrically-inclined.

7   See Rojola 2002, 84.

8   Lejeune's essay was translated into English in 1989 for inclusion in a collection of his essays, but his original text was published already in 1973.

9   Doubrovsky 1993.

10 Genette 1993, 75–77.

11 Haapanen 1998b.

12 For a more comprehensive presentation of Saisio's trilogy, consult my doctoral thesis: *Elämästä autofiktioksi. Lajitradition jäljillä Pirkko Saision romaanisarjassa Pienin yhteinen jaettava, Vastavalo ja Punainen erokirja (From Real Life to Autofiction: Tracking the genre tradition in Pirkko Saisio's novel series Pienin yhteinen jaettava, Vastavalo and Punainen erokirja)*, set to be submitted in autumn 2011. I have also examined the link between Saisio's *Pienin yhteinen jaettava* and autofiction in shorter form in an earlier article. (Koivisto 2005.)

13 Later translated into Finnish under the name *Otteita kumouksellisista kokouksista* (2009).

14 Lejeune 1989, 26–28.
15 Read an in depth analysis of Kauranen's mother series and her correlation to Marguerite Duras, beginning with the similarity in cover art for *Ihon aika* and *L'Amant,* in my article (Koivisto 2004). Duras is a popular author in Finland and almost all of her novels and prose have been translated into Finnish. Her method for combining personal narrative with fiction has inspired several Finnish authors. Like Kauranen, Pirkko Saisio has also mentioned Duras as an influence (Saisio 2003b).
16 Rojola 2002.
17 Lehtonen 2001, 133–141.
18 Salin 2008, 216–233; 220–221 in particular.
19 For more information on the discourse and its origin, see the 2010 collection of essays "Mitä Houellebecq tarkoittaa?" (What does Houellebecq mean?) edited by Timo Hännikäinen (2010).
20 Makkonen 1996, Rojola 2002.
21 Numerous works of Finnish literature relay experiences from the Russian occupation of Finnish territory during the war. In addition to Kilpi, several other authors walk the line between autobiography and fiction, including Anu Kaipainen, whose last work of autofiction describes her childhood as an evacuee. Raisa Lardot has also written a wrenching novel about evacuation. The Karelian expulsion literature corresponds to stories about the Holocaust found in autofiction from continental Europe, even if the experience of the Finns is by no means as dramatic in scale.
22 Niemi 1999, 169–170, 179.
23 Makkonen 1995.
24 Hypén 2002; 32–34, 37–39.
25 Tikkanen 1978.

References

Holappa, Pentti 1998: *Ystävän muotokuva.* [Portrait of a friend.] Helsinki: WSOY.

Holmberg, Anniina 2009: *Kaiku.* [Echo.] Helsinki: Siltala.

Hotakainen, Kari 1997: *Klassikko.* [Classic.] Helsinki: WSOY.

Härkönen, Anna-Leena 2001: *Heikosti positiivinen.* [Slightly positive.] Helsinki: Otava.

Härkönen, Anna-Leena 2004: *Loppuunkäsitelty.* [Concluded.] Helsinki: Otava.

Itkonen, Juha 2010: *Seitsemäntoista.* [Seventeen.] Helsinki: Otava.

Jansson, Henrik 2007: *Protokollsutdrag från subversiva möten.* [Excerpts from minutes of subversive meetings.] Vasa: Scriptum.

Kauranen, Anja 1989: *Kiinalainen kesä.* [Chinese Summer.] Helsinki: WSOY.

Kauranen, Anja 1993: *Ihon aika.* [The time of skin.] Helsinki: WSOY.

Kauranen, Anja 1996: *Syysprinssi.* [The Autumnal Prince.] Helsinki: WSOY.

Kaipainen, Anu 2007: *Vihreiksi poltetut puut.* [Wood burnt green.] Helsinki: WSOY.

Kihlman, Christer 1971: *Ihminen joka järkkyi.* [*The Quaking Man.*] Translated in Finnish by Pentti Saaritsa. Helsinki: Tammi.

Kilpi, Eeva 1998: *Muistojen aika.* [Era of Recollection.] Helsinki: WSOY.

Kilpi, Eeva 2001: *Rajattomuuden aika.* [Era of Infinity.] Helsinki: WSOY.

Latvala, Taina 2009: *Paljastuskirja.* [Book of Revelation.] Helsinki: WSOY.

Niklander, Hannu 1999: *Aurinko katsoo taakseen.* [The Sun looks Back.] Jyväskylä: Atena.

Niklander, Hannu 2003: *Radan varrella varjo.* [A Side of the Shadow on the Tracks.] Jyväskylä: Atena.

Niklander, Hannu 2006: *Kuu jättää jäljen*. [The Moon Leaves a Trace.] Jyväskylä: Atena.

Saisio, Pirkko 1998: *Pienin yhteinen jaettava*. [The smallest common multiple.] Helsinki: WSOY.

Saisio, Pirkko 2000:*Vastavalo*. [Counterlight.] Helsinki: WSOY.

Saisio, Pirkko 2003a: *Punainen erokirja*. [The Red Book of Separation.] Helsinki: WSOY.

Sandström, Peter 2004: *Manuskrift för pornografiska filmer*. [Manuscripts for pornographic films.] Helsingfors: Schildts.

Siirilä, Jussi 2010: *Historia on minut vapauttava*. [History shall vindicate me.] Helsinki: Gummerus.

Snellman, Anja & Jokisalo, Ulla 1998: *Side*. [Bond.] Helsinki: Otava.

Tapper, Harri 1998: *Missä kurkien aura on*. [Where cranes plough the sky.] Jyväskylä: Atena.

Turkka, Jouko 1994: *Häpeä*. [Shame.] Helsinki: Otava.

Vimma, Tuomas 2004: *Helsinki 12*. Helsinki: Otava.

Vimma, Tuomas 2005: *Toinen*. [Second.] Helsinki: Otava.

Vimma, Tuomas 2008: *Gourmet*. Helsinki: Otava.

Väisänen, Hannu 2004: *Vanikan palat*. [Pieces of Hard Bread.] Helsinki: Otava.

Väisänen, Hannu 2008: *Toiset kengät*. [Other Shoes.] Helsinki: Otava.

Väisänen, Hannu 2010: *Kuperat ja koverat*. [Convex and Concave.] Helsinki: Otava.

Abbott, Porter H. 1988: Autobiography, Autography, Fiction. Groundwork for Taxonomy of Textual Categories. *New Literary History*. Vol. 9: 3, 1–19.

Doubrovsky, Serge 1993: Autobiography / Truth / Psychoanalysis. Transl. Logan Whalen and John Ireland. *Genre*, Vol XXVI, 1, spring 1993, 27–42.

Foucault, Michel 1998: *Seksuaalisuuden historia*. [*The History of Sexuality*.] Transl. by Kaisa Sivenius. Helsinki: Gaudeamus.

Gasparini, Philippe 2004: *Est il je? Roman autobiographique et autofiction*. [*Is it I? Autobiographical novels and autofiction*.] Paris: Editions du Seuil.

Genette, Gérard 1993: *Fiction & diction*. Transl. Catherine Porter. Ithaca, London: Cornell University Press.

Haapanen, Irmeli 1998: *Minuuden askartelija*. [Crafting the ego.] Online archive of the newspaper Turun Sanomat at http://www.ts.fi/arkisto/haku.aspx?ts=1,0,0,0:0: 20871,0. Visited 6 June 2011.

Hännikäinen, Timo 2010 (ed.): *Mitä Houellebecq tarkoittaa?* [What does Houellebecq mean?] Turku: Savukeidas.

Koivisto, Päivi 2004: Anja Kauranen-Snellmanin omaelämäkerralliset romaanit autofiktioina. [Anja Kauranen-Snellman's autobiographical novels as autofiction.] In: Tuomo Lahdelma, Outi Oja, Keijo Virtanen (eds.), *Laji, tekijä, instituutio*. [*Genre, author, and institution*.] KTSV 56 (2003). Helsinki: SKS, 11–31.

Koivisto, Päivi 2005: Minähän se olen! [Here I am!] In: Pirjo Lyytikäinen, Jyrki Nummi & Päivi Koivisto (eds.), *Lajit yli rajojen*. [*Genres across borders*.] Helsinki: SKS, 177–205.

Lehtonen, Mikko 2001: *Post scriptum. Kirja medioitumisen aikakaudella*. [Post scriptum: A book on the era of mediazation.] Tampere: Vastapaino.

Lejeune, Philippe 1989: *On Autobiography*. Edited with foreword by Paul John Eakin. Transl. Katherine Leary. Minneapolis: University of Minnesota Press.

Website of the Life Story Association: http://www.elamantarina.fi/ Accessed 29 May 2011.

Makkonen, Anna 1995: Pamfletista tunnustukseen: lajimurros 1960–70-luvulla. Esimerkkinä Christer Kihlmanin *Ihminen joka järkkyi*. [From pamphlet to confessional: genre change in the 1960s and 70s: with examples from Christer Kihlman's *Mannen som skalv*. (The Quaking Man).] In: Markku Ihonen & Yrjö

Varpio (eds.), *Helmi simpukka joki. Kirjallisuushistoria tänään.* [Pearl Mussel River. Literary History Today.] Tietolipas 137. Helsinki: SKS, 102–114.

Makkonen, Anna 1996: Paljastuksia kaikilta vuosilta. [Revelations throughout Time.] In: Mervi Kantokorpi (ed.), *Muodotonta menoa. Kirjoituksia nykykirjallisuudesta.* [Formless goingson: Musings on contemporary literature.] Helsinki: WSOY, 98–115.

Niemi, Juhani 1999: Kirjallisuus ja sukupolvikapina. [Literature and Generational Rebellion.] In: Pertti Lassila (ed.), *Suomen kirjallisuushistoria 3. Rintamakirjeistä tietoverkkoihin.* [Finnish Literary History 3. From Letters from the Front lines to Network Communications.] Helsinki: SKS, 158–171.

Rojola, Lea 2002: Läheisyyden löyhkä käy kaupaksi. [The reek of proximity sells big.] In: Markku Soikkeli (ed.), *Kurittomat kuvitelmat. Johdatus 1990-luvun kotimaiseen kirjallisuuteen.* [*Undisciplined imaginings: An introduction to Finnish literature of the 1990s*]. Turku: Turun yliopiston taiteiden tutkimuksen laitoksen sarja A, No. 50, 69–100.

Saisio, Pirkko 2010: Muutama sana sivupersoonista. [A few words about alter egos.] In: Pirkko Saisio under the pseudonym of Eva Wein, *Puolimaailman nainen; Kulkue.* [Demi-monde; Parade.] Helsinki: Tammi, 5–14.

Saisio, Pirkko 1993: Elämää Jukka Larssonin ja Eva Weinin varjossa. [My life as Jukka Larsson and Eva Wein.] In: *Jukka Larsson. Kärsimystrilogia.* [From Trilogy of Suffering by Jukka Larsson.] Helsinki: WSOY, 419–439.

Saisio, Pirkko 2001: Pirkko Saisio. In: Ritva Haavikko (ed.), *Miten kirjani ovat syntyneet?* 4. [What inspired my books? 4.] Helsinki: WSOY, 336–369.

Salin, Sari 2008: *Narri kertojana.* [The Jester as Narrator.] Helsinki: SKS.

Sennett, Richard 1977: *The Fall of Public Man.* New York: Alfred A. Knopf.

Tarkka, Pekka 1992: Finis Finlandiae. [The End of all things Finnish.] *Helsingin Sanomat* 20.11.1992.

Unprinted sources

Saisio, Pirkko 2003b: Kirja A & Ö. Kirjailija Pirkko Saisio Tuula-Liina Variksen vieraana. [The A to Z of Books: Pirkko Saisio as a guest of Tuula-Liina Varis, Tv-programme.] Helsinki: Ikoni & Indeksi.

Kristina Malmio

Phoenix-Marvel Girl in the Age of *fin de siècle*

Popular Culture as a Vehicle to Postmodernism in *Diva* by Finland-Swedish author, Monika Fagerholm

Four years after the success of the novel *Underbara kvinnor vid vatten* in 1994, [*Wonderful Women by the Water*], Monika Fagerholm (b. 1961) published *Diva*, a novel with the intriguing subheading: "En uppväxts egna alfabet med docklaboratorium (en bonusberättelse ur framtiden)" [The Alphabet of an Adolescence with a Laboratory of Dolls (A Bonus Tale from the Future)].[1] *Diva* is a broad tale, altogether 445 pages, written solely from the perspective of its protagonist, a 13-year-old schoolgirl named Diva. The book depicts Diva's life, family and friends in a suburb of Helsinki, Finland in the 1970s. She is surrounded by many people, primarily her schoolmate SannaMaria and SannaMaria's mysterious, mute sister Kari, and Franses Fagerström, an older girl with a boyfriend and a dog. Diva's mother and her two, older brothers, her teacher Daniel, and boyfriend Leo are also of importance. Diva is not an "ordinary" teenage girl (see also Heinonen 2003, 157); she describes herself as tall and beautiful, a mathematical genius, extraordinarily intelligent, always hungry, and always Lucia at her school.[2] She is intellectually aware, familiar with philosophy and literature, sexually precocious, at times very adult, at times most adolescent. She is an omnipotent and self-reflexive character, who transgresses many boundaries in the novel, which likewise transgresses many conventions, in an omnipotent and self-reflexive way.

The novel's consequent confrontation with various established norms has been emphasised. For example, Amanda Doxtater remarks that *Diva* criticises traditions and explores strategies of how to exist within or against traditions, and especially how to redefine the relation between the female reader and the literary canon (Doxtater 2004, 125). The content and the narrative of the book are – as many writers have already pointed out – tricky to describe, because the novel is not a novel *about* Diva and her life and family; the novel and the protagonist are the same. *Diva* is Diva, and vice versa. "Solipsism in puberty", were the words used by the critic Pia Ingström in *Finlands svenska litteraturhistoria* II [Finland-Swedish Literary History 2] (Ingström 2000, 326) to describe the novel. According to the reviewer Johan Kjellberg (1998), it is a look inside the head of a teenage girl. The novel is a book about Diva's diary, and simultaneously also the diary (Kurikka 2005,

59–60). Besides being a depiction of the adolescence of a young girl, Diva, the novel is also a book in the genre "books for girls", and a self-conscious novel about writing (see Kurikka 2005, 57). The protagonist creates herself through her narration, in her narrative and she does it in a language that combines the many languages by which she is surrounded (see Stenwall 2001, 200). Diva's "babbling" is a mixture of words she has herself created – clichés, words and phrases from her mother, brothers and friends, the language and citations of her teachers, dialogues from films, typographic experiments (such as the use of bold type and capital letters, and a vignette with a small dog at the beginning of each chapter), and so on. This is all mediated through the consciousness of Diva herself, or, rather, two Divas. Kaisa Kurikka characterises the novel's narrative structure as "utterly complicated" and describes its two narrators in the following manner:

> One of them is Diva at the age of 13 telling her own story in the middle of everything; she is the Diva experiencing life while the story is being told. The other narrator is also Diva, but this time she is narrating the story from an unspecified time in the future. Both of the narrators use present tense (or sometimes future tense) as if they were in the middle of the events they are telling about, but the "later" Diva sometimes tells about her life retrospectively as if from a distance. Both narrators tell the same story, the younger Diva in a bit more elliptic and fragmented manner, the older Diva sometimes commenting on the happenings while she is telling about them. (Kurikka 2008, 59, see also, Kurikka 2005, 60.)

The postmodern features of the novel have been put forward in almost all texts written about the novel (e.g., Hedman 1998; Laitinen 2000; Stenwall 2001; Ingström 2000; Kurikka 2005). Scholars have commented upon the fragmented, mobile and many-voiced identity of the protagonist; the novel's heavy intertextuality with references to both high and low culture, and the consequent use of parody and irony have also been observed (see e.g., Heinonen 2003; Stenwall 2001;Laitinen 2000). The self-reflexiveness of *Diva* has been pointed out as one of its postmodern traits (Kurikka 2005, 57). By 1998, many of the features and literary strategies used by Fagerholm in the novel had already been employed in contemporary postmodern culture, especially in international and national literature and film. The novel is postmodern, or poststructuralist, according to the reviewer Kaj Hedman who also remarked: "Den kan upplevas som en tidsinlaga, som skriven efter moderecept. Men så enkelt är det inte. Snarare kan man få ett intryck av att Monika Fagerholm på ett skickligt sätt utnyttjar modefenomen för sina egna syften" (Hedman 1998) (It can be apprehended as up to date, written after a favourite recipe. It is, however, not that simple. Rather one thinks that Monika Fagerholm in a skilful manner makes use of an up-to-date phenomenon for her own purposes).

The novel has numerous textual traces for a reader to follow. In the novel, the intertextual allusions to other texts, authors and forms of culture cover a wide range: they include literature for children and youth as well as modernist prose, mass culture and high literature (Kåreland 2004,

127; Doxtater 2004; 128, 132; Heinonen 2003; 160; Kurikka 2005, 64, 71). Popular culture in its many forms – pop songs and films–is also alluded to in the novel. *Diva's* fanciful language universe is structured by repetition – certain citations are repeated in an almost ritualistic manner – a literary strategy Fagerholm used earlier in the novel *Underbara kvinnor vid vatten* (see also, Ingström 1995, 203). The repeated citations, then, become the emblems of the novel.[3] However, while ordinary novels usually have one or two emblems, Fagerholm's novel is characterised by a vast number emblems, used many times. One of the many repeated intertexts in *Diva* is that of Phoenix-Marvel Girl, a fictional comic book super heroine from comic strips published by the American media company, Marvel Comics.

In this article, I will examine Phoenix-Marvel Girl as an intertext (see Genette 1997, 1–2) to Diva, the protagonist; the narrator, and *Diva*, the novel, in order to discuss the significance of popular culture for the novel.[4] Phoenix-Marvel Girl has been mentioned in many analyses, but the significance of the super heroine or of popular culture for the novel has not yet been thoroughly analysed. I will show that the Phoenix Marvel-Girl has many (more) functions in the novel, and that there are several parallels between Diva and Phoenix-Marvel Girl that have not yet been discussed. Phoenix Marvel-Girl may also be Diva's idol, a super heroine with whom she identifies herself, as Åsa Stenwall (2001, 205, 229) has argued, but I think that is only a part of the significance of Phoenix-Marvel Girl for the novel. What I want to show is how the powers and abilities of Phoenix-Marvel Girl (generic conventions that occur in science fiction) are used in the story telling in *Diva*.[5]

In addition to intertextuality, I will also examine the importance of the novel within Finland-Swedish literature and consider *Diva* as a turning point, a node, within Finland-Swedish literature. Here the novel's use of popular culture is of central importance. *Diva* has been hailed as *the* new book of girls, but it is as much *the* new novel of Finland-Swedish literature, a novel that goes profoundly against the tradition of Finland-Swedish novels. The novel stages a struggle between modernism and postmodernism, and, by the use of popular culture, breaks the tradition of the so-called "narrow room" of Finland-Swedish literature in an almost grandiose way. With the powers of Phoenix-Marvel Girl, Finland-Swedish literature enters the age of mass communication, globalisation, and the Internet. It can be described as a science fiction novel written in a period of *fin de siècle*. According to John Docker, postmodernism as well as other *fin de siècle* periods in history are characterised by the following features:

> *Fin de siècle* periods are unusually intellectually turbulent and self-questioning, a curious effect, as if self-fulfilling prophecy, of the very self-consciousness of being at the end of a century. *Fin de siècle* periods are liminal, jumping out from between centuries, looking back on the old and forward to the new, placing past, present and future in unexpected, unforeseen, suddenly different relationships. Such periods are usually awash with futuristic glimmerings, prophecies, the new

and unpredicted. Yet also and equally are they times of Gothic, forebodings, sinister omens, *unheimlich*, forecasts of disaster, history as relentless drift into living death (Docker 1994, 103–104).

Docker's description of what is typical of fin de siècle periods is not only a depiction of postmodernism, but also could be a description of the characteristics of Fagerholm's *Diva*. The novel's fluctuation between present and future tense is a way to deal with questions of time, past, present, and future. *Diva* is indeed intellectually "unstable" and highly self-reflexive, and in a performative way, occupied with creating a prediction and simultaneously fulfilling it.

A Masterpiece and a Disappointment

"Surprise me", Diva's mother tells her, "Så vill jag att du ska vara för mig, Diva. **Ny. Fantastisk. Annorlunda.**" [That is how I want you to be for me, Diva. **New. Fantastic. Different.**] (Fagerholm 1998, 33. Emphasis in the original). Both the novel and the protagonist strive to fulfil this request. Diva, as well as *Diva*, have in common the ambition to be extraordinary and the novel was received as such. When it first appeared in 1998, the reviewers pointed out that the novel was in many ways new and different. For example Åsa Stenwall, the first to write a longer essay on the novel, declared: "Diva kräver inte en ny läsart. Diva kräver revolution" (Stenwall 2001, 241) (Diva does not demand a new kind of reading. Diva demands a revolution).

The critics were of opposite minds: the novel was called both a masterpiece and a disappointment (Kåreland 2004, 122), a modern classic (Sundström 2004) and an interesting failure (Beckman 1998). The comments varied; the critics were amused, confused and irritated. They emphasised the novel's new, experimental form and language, and the way the generic conventions of books for girls were used, parodied and recreated in it (see e.g., Kåreland 2004). The protagonist was perceived as something not before seen, an extraordinary girl character in the overall history of the novel (see e.g., Möller 1998). The commentators also remarked that this was the first time a suburb was the milieu of such an experimental novel. Overall, the critics and the scholars were united in their estimation that such a huge and experimental novel about a thirteen-year-old girl, had never before been written in Finland-Swedish literature. The closest examples of a book similar to *Diva*, were found in *The Catcher in the Rye*, the novel by J.D. Salinger published in 1951. Actually, this is a comparison put forward by the novel itself, and by the author. *Diva* includes repeated allusions to the story of Holden Caulfield, a teenage rebel and Fagerholm herself mentioned the importance of Salinger's novel in interviews (see Kåreland 2004, 130–131).

The Many Identities of Diva

The opening passage of the novel illustrates perfectly the hybrid nature of both the text and its protagonist. After the title "**Phoenix-Marvel Girl**" (bold type in the original), the first-person narrator boldly declares: "Jag är Diva, allt jag berättar är sant. Slut ögonen, dröm om det vackraste som finns. Öppna ögonen igen. Se mig. Flickkvinnan. DivaLucia. Tretton år, strax fjorton. BabyWonder. Hon man trodde inte fanns" (Fagerholm 1998, 11) (I am Diva, everything I tell you is true. Shut your eyes, dream of the most beautiful thing in existence. Open your eyes again. See me. The Girl-woman. DivaLucia. Thirteen years, almost fourteen. BabyWonder. The girl you didn't think existed. *Doxtater's transl.*). The protagonist is described in a series of both "real" and fictional figures: she is Phoenix-Marvel Girl, Diva, girl and woman, Lucia, BabyWonder. She invites the readers to dream, and see with their own eyes. This begins a constant play between "reality" and culture, literature and fantasy that continues throughout the novel. The boundaries of so-called reality are repeatedly transgressed (see also Stenwall 2001, 209). Gérard Genette defines 'intertextuality' as "a relationship of co-presence between two texts or among several texts". A text is actually present in another text in forms of quotations, or allusions. (Genette 1997, 1–2.) Why do I think, then, that Phoenix-Marvel Girl is of special importance among the many intertextual allusions in the novel? After all, the novel is heavily intertextual. There are, I argue, several ways in which its centrality is put forward in the text.

First, the title of the opening passage of the novel is that of "Phoenix-Marvel Girl". It denotes that the identity of Phoenix Marvel-Girl is (even literally) above all the other representations mentioned in the passage. The passage is not only the opening episode of the novel, and therefore of central importance, but it also summons the many "embodiments" of the protagonist in the novel. Besides Phoenix-Marvel Girl, the speaking "I" identifies herself as "Diva", a nickname with many allusions attached to it. Diva, read literally, is a woman who pretends or a star who takes everything out of being a star. In the novel, Diva is the name of a dog in a play called 'Best in Show'. It is also the name of a doll with golden hair made of yarn, with green buttons as eyes, and without clothes. "**Saknar inte likhet**" (Is not without likeness), the protagonist comments ironically, when she sees the doll (Fagerholm 1998, 29). Diva describes herself as both girl and woman, and a combination of Diva and Lucia in the same person. While a diva stands for a somewhat pretentious female star or aspiring star, Lucia is the opposite, the symbol of light, purity and innocence. They are connected by the fact that both are at the centre of other people's attention. In addition, Diva is "BabyWonder", perhaps a combination of a small child and Wonder Girl (see Rovin 1985, 337). The "names" of the representations, "girlwoman", "DivaLucia" and "BabyWonder", are written as one word to emphasise the hybrid nature of Diva. The elements and combinations that constitute her "identity" are unpredictable, and already the opening of the novel exposes a postmodernist attitude (see Docker 2004, xvii–xviii). All in all, Diva's story opens with a list of almost parodic combinations of representations of girls and women (see also Kurikka 2005, 64).

Phoenix-Marvel Girl is not only the title of Diva's introduction of herself, but also an intertextual trace that is repeated in the narration. At the end of the novel, Fagerholm gives the reader a list of references. "The Encyclopedia of Super Heroes" written by "Jeff Raven" [sic!] is one of the books mentioned (Fagerholm 1998, 447). *The Encyclopedia of Superheroes* is a book that tries to make science out of comics with an introduction in which Jeff Rovin relates the development of the gods in ancient mythologies to the super heroes of the 1980s. In the book, a number of "Super heroes" are introduced in a systematic manner.[6] With the allusion to Phoenix-Marvel Girl, Fagerholm, then, enters a dialogue with Rovin's book, Marvel Company and international popular culture.

At three places in the novel, there are more or less extensive, direct citations from Rovin's book[7] within which the Marvel Girl is described; in other places in the novel, the protagonist Diva refers to Phoenix-Marvel Girl. Altogether, most of the Phoenix-Marvel Girl intertexts occur at the end of the novel.

Phoenix-Marvel Girl as a Paratext

In the three major citations, the descriptions of Phoenix-Marvel Girl from the Rovin book are placed as epigraphs of the chapters to come. They are not translated into Swedish, but cited in English, and therefore differ from the rest of the text. When one scrutinises the graphic appearance of the passages that include references to Phoenix-Marvel Girl, one notices, however, that even all the other chapters within major chapters appear the same. In that sense, the novel consists of all prefaces (see even Kurikka 2005, 59).[8] Yet, the opening passages that refer to Phoenix-Marvel Girl are, I argue, what Genette calls 'paratexts' (Genette 1997). Paratexts – titles, subtitles, prefaces, postfaces, book covers, and many other kinds of secondary signals – provide texts with variable settings and sometimes a commentary. Paratexts are of importance, Genette argues, because they are "probably one of the privileged fields of operation of the pragmatic dimension of the work – i.e., of its impact upon the reader" (Genette 1997, 3). The fact that the chapters or passages that refer to Phoenix-Marvel Girl, are at the beginning of the chapters, makes them more significant than the following passages, and give them the status of paratexts. Moreover, the long citations from the Rovin book differ from the overall text, and can even therefore be considered as paratexts, or to put it differently, as epigraphs to the chapters.

As already mentioned, Kurikka alternates her commentary between two narrators in *Diva*, the younger Diva who experiences, and the older, "later" Diva, who narrates the story in an unspecified future (Kurikka 2008, 59). It is often difficult, she remarks, if not impossible, to distinguish between the two narrators (Kurikka 2005, 60).[9] I will make this even more complicated; I think there is yet another narrator in the story, the one who narrates the title of the book, and the headings of the chapters, texts that are situated "outside" the actual narration. This is the narrator of the paratexts, a narrator who might be identical with the younger or older Diva, who narrates her story in the present and in the future, but not necessarily. The references to Phoenix-Marvel Girl within the story belong to Diva herself. However, this distinction between the narrator and the two Divas, narrating the story, is arbitrary and used only for the analysis. In the story, the narrator levels between the younger Diva and the older Diva are transgressed repeatedly. However, in the case of the titles, it is clear: they are narrated by a narrator.

The first one to call Diva "Phoenix-Marvel Girl", is the narrator in the title of the passage; the other representations listed under the heading Phoenix-Marvel Girl, those of a woman and a girl, Lucia and BabyWonder, are made by the first-person narrator, who declares: "I am Diva, [...] See me. The Girl-woman. DivaLucia. Thirteen years, almost fourteen. BabyWonder". In the paratexts to come, Phoenix-Marvel Girl is presented by a narrator, who quotes Rovin. Besides the allusions to Phoenix-Marvel Girl made by the narrator, Diva herself mentions the comic strip heroine several times.[10] Not only the fact that the opening passage of the novel has the title "Phoenix-Marvel Girl", but also the broadness of the citations from Rovin's book, and their placement at the beginning of the chapters, signals that Phoenix-Marvel Girl is – among the many references and intertexts of the novel – of central importance.

The Narrator's References to Phoenix-Marvel Girl

Critics and scholars have perceived Phoenix-Marvel Girl only in relation to the protagonist, Diva (Sundström 1998; Laitinen 2000; Stenwall 2001). I, however, argue that the intertext to the comic strip super heroine has different functions for the protagonist, the narrator and the novel *Diva*. When one scrutinises the intertextual occurrences and use of Phoenix-Marvel Girl in *Diva*, one notices that the protagonist Diva's references to Phoenix-Marvel Girl are different from those of the narrator who uses the comic series heroine in the paratexts, and that that in turn differs from the significance of Phoenix-Marvel Girl for Monika Fagerholm, the writer. The role of the narrator is clearly an informative one. She accounts for the central information about Phoenix-Marvel Girl. In the paratexts that consider Phoenix-Marvel Girl, her story and powers are only gradually revealed to the reader, who is unfamiliar with Marvel Comics and the X-Men series within which Phoenix-Marvel Girl is one central figure. After the first mention of her name at the beginning of the novel, the narrator makes the next allusion to Phoenix-Marvel Girl on page 53. The paratext, an extensive citation from *The Encyclopedia of Super Heroes*, begins chapter 2, called "Schopenhauers lilla gröna hund (Mina delvis vilda år med Franses Fagerström)" (Fagerholm 1998, 51) [Schopenhauer's little green dog. (My semi-wild years with Franses Fagerström)].

Here under the title "**Marvel Girl**", a direct citation from the Rovin book is presented with the following topics: Alter Ego; First Appearance; Occupation; Costume; Tools and Weapons, and Quote.[11] One of the typical features of the super heroes is, Rovin writes, that "they achieve anonymity by assuming a mortal identity or alter ego" (Rovin 1985, ix). Phoenix-Marvel Girl lives under the pseudonym Jean Grey, and she is a student and a model. Her occupations are, then, the same as those Diva sees as hers, and she is, Heinonen writes, the double of Diva (Heinonen 2003, 163). Jean Grey first appeared in 1963 in X-Men, a Marvel Comics series. Her "Tools and Weapons" are "None", and the declaration typical of her, "The quote", is: "What kind of school *is* this, sir?" (Fagerholm 1998, 53, Rovin 1985, 182, xi). The detailed description of the outfit of the Marvel Girl in the Rovin text is quoted in full by the narrator. The account of the two, various costumes, reveal for those unacquainted with the comic-strip character, that Jean Grey in fact has two different "embodiments". She wears different suits when she is Marvel Girl and when she is Phoenix. It is also important to note that nowhere does Rovin use in his description the composite name, "Phoenix-Marvel Girl", which the narrator uses to open Diva's story. In *The Encyclopedia of Superheroes*, Jean Grey is either "Marvel Girl", or "Phoenix", which is her later incarnation.

The second major citation from Rovin's book comes on page 373, as a paratext to chapter 4 with the title "Det senare alfabetet" (The Later Alphabet), under the heading "**Phoenix-Marvel Girl**". Here the biography of Phoenix-Marvel Girl is presented. Jean is a mutant, and after she witnesses her friend's death at the age of ten, Jean's latent telepathic powers come to the surface. She is taken to see Professor X, who manages to turn off her telepathic powers until she matures sufficiently to handle them. He also shows her how to use another latent power, telekinesis, the ability to move objects on the ground and through the air without touching them. Later on, after Jean Grey has tried to live a normal life, she is drawn into an adventure in which she is killed:

> […] After several years, Professor X lifts the blockade he'd used on her telepathy, making Jean all the more powerful. In time, she decides to leave the group[12] to pursue a nonsuper life. Still, she manages to become embroiled in an adventure involving the super-robot Sentinels, and dies in the crash of a spaceship; however her intense adrenal state at the time, and her mental powers allows Jean to tap the "phoenix force", the collective emotional output of all sentient things in the universe. Using the force to revive her body, she becomes the Phoenix; able to soar through space and fire blasts of energy mighty enough to send most any other superhero or villain through a wall, she reaffiliates herself with the X-men (Fagerholm 1998, 373, a direct citation from Rovin).

Here, in a paratext almost at the end of the novel (on page 373 of 445), some of the central characteristics of Jean Grey and Phoenix are presented. She is associated with energy and fire, and possesses supernatural powers and abilities. Jean Grey's central transformation is also explained. Only after her death, does she become Phoenix. The story of Jean Grey includes a long series of transformations and deaths followed by resurrection and the possession of mightier powers than before. Phoenix-Marvel Girl also has many different incarnations and names (see http://www.marvel.com/universe/Phoenix_(Jean_Grey)).[13]

Characters with such super powers as those shown by Phoenix-Marvel Girl are common in popular culture. Patricia Waugh in her book, *Metafiction. The Theory and Practice of Self-Conscious Fiction* has commented upon the use of popular forms in self-reflexive novels. Her central idea, based on the Russian formalist views of literary evolution, is that the defamiliarisation of popular forms in new contexts "[…] uncovers aesthetic elements that are appropriate for expressing the serious concerns of the new age" (Waugh 1984, 79). Popular forms are applied in metafictions because a large audience has access to them and is already familiar with them (Waugh 1984, 86).[14] For example, the use of detective-story plots in metafictions provides readers with the satisfaction that is attached to the predictable (Waugh 1984, 82). The use of popular forms in 'serious' fiction is crucial for "undermining narrow and rigid critical definitions of what constitutes, or is appropriately to be termed 'good literature'"; Waugh writes and argues, that the continuing assimilation of popular forms into 'serious fiction' ensures the renewal of the novel genre (1984, 86).

Waugh's arguments raise many questions and comments related to *Diva*. First, is Phoenix-Marvel Girl actually defamiliarised in the novel? The answer is both yes and no. On the one hand, a Finland-Swedish experimental novel is an unusual context in which a science fiction comic book character might occur. One can argue, then, that an almost parodic transcontextualisation (see Hutcheon 1985, 31–32) of Phoenix-Marvel Girl takes place in the novel. On the other hand, the novel is about a thirteen-year-old-girl. Like many children and teenagers, Diva reads comics, and the comic-strip super heroine, Phoenix-Marvel Girl, belongs to the world of youngsters. Such reading is a dimension of her childish qualities. In this context, Phoenix-Marvel Girl is not defamiliarised, but represents a "realistic" element of the life and consciousness of a young girl in the 1970s, the setting of the story. One of the obvious functions of Phoenix-Marvel Girl in *Diva* is, then, to contribute to the creation of a teenage world, to depict the mental landscape of a teenage girl. The fact that the passages from the Rovin book are in Fagerholm's book cited in English marks a change. Such large parts of text written in English seldom occur in Finland-Swedish novels. The English citations are, however, a comment on the fact that the popular culture by which the country is surrounded is mostly American or English. English is also the language of the culture of youth.

According to Waugh, popular forms are brought into play because there already exists an audience familiar with them. The fact that Fagerholm cites whole passages from *The Encyclopedia of Superheroes* can, however, be taken as a sign that she is unsure of how well her readers actually are acquainted with Phoenix-Marvel Girl, an American comic strip, TV and feature film character.[15] In the Finland-Swedish literary context, the allusions to Phoenix-Marvel Girl do not assume, I think, a large audience already familiar with the comic-strip character. However, the allusions to Phoenix-Marvel Girl do undermine a rigid notion of what "good" literature contains by introducing popular culture into the Finland-Swedish novel. One of the typical features of postmodernism is the breakdown of the distinction between art and popular culture. It has become increasingly difficult to agree upon criteria that serve to differentiate art from popular culture and to maintain a barrier between art and popular culture. (Strinati 2004, 207–208.) The presence of Phoenix-Marvel Girl explodes the limits between the serious literature and popular culture in the novel. The allusions to a character at home in popular culture, partly create and emphasise the postmodern characteristics of the novel. The use of popular culture is a regular feature in postmodern novels (see e.g., Strinati 2004, 208; Waugh 1984, 22, 81).

The third and final paratext, within which Phoenix-Marvel Girl occurs, is only a very short one, at the beginning of the last chapter, "Men jazzslingorna" (But jazz loops). It has, once again, the title "**Phoenix-Marvel Girl**", written in the text in bold type, and is found on page 431. Here Fagerholm cites only the following, concluding lines from Rovin's description of Marvel Girl. "Comment: As Phoenix, Jean enjoys cult status. Had she not died, according to What if # 27, Jean would eventually have lost control of her emotions and one day destroyed the universe."

The Diva-narrators with the Powers of Phoenix-Marvel Girl

The paratexts in *Diva* promote the importance of Phoenix-Marvel Girl for an understanding of the novel. The question is, then, why does the author draw the reader's attention repeatedly to Phoenix-Marvel Girl, and why her, of all the different popular culture heroines?

Feminist scholars and critics have been fascinated by the omnipotent qualities of both the protagonist Diva and the novel. It has been pointed out that *Diva* is a novel about a girl without limits (Stenwall 2001, 203), that Diva blasts the boundaries of what a girl may do, and Fagerholm blows up the limits of the genre (Sundström 2004). Kurikka argues that *Diva* is a utopian text; it creates a new room, at the same time both a non-place and a happy place when it is read in relation to earlier stories about young girls (Kurikka 2005, 69–70, see also Stenwall 2001, 203). Mainly the novel has been read in relation to a genre called 'books for young girls', a genre that typically has a young, female protagonist, and depicts her life at home and school, her parents, eventual boyfriend and mates.

What I want to claim here, is that the narrator's and the author's literary strategies remind the reader of the capacities of Phoenix-Marvel Girl on many points. Many of the omnipotent qualities of the novel pointed out by scholars are actually related to Phoenix-Marvel Girl. Jean Grey possesses great, limitless powers, which enable her to communicate with others telepathically, to read minds, influence and control the minds of others, project her thoughts into the minds of others, initiate astral travel, and mentally astonish opponents with "pure psionic force". She also holds telekinetic powers, allowing her to levitate and manipulate objects and others, generate force fields, fly, and produce huge explosions. She can telepathically take away or control people's natural bodily functions and senses, like sight, hearing, smell, taste, or even mutant powers. Another result of her telepathy is that she is gifted with "total recall", a memory with extreme accuracy and abundant volume. She can even create star gates that can transport her to anywhere in the universe immediately. (http://www.marvel.com/universe/Phoenix_(Jean_Grey), http://en.wikipedia.org/wiki/Jean_Grey) Many of her capacities are connected to the fact that she is the heroine of a science fiction comic series.

The comic-strip character can read minds, and so can the two narrating Divas. "SannaMaria är genomskinlig, öppen som en bok", Diva remarks (Fagerholm 1998, 109) (SannaMaria is transparent, open like a book). She knows, for example, what and how SannaMaria thinks when she is being observed. When Diva's mother tries to turn her mind against her friend Franses, Diva reminds herself of being Phoenix Marvel-Girl, and therefore being able to see through her (Fagerholm 1998, 87). Everything in the story is communicated through the mind of Diva, and she is also, more or less, in the head of the persons she depicts as she describes their thoughts, emotions, and memories. This is, of course, typical of all omniscient narrators, who are in total control of their stories. But, Diva's all powerful narration also reminds of and relates to the telepathic skills of Phoenix-Marvel Girl, and all her omnipotent qualities and strategies can be seen as expressions of the Phoenix-Marvel Girl dimension in her.

Phoenix-Marvel Girl is able to travel in time and space. In *Diva*, as the two narrating Divas in the story mix present and future tense with constant repetitions of the already-happened, boundaries of time and space are also transgressed. As in Jean Grey's telekinetic travels, the many journeys in time that occur in the narration are not limited by 'natural' boundaries of time and place, or by the conventions of literary realism. The protagonists move frequently between different levels of time, as in the following passage from the novel: "Och jag kommer att ha fyllt många sidor i min dagbok och dem kommer vi att gå igenom med en frenesi som skulle imponera även på den mest blaserade sexolog. [...] Men ännu är det sportlov, jag ligger i min säng, jag kan inte sova." (Fagerholm 1998, 157) [And I will be writing many sides in my diary and we will be going through them with such a frenzy that could make an impression even on the most blasé sexologist. [...] But it is still the sports holidays,[16] I lie on my bed, I am not able to sleep.]. Elsewhere, Diva remarks that SannaMaria stands at a table in "a future which will soon be here, just in some years (Fagerholm 1998, 202) and continues, after a description of what happens in the future, that "**Och nu**, [...], I detta NU när inget av det där ännu har hänt." (Fagerholm 1998, 203) (And now [...], in this NOW when nothing of that yet has happened.). Or, when she declares that: "Jag är inte längre här när det händer. Men det är en historia som redan finns." (Fagerholm 1998, 422) (I am not anymore here when this happens. But it is a history that already exists.). The "unnatural", non-linear temporal movements are characteristic of the style of the novel. They show and emphasise the two narrators' power to transcend time and place. The Phoenix-Marvel Girl-like abilities of the narrators to travel in time and space relate the novel, not only to science fiction, but also to postmodernity. Confusion over time and space is typical of postmodern culture; it is less likely to reflect a coherent sense of space or time. Dominic Strinati concludes that: "Because of the speed and scope of modern mass communications, and the relative ease and rapidity with which people and information can travel, time and space become less stable and comprehensible, and more confused and incoherent" (Strinati 2004, 208).

The way in which the replies and language of other characters are cited and repeated in Diva's narration, as well as her detailed descriptions of all the things that have happened, is like a literary adaptation of the Phoenix-Marvel Girl's telepathic, telekinetic skills and her capacity of "total recall". The novel can be seen an expression of incredible memory, the talent of being able to memorise with extreme accuracy and abundant volume. Diva's story is like a super diary, the diary of an omnipotent mutant, with a memory that is one thousand times more precise and detailed than the memory and diaries of "ordinary" people.

There are many parallels, then, between the narration style in *Diva* and the fantastic capacities of Phoenix-Marvel Girl. The omnipotence of Diva, pointed out by many scholars and writers, both relates to and reminds of the omnipotence of Jean Grey and Phoenix-Marvel Girl. One can argue that Monika Fagerholm transfers and transforms the omnipotent, supernatural powers and skills offered by the heroine of a science fiction comic-strip book into narrative possibilities actualised in a Finland-Swedish suburban reality of the 1970s. This surely is a defamiliarisation of Phoenix-Marvel Girl, the comic strip heroine, in the sense Waugh means (Waugh 1984, 79). The use of the popular comic strip heroine in a new, Finland-Swedish context, "uncovers", as Waugh argues, "aesthetic elements that are appropriate for expressing the serious concerns of the new age". Stenwall (2001, 204, see also 229) interprets Phoenix-Marvel Girl as the idol of Diva. I think that Phoenix-Marvel Girl is not only the idol of Diva and *Diva*, but also of the author, Monika Fagerholm.

Diva's Use of Phoenix-Marvel Girl

I will now discuss the way in which the protagonist uses allusions to Phoenix-Marvel Girl. The similarities between the protagonist Diva and Phoenix-Marvel Girl have already been mentioned. Both are students and later models; they have paranormal capacities and face the death of their friend (Heinonen 2003, 163). In the novel, Diva is taken to see a school psychologist as Jean Grey is taken to Professor X. According to Kurikka (2005, 63), Diva is never modest, and she does not dream of superheroes because she considers herself to be one. "Phoenix Phoenix Marvel-Girl" is according to Diva, her own special mantra (Fagerholm 1998, 250). By repeating the mantra to herself, she tries to produce or produces supernatural powers.[17]

There are however even differences between the protagonist and Phoenix-Marvel Girl that have not yet been examined. In the parts where Diva alludes to Phoenix-Marvel Girl, she repeats the facts the narrator cites about Phoenix-Marvel Girl from Rovin's book. The protagonist Diva is, however, not at all as super as Jean Grey (or the narrator, and the author). When one looks at the situations within which Diva herself associates to Phoenix-Marvel Girl, one notices that the allusions occur when Diva tries to master her emotions in conflicts with her mother, brother, or friends. The intertextual references to Phoenix-Marvel Girl take place in situations characterised by a struggle for power, when someone tries or actually exorcises physical or mental power over the protagonist. These circumstances are characterised by the fact that she is all but omnipotent. The omnipotence of Phoenix-Marvel Girl, is, then, opposed to the protagonist's actual lack of powers. The allusions, when used by the protagonist, put forward the darker side of the story – Diva's smallness and lack of all kinds of power (see also Kåreland 2004, 136; Stenwall 2001, 226). She fears breaking apart due to her anger, sadness or disappointment, and identifies with the Phoenix-Marvel Girl. "**Jag är Phoenix-Marvel Girl**" [I am Phoenix-Marvel Girl], Diva whispers to herself when she has struggled with her brother, has been hit in the nose, bleeds, and has lost (Fagerholm 1998, 129). She asks her friend, Franses, whether she thinks Diva is Phoenix Marvel-Girl, and Franses crudely replies: "Du är full av skit [...] Jag tror inte på ett ord av det du berättar för mig." [You are full of shit [...] I don't believe a word of what you are saying.], and asks her to be quiet (Fagerholm 1998, 243). Before this passage, there is one, in which Franses has told Diva that she is crazy, and Diva feels sad and betrayed. She imagines herself rushing into the arms of her mother, and thinks: "**Phoenix-Marvel Girl. Tools and Weapons: None**" (Fagerholm 1998, 184). Even in this situation, she refers to Phoenix-Marvel Girl, but is her opposite.

The name, Phoenix-Marvel Girl, is repeatedly mentioned in bold type, which furthermore emphasises its significance in the story (although many citations in the text are written in bold type). The comic strip super heroine is, then, an important cultural resource with which Diva encourages herself, and one more component in the list mentioned at the beginning of the story, the one that includes DivaLucia, and so on. Diva even tries to act like Phoenix-Marvel Girl. She makes an effort to use the power of thought to make Daniel, her teacher with whom she is in love, to come to her, but fails. She, then, fantasises how she breaks a window:

> **Hur skall det uttryckas:** jag slår näven genom glasrutan som spricker i tusen bitar för glaset har en elektronisk spänning i sig som gör att det inte skärvas utan smulas. "Phoenix, alltså. Marvel Girl. Naturligtvis är det en fantasi." Det händer inte. Ingenting händer. (Fagerholm 1998, 112.) (How to express it: I hit my fist through a window that cracks into thousand pieces because of the

electric tension in the glass that makes the glass break not into pieces but to scrap. "Phoenix, that is. Marvel Girl. Of course it is fantasy." It does not happen. Nothing happens.)

Diva also looks at her teacher's cat with a "phoenix gaze", a kind of X-ray vision (Fagerholm 1998, 388), and acts like a heroine on a small scale. By mistake she drops her (or Franses') dog in the middle of rush hour traffic, but then stops the cars and lifts the dog up. She then thinks she has saved the dog's life and says to herself: "**Phoenix-Marvel Girl**" (Fagerholm 1998, 287). This passage is an example of a parodic transcontextualisation of the comic strip heroine; the smallness of Diva's action is opposed to the immense powers of Phoenix-Marvel Girl in her struggle to save the world. In another passage, Diva feels herself threatened by Franses' boyfriend, in a competition for the love of Franses. She thinks: "**Försök ta på henne så får du se.** FJÅNG PÅFF, jag är Phoenix-Marvel Girl." (Fagerholm 1998, 392.) (Try to touch her and you will see. FJÅNG PÅFF, I am Phoenix-Marvel Girl.) She here uses words that imitate the conventions of how the sounds of punches are represented in the comic strip world.

In the world of Diva, Phoenix-Marvel Girl is also a comic strip character that represents "bad" American popular culture. Diva's mother hates, according to Diva, Phoenix-Marvel Girl. In a very metaliterary passage with the heading "De förbjudna uttrycken" (The forbidden expressions), Diva is awake in the middle of the night. She contemplates herself and her development, discusses the irony of teenage girls, how it differs from her mother's use of irony which is from books on literary theory, and which she uses above all, when Diva tries to act as an Ordinary Teenager. Diva describes herself and Sebbe Nsson, a schoolmate, standing together on the roof of their school watching the stars, then, seemingly abruptly, turns to a discussion on culture and literature:

> Stått på Östra läroverkets tak, ett huvud för sig bredvid ett annat huvud för sig, medan Vintergatan sprängt sig över dessa huvuden som ett bevis på att det oerhörda kan vara sant.
> **Phoenix** alltså. **Phoenix-Marvel Girl.**
> Min mamma HATAR Phoenix-Marvel Girl. Hon tycker att jag i stället för att sitta med näsan begraven i dåliga seriemagasin ska läsa seriös litteratur och börjar varmt rekommendera vissa verk av den storartade författaren Stendhal som är hennes speciella favorit på grund av det sinistra tonfallet ... [...] man kan inte vara ung och söt och lyssna på henne, jag lyssnar inte på henne, men inte för att jag är ung och söt utan för att jag mediterar med mitt eget speciella mantra och mitt eget speciella mantra ÄR Phoenix Phoenix-Marvel Girl. (Fagerholm 1998, 250).[18]
> [Standing on the roof of the Östra läroverket [the name of the school], a head of one's own standing next to another head of one's own, while the Milky Way explodes above these heads as a proof that the unprecedented can be true.
> **Phoenix** that is. **Phoenix-Marvel Girl.**
> My mother HATES Phoenix-Marvel Girl. She thinks that I should, instead of sitting buried in bad serial comics, read serious literature and recommends

warmly the works of the magnificent author Stendhal, who is her absolute favourite because of his sinister style ... [...] one cannot be young and sweet and listen to her, I do not listen to her, but is not because I am young and sweet but because I am meditating on my own special mantra and my own special mantra IS Phoenix Phoenix Marvel-Girl].

"Milky Way" and "explodes" are the words in the passage that associate to the comic strip heroine. Diva is familiar with Phoenix-Marvel Girl from comic strips, which she reads with great intensity. Her mother, (who in certain parts of the novel, I think, can be interpreted as the double of the author) however, prefers Henry Miller, Stendhal, and other authors of high literature, and, according to Diva, hates Phoenix-Marvel Girl. In the passage above, the relation between "high", established literature, and "low", popular culture, is posited in a self-reflexive and, also, self-ironic manner. The culture of European, educated adults is opposed to the American popular culture of teenagers. This opposition is also present elsewhere in the novel. Diva's friend Franses obviously represents the popular and her boyfriend Leo high culture. According to Diva, Franses' hobbies are to bite her nails, to be with her boyfriend, to sing songs from musicals, to run out in the night, to be a scout in the woods, and engage in a circus life (Fagerholm 1998, 58). She belongs to the suburb, and on her underpants is written, "Love is". She likes to draw Diva, but she is no good. Franses is, according to Diva's mother, somebody Diva should look out for, because she is an "untalented careerist" (Fagerholm 1998, 86). Leo, on the other hand, lives in the centre of the city, prefers French new-wave films, Eisenstein, experimental films by Michelangelo Antonioni, and other classics, shown in the "serious darkness of the film archives" (Fagerholm 1998, 74). He plans a career as a film director, and is very serious. Diva's mother, who prefers high culture, consequently, dislikes Franses and favours Leo. In the novel, Diva's oscillation between her love for Franses, and for Leo, is also a fluctuation between popular culture and "high" literature. While modernist critical theory saw mass culture as the main danger to civilisation, postmodern theorists are, at least some of them, by contrast optimistic (Strinati 2004, 207–208; see also Docker 1994, xvii, and Doxtater 2004, 126–128). According to John Docker, postmodernism "... does not ascribe to popular culture phenomena any single commanding meaning or purpose." Instead, it is

[...] interested in a plurality of forms and genres, a pluralising of aesthetic criteria, where such forms and genres may have long and fascinating histories, not as static and separate but intertwined, interacting, conflicting, contesting, playing off against each other, mixing in unpredictable combinations, protean in energy, moving quickly between extremes, from pathos to farce, intensity to burlesque, endlessly fertile as narrative, theatricality, and performance (Docker 1994, xvii–xviii).

In the background of postmodernism, lurks literary modernism, and its ideas about popular culture, Docker argues. The features in *Diva* that actually signal the novel's relation to literary modernism are the requirements uttered by Diva's high culture mother, that one should be "New. Fantastic. Different". They are the project and evaluative criteria of modernist art. Literary modernism drew a barrier between "high" and "low" culture, and grounded on a hierarchical apprehension of culture, where the highly educated elite, high above the common readers, apprehended as uneducated and less civilised, were engaged in the cultural cultivation of the less privileged (see e.g., Docker 1994, 26–31, 169, Strinati 2004, 2–10). The entrance of Phoenix-Marvel Girl and by that even of popular culture in *Diva,* and Finland-Swedish literature, signals a new era. Diva's world consists of endless combinations of both popular and high culture. Neither of them dominates, and Diva moves unlimitedly in a very postmodern way between the two cultural poles. The gap between the aesthetic preferences of the different generations, Diva's mother and Diva herself, is also the gap the novel is about to overcome. Diva, the protagonist, can be read as a personification of a literature about to mature, still in the middle of a struggle between modernism and postmodernism (see also Stenwall 2001, 222).

Later on, Diva has a conversation with her mother in which she takes over central passages from the story of Phoenix-Marvel Girl and her paranormal powers. The mother reveals that she is afraid of her children becoming grown up and losing them. She then asks if Diva likes her new boyfriend, called "Räddaren".[19] Diva asks, in a crude, teenage way, if it matters, and her mother asks if she always has to be devious. Diva replies, then, that she is going to travel far away with Franses, but then she remembers that she is not friends with Franses anymore. She also realises that the fact that their friendship has ended will make her mum glad because she does not like Franses, so Diva quickly changes the subject to Phoenix-Marvel Girl. She offers her mother a story about herself as Jean Grey about to become a superhero with paranormal powers. As long as she tells the story, she identifies herself with Phoenix-Marvel Girl; she says that she is "**Jane** [sic!] **Grey**" (Fagerholm 1998, 395) and imitates the characteristic reply of the comic strip heroine. Diva also relates to the biography of Jean Grey. "Reality" enters, when Diva asks herself to stop fantasising, making up stories, considering herself to be a Phoenix-Marvel Girl. Some pages later, when the reply is repeated, it is revealed that it is her mother (Fagerholm 1998, 399), who wants her to quit, and that Diva has told her mother about Phoenix-Marvel Girl just to have something to talk about (Fagerholm 1998, 400).[20] Here Phoenix-Marvel Girl is associated with the protagonist's childish fantasies and with a tension between a fantasy world and "reality" (see Rönnholm 1998).

The tension between childish fantasies and the reality put forward by other people is central to the theme of explosion, taken up by Diva several times in accordance with Phoenix Marvel-Girl. Diva's prolonged, highly self-reflexive considerations on culture, literature, the irony of schoolgirls and the necessity of writing a novel with sympathetic, warm and strong heroines with whom everyone can identify, closes with a conclusion that she is never going to write a book (although the novel is about her writing her own story in the form of a diary). Instead, she will end up in a novel about photo models in the future, but that is not, according to her, going to affect her courage to face life. This leads her to discuss her relation to the World and Reality, and she mentions that she does not agree with "our discussions with each other". The narration, rich in associations used in *Diva*, leads Diva from thoughts on literature and culture to communication, therapy, and reality, and further on to Phoenix-Marvel Girl. She then adds: "Men man måste fortsätta **konversera** i alla fall om man inte tänkt spränga världen eller sig själv i bitar./ Phoenix. Phoenix Marvel-Girl." (Fagerholm 1998, 253). (One has to continue with conversation after all if one does not intend to explode the world or oneself into pieces. Phoenix. Phoenix-Marvel Girl.) Communication is there in order not to blast the world, and the mantra to calm her.

Later, Diva repeats the idea of explosion, a theme connected to thoughts on destruction. She returns to the destiny of Phoenix-Marvel Girl, who broke into pieces, when she understood that her paranormal powers, originally trained and channelled right by the Professor X to serve a good cause, had grown too great for her to control (Fagerholm 1998, 396). Phoenix-Marvel Girl fights for a good cause, and rescues the world by exploding into pieces, in a self-conscious act. She represents not only omnipotent powers and a mastery of time and space, but also self-destruction, death and resurrection. The explosion of oneself, or the world – the dilemma Jean Grey is confronted with due to her supernatural powers – is in the case of Diva transformed into a fear of mental explosion because of lack of power.[21]

Popular Culture and the "Resurrection" of the Finland-Swedish Novel

I have above discussed the significance of Phoenix-Marvel Girl as an intertext in *Diva*. Phoenix-Marvel Girl is the protagonist's idol, her object of identification and the origin of her fantasy of omnipotence. Phoenix-Marvel Girl gives the narrators and the author vehicles typical of science fiction out of which to create something new, fantastic and different. It enables the author to transgress many literary boundaries. The comic strip heroine also stands for the "bad" popular culture that usurps the time and interest of youngsters, and is, in the eyes of their parents, a threat to their development. Phoenix Marvel Girl, the comic strip character with telekinetic and telepathic powers, who dies several times and is born anew with even greater powers than before, is also a metaphor for the entire novel, and even for the project of the author. Phoenix-Marvel Girl is, then, one of the many possible interpretative keys offered by the novel itself.

However, there are still some passages on which to comment in the relation between the novel and the comic strip heroine. Waugh argues that certain popular forms are more likely than others are at particular times to be taken up as modes of serious expression. She concludes: "The choice depends upon each set of historical and cultural circumstances" (1984, 80).

Why, then, use Phoenix-Marvel Girl? What exactly are "the serious concerns of the new age" (Waugh 1984, 79) that Phoenix-Marvel Girl connects to in *Diva*? I want to argue, that the intertextual relation to Phoenix Marvel Girl not only structures the novel in a profound way, but also creates one dimension of its significance as a node in Finnish literature.

Phoenix-Marvel Girl, an American Marvel Comics heroine occurs in a Finland-Swedish novel. There is, I think, both a Finland-Swedish and a global dimension in the use of Phoenix-Marvel Girl in *Diva*, and the two aspects are intertwined. Marvel Comics was founded in 1939 as Timely Comics. It is the largest American comic book publishing company, a media company owned by Marvel Publishing, which is a subsidiary of the huge, international conglomerate, Marvel Entertainment. Marvel Entertainment produces comics, movies and toys. Phoenix-Marvel Girl represents international popular culture produced in the USA; she also stands for popular culture and mass communication, and for its power in the lives of people in the postmodern age. Postmodernism, Dominic Strinati writes: "describes the emergence of a society in which the mass media and popular culture are the most important and powerful institutions, and control and shape all other types of social relationships" (Strinati 2004, 205).[22] According to Docker, postmodernism is an apocalyptic genre that "creates a new historical period, 'postmodernity', a period of the post-industrial, a new age of information, computers, mass media, mass communication" (Docker 1994, 104). In the novel, Diva is everywhere present; like Phoenix-Marvel Girl she has "total recall" and through her many, repeated intertextual allusions, she creates a network able to transcend all boundaries of time and place. Thus, she actually resembles the Internet and modern mass communication in the global world. In an interview in *Svenska Dagbladet*, shortly after the publication of *Wonderful Women by the Water*,[23] Fagerholm mentioned two major aspects, which according to her had transformed Finland significantly in a very short time – the fall of the Soviet Union and membership in the European Community. These changes had a strong impact even on Finland-Swedish culture. Besides these, she mentions the ongoing internetisation of society (Werkelid 1995).

In Finland-Swedish literature, popular culture is somewhat of a special case. In maintaining of Finland-Swedish minority culture and Swedish language in Finland, literature has been of special importance. In this context, the writing of popular literature has been problematic, when every individual act of writing was received as an effort for the whole culture in its totality, John Sundholm argues (Sundholm 2000, 175). The popular literature read in Swedish in Finland, has been imported mainly from Sweden, and few Finland-Swedish authors have written so-called popular literature. Maybe the novel *Diva*, with its comments upon the cult status of Jean Grey and Kari, makes a self-reflexive and self-ironic comment upon its own literary position to come. The explosion of the traditional conventions within the Finland-Swedish novel, that takes place in Fagerholm's novel, seems to have guaranteed *Diva* a place on the list of the important books within Finland-Swedish literature.[24]

Within the context of Finland-Swedish literature, the use of the "unnatural" possibilities offered by American popular culture, and of science fiction, *Diva* breaks the limits of national literature. The tradition of the "narrow room", a metaphor used by the Finland-Swedish author and scholar Merete Mazzarella (Mazzarella 1989) to describe the claustrophobic state of Finland-Swedish literature at the end of the 19th and at the beginning of the 20th century, is literally blasted by the powers of the Phoenix Marvel-Girl, and international popular culture. Phoenix-Marvel Girl's capacities are in the novel used to explode the Finland-Swedish novel tradition, and open the way for Finland-Swedish literature to enter the 21st century and postmodernism. In the 20th century, Finland-Swedish literature existed in a double minority position, as a marginal literature in relation to both Finnish and Swedish literature, Thomas Warburton (1984, 11) argued. *Diva* puts a definite end to looking towards Sweden in Finland-Swedish literature. Fagerholm's use of the comic strip character provides her with a literary strategy and style, able to break with the conventions of Finland-Swedish literature and Finnish "normal" prose and its long traditions of programmatic demands of realism (Mazzarella 2002). The novel opens up, I argue, the windows of Finland-Swedish literature to the world.

The use of Phoenix-Marvel Girl is contradictory in *Diva*. On the one hand, in the context of *Diva*, a highly experimental, postmodern novel, the author uses Phoenix-Marvel Girl for the good cause to rescue the Finland-Swedish novel by renewing its tradition. On the other hand, popular culture is used to fight for literature in a postmodern world that, according to Strinati, is a world within which mass communication and popular culture have become all too important.[25] Nevertheless, a break in tradition has been accomplished and Finland-Swedish literature can become part of the international postmodern tradition that incorporates popular culture as a literary motif.

Notes

1   All translations of the novel are mine except two, which are by Amanda Doxtater, and so marked.

2   The Festival of Lucia is celebrated annually on the 13th of December when a young, often blonde, girl dressed in a long, white dress with candles in her hair, appears in public as Saint Lucia, a martyr who died in Syracusa, Italy in the 13th century. The Italian tradition has been adopted in Sweden and other Nordic countries. She symbolises the light in the middle of darkness of the winter.

3   The way the text emphasises repetition and difference, makes its comprehension of signs and signification very poststructuralist indeed, Kurikka argues (2005, 61, see also 69).

4   For a definition of and a discussion on the concept 'popular culture', see Strinati 2004, xvi–xvii.

5   According to Jeff Rovin, "[…] superheroes have at least one superpower, whether physical or attributable to a weapon, instrument, or conveyance: they work actively and magnanimously for the common good; their values are neither vindictive nor selfish; they tend to operate on earth, though they may not be from this world;

they achieve anonymity by assuming a mortal identity or alter ego; and they were a distinctive costume" (Rovin 1985, ix).

6   Rovin seems to imitate the way comic book figures are introduced on the Internet pages of Marvel Comics (http://www.marveldirectory.com/individuals/j/jeangrey. htm). On other pages, the picture of Jean Grey is followed by a table of "power grids", where her intelligence, strength, speed, durability, energy projection, and fighting skills are measured on a scale from 1 to 7. She gets six points at every other level except "energy projection" which is at maximum level. After that, comes a description of her identity traits with headings like Universe, Occupation, Citizenship, Place of Birth, and so on (http://marvel.com/universe/Phoenix_ (Jean_Grey)).

7   Actually, Fagerholm cites almost completely Rovin's description of "Marvel Girl" (see Rovin 1985, 182).

8   The novel also has a heading "Prologerna" [The prologues] at the beginning (Fagerholm 1998, 9).

9   Kurikka remarks that it is impossible to distinguish between the "I-Diva-who-experiences"and the narrating I, which Kurikka does not want to call "Diva", although the narrating I is Diva, but later. (Kurikka 2005, 60.)

10 There are also other places in the text where the comic book world is present. For example, in Chapter 2, there is a long passage in which words are written as sounds in comic books occur. Here, the conventions of the comic books are partly imitated (Fagerholm 1998, 94–106). However, I will focus on the passages in which Phoenix-Marvel Girl is explicitly mentioned.

11 Rovin writes that his list is made up in order to distil the qualities that have made each superhero compelling and unique and to catch the sense of wonder attached to the character (Rovin 1985, xi).

12 The group Jean Grey belongs to is that of X-Men, "a team of justice-upholding mutants" (Rovin 1985, 182).

13 The story of Jean Grey is complicated indeed: "After Jean and the X-Men defeated scientist Stephen Lang and his robotic Sentinels on his space station, the heroes escaped back to Earth in a shuttle through a lethal solar radiation storm. Dying from radiation poisoning, Jean was saved by the cosmic entity known as the Phoenix Force who created a duplicate body complete with memories and personality, absorbed a portion of her consciousness and cast her into suspended animation in a strange cocoon at the bottom of Jamaica Bay. For months, the Phoenix believed itself to be the real Jean and saved the universe by healing the M'Kraan Crystal. Mental manipulation by Mastermind caused Phoenix to go insane and become Dark Phoenix. Ultimately, the portion of Jean's consciousness within Phoenix resurfaced, causing it to commit suicide. This portion of Jean Grey's consciousness then journeyed to the afterlife to meet a manifestation of Death. Death explained the Phoenix Force to Jean, who now wore a White Phoenix costume, before this portion of her consciousness and residual Phoenix energy was sent to Jean's original body in the cocoon, where it was rejected, and then to her clone, Madelyne Pryor". <http://www.marvel.com/universe/Phoenix_(Jean_Grey)>, see also <http://www.marveldirectory.com/individuals/j/jeangrey.htm>

14 Heidi Hansson offers a similar explanation, when she argues that the main reason why mass-market romance is used in postmodern romances is that "the choice of a popular form establishes a common basis for reader and writer". Popular romances have a large readership, which suggests that postmodern romances are intended for a larger audience than the cultural elite. (Hansson 1998, 163)

15 Jean Grey has occurred, among other things, as a character in the X-Men animated television series in the middle of the 1990s. See "Jean Grey in other media", <http://en.wikipedia.org/wiki/Jean_Grey_in_other_media>. Also, a new feature film, *X-Men Origins: Wolverine*, "based on the popular Marvel Comics", was launched in 2009.

16 This is a typically Finnish/Swedish holiday that takes usually place in February.

17 *Diva* is much about the performativity of language, the power of language to make things happen (see also Heinonen 2003).

18 The extended citations from the novel are due to the associative style of the novel and stream-of-consciousness narration.

19 The Savour is an intertext to Salinger's novel, whose title in Swedish, is *Räddaren i nöden*.

20 On other occasions, Sebbe Nsson and Franses ask Diva to quit. The parallelism of the passages in the novel is characteristic. Repeatedly, the narrator returns to earlier passages, and recounts them anew, in a slightly different version.

21 Åsa Stenwall's interpretation of Diva's identification with Phoenix-Marvel Girl, and her self-destruction in order to save the World, is a Freudian one. In order not to explode like Phoenix-Marvel Girl, Diva is forced to develop a superego that controls normal instincts, aggressiveness, and sexuality. The question is whether Diva's explosive force, "blast effect", in the end is too dangerous. Whatever her adult destiny will be, it will certainly include reduction, Stenwall concludes (Stenwall 2001, 228–229).

22 In an interview in 2002, Fagerholm openly criticised popular culture and mass media: "... populärkulturen tar så mycket utrymme i våra liv och är absolut inte ute efter att förnya strukturer, utan snarare befästa de gamla och kommer effektivt att hindra nya strukturer från att bli synliga och få plats i samhället" (Jordebo 2002). [... popular culture takes up so much space in our lives and is definitely not out to renew structures, but to recreate the old ones and will effectively prevent the new structures from becoming visible and gaining a place in the society].

23 In this novel, popular culture is used abundantly, both in order to create a fictive 1960s and an age of consumer innocence and in order to create a postmodern novel. In an interview on this novel Fagerholm said: "Poängen är att yta och djup inte är motsättningar. Jag vill inte heller ha någon indelning i högt och lågt. Det som intresserar mig är hur allt det som Bella och Rosa ägnar sig åt är betydelsebärande i sig." [The point is that the surface and the deep are not opposites. What interests me is to look at how the activities of Bella and Rosa (the protagonists of the novel) are significant as such] (Korsström 1995).

24 The fact that only ten years after it was published, the novel has been the object of many studies can be seen as a sign of its impact. Several Master's theses and articles have already been written about the novel, and there will be more to come. For example, several feminist interpretations have been made on *Diva* (see e.g., Laitinen 2000; Stenwall 2001; Heinonen 2003; Doxtater 2004; Kåreland 2004).

25 For a critique of this apprehension of postmodernism, see Strinati 2004, 221–224.

References

Fagerholm, Monika 1998: *Diva. En uppväxts egna alfabet med docklaboratorium (en bonusberättelse ur framtiden).* [The Alphabet of Adolescence with a Laboratory of Dolls (a bonus tale from the future).] Helsingfors: Söderströms.

Beckman, Åsa 1998: Skapa ett eget alfabet. [Creating One's Own Alphabet.] *Dagens Nyheter* 23.10.1998.

Docker, John 1994: *Postmodernism and Popular Culture. A Cultural History.* Cambridge, Melbourne, New York: Cambridge University Press.

Doxtater, Amanda 2004: Women Readers, Food and the Consumption of Text: Karin Boye's Kris and Monika Fagerholm's Diva. In: Helena Forsås-Scott (ed.), *Gender*

– Power – Text. Nordic Culture in the Twentieth Century. Norvik Press Series A: NO 25. Norwich: Norvik Press.

Genette, Gérard 1997: *Palimpsests. Literature in the Second Degree*. Lincoln and London: University of Nebraska.

Hansson, Heidi 1998: *Romance Revived. Postmodern Romances and the Tradition*. Acta Universitatis Umensis, Umeå Studies in Humanities 141. Umeå: Umeå University.

Hedman, Kaj 1998: Fagerholm ser allt ur "Divas" synvinkel. [Fagerholm views everything through "Diva's" perspective.] *Österbottningen* 11.11.1998.

Heinonen, Niini 2003: Kun kerrankin tyttö saa puhua. Performatiivinen identiteetti ja henkilökuvaus Monika Fagerholmin *Diivassa*. [For Once a Girl is Allowed to Talk. The Performative Identity and Character Portrayal in Monika Fagerholm's *Diva*.] In: Pirjo Lyytikäinen and Päivi Tonteri (eds.), *Romaanihenkilön muodonmuutoksia. Kuusi kirjoitusta henkilökuvauksesta*. [The Metamorphoses of Novel Characters.] Helsinki: Suomalaisen Kirjallisuuden Seura, 154–181.

Hutcheon, Linda 1985: *Theory of Parody. The Teachings of Twentieth Century Art Forms*. London: Methuen.

Ingström, Pia 1995: Jag, mitt livs tappra hjältinna. [Me, the Brave Heroine of My Life.] In: Michel Ekman and Peter Mickwitz (eds.), *Rudan, vanten och gangstern. Essäer om samtida finlandssvensk litteratur*. [The Carp, the Glove, and the Gangster. Essays in Contemporary Finland-Swedish Literature.] Helsingfors: Söderströms förlag, 180–208.

Ingström, Pia 2000: Den nyaste prosan. [Latest Prose Fiction.] In: Claes Zilliacus, Michel Ekman (eds.), *Finlands svenska litteraturhistoria. Andra delen: 1900-talet*. [Finland-Swedish literary history: the Twentieth Century.] Helsingfors, Stockholm: Svenska litteratursällskapet i Finland, Bokförlaget Atlantis, 318–326.

Jordebo, Lena 2002: Litteratur ska visa på utopier. [Literature should point out utopias.] *Dagens Nyheter*, 14.12.2002.

Kjellberg, Johan 1998: En intellektuell Pippi Långstrump. Monika Fagerholms nya roman *Diva* har en stark kvinnlig berättare. [An Intellectual Pippi Långstrump. Monika Fagerholm's New Novel *Diva* has a Strong, Female Narrator.] *Vasabladet* 18.10.1998.

Korsström, Tuva 1995: Från seger till seger med Underbara kvinnor vid vatten. [From Victory to Victory with Wonderful Women by the Water.] *Hufvudstadsbladet* 6.2.1995.

Kurikka, Kaisa 2005: Tytöksi tulemisen tila. Monika Fagerholmin Diva utopistisena tekstinä. [Becoming Girl. Monika Fagerholm's *Diva* as a Utopian text.] In: Anna Helle and Katriina Kajannes (eds.), *PoMon tila. Kirjoituksia kirjallisuuden postmodernismista*. [Conditions of PoMo. Writings on Postmodernism in Literature.] Jyväskylän ylioppilaskunnan julkaisusarja numero 74. Jyväskylä: Kampus Kustannus, 56–72.

Kurikka, Kaisa 2008: To use and abuse, to write and rewrite: metafictional trends in contemporary Finnish prose. In: Samuli Hägg, Erkki Sevänen and Risto Turunen (eds.), *Metaliterary Layers in Finnish Literature*. Studia Fennica Litteraria 3. Helsinki: Finnish Literature Society, 48–63.

Kåreland, Lena 2004: Flickbokens nya kläder. Om Monika Fagerholms *Diva*. [The New Clothes of the Book for Girls.] In: Eva Heggestad and Anna Williams (eds.), *Omklädningsrum. Könsöverskridanden och rollbyten från Tintomara till Tant Blomma*. [Changing Room. Gender Transgressions and Changes of Roles from Tintomara to Aunt Blomma.] Lund: Studentlitteratur, 121–137.

Mazzarella, Merete 1989: *Trånga rummet. En finlandssvensk romantradition*. [The Narrow Room. A Finland-Swedish Novel Tradition.] Helsingfors: Söderström.

Mazzarella, Merete 2002: Vad är finlandssvensk litteratur? [What is Finland-Swedish Literature?] In: Satu Gröndahl (ed.), *Litteraturens gränsland. Invandrar- och minoritetslitteratur i nordiskt Perspektive*. [The Borderland of literature. Immigrant and Minority Literature in the Nordic perspective.] Uppsala: Centrum för multietnisk forskning, 224–230.

Möller, Anna-Lena 1998: En finlandssvensk Diva. [A Finland-Swedish Diva.] *Vasabladet* 23.10.1998.

Ritamäki, Tapani 1994: 60-talet du aldrig vetat om. [The 1960s You Did not Know about.] *Ny Tid* 1.12.1994.

Rovin, Jeff 1985: *The Encyclopedia of Superheroes*. New York and Oxford: Facts on File Publications.

Rönnholm, Bror 1998: Vara sitt eget konstverk. [To be One's Own Piece of Art.] *Åbo Underrättelser* 23.10.1998.

Stenwall, Åsa 2001: *Portföljen i skogen. Kvinnor och modernitet i det sena 1900-talets finlandssvenska litteratur*. [Briefcase in the Wood. Women and Modernity in the late 20th Century Finland-Swedish Literature.] Helsingfors: Schildts.

Strinati, Dominic 2004: *An Introduction to Theories of Popular Culture*. Second Edition. London and New York: Routledge.

Sundholm, John 2000: Den klassiska detektivromanen. [Classical Detective Novel.] In: Clas Zilliacus, Michel Ekman (eds.), *Finlands svenska litteraturhistoria. Andra delen: 1900-talet*. [Finland-Swedish Literary History: the Twentieth Century.] Helsingfors, Stockholm: Svenska litteratursällskapet i Finland, Bokförlaget Atlantis, 175–176.

Sundström, Charlotte 1998: Om HENNE man trodde att inte fanns. [About HER You did not Know Existed.] *Ny Tid 6.11.1998*.

Sundström, Charlotte 2004: Mellan allt och inget. [Between Everything and Nothing.] *Ny Tid* 51–52/2004.

Warburton, Thomas 1984: *Åttio år finlandssvensk litteratur*. [Eighty Years of Finland-Swedish Literature.] Helsingfors: Schildt.

Waugh, Patricia 1984: *Metafiction. The Theory and Practice of Self-Conscious Fiction*. London and New York: Methuen.

Werkelid, Carl Otto 1995: "Mellanfallarna" får upprättelse. [Those In-between Get their Revenge.] *Svenska Dagbladet* 15.5.1995.

Österlund, Mia 1999: En Diva för årets alla dagar. [A Diva for all the Days of the Year.] *Astra Nova* 1–2/1999.

Unpublished sources

Laitinen, Nelly 2000: Att vara sig själv nog. Monika Fagerholms Diva som litterär artefakt och autonomt miniatyruniversum. [To be Oneself Enough. Monika Fagerholm's *Diva* as a Literary Artefact and an Autonomous Miniature Universe.] Helsingfors: University of Helsinki, Department of Nordic Literature. [Unpublished Master's Thesis.]

Internetpages

http://www.marvel.com/universe/Phoenix_(Jean_Grey)
http://en.wikipedia.org/wiki/Jean_Grey
http://www.marveldirectory.com/individuals/j/jeangrey.htm)
http://en.wikipedia.org/wiki/Jean_Grey_in_other_media

Further Reading

Haasjoki, Pauliina 2005: Ei kahta ilman kolmatta: ambivalenssi, biseksuaalisuus ja lukeminen. [Misfortune Never Comes Alone: Ambivalence, Bisexuality and Reading.] In: Olli Löytty (ed.): *Rajanylityksiä: tutkimusreittejä toiseuden tuolle puolen.* [Crossing Boundaries: Research Routes beyond Otherness.] Helsinki: Gaudeamus, 181–202.

Haasjoki, Pauliina 2005: Mitä tiedät kertomuksestani?: biseksuaalinen ambivalenssi ja queer-lukeminen. [What do You Know about my Story?: Bisexual Ambivalence and Queer-reading.] *Naistutkimus.* [Women Studies.] 18 (2), 29–39.

Haasjoki, Pauliina 2010: Kaikkivoipaisesti queer. Omnipotenssi, seksuaalisuus ja ambivalenssi Monika Fagerholmin *Diivassa.* [All-powerfully queer. Omnipotence, Sexuality, and Ambivalence in Monika Fagerholm's *Diva.*] SQS 1–2/2010, <http://www.helsinki.fi/jarj/sqs/sqs12_10/sqs122010haasjoki.pdf>.

MARI HATAVARA

History After or Against the Fact?
Finnish Postmodern Historical Fiction

Aikamoinen kollo ja kusipää minusta tuli (*SH*, 32).

Quite a jerk and an asshole I grew out to be (all translations the author's).

The speaker of this line, the narrating 'I' in Juha Seppälä's historical novel, *Suomen historia* (1998, "Finnish History" = *SH*) is, allegedly, Marshal Carl Gustaf Emil Mannerheim (1887–1951), who depicts his own youth and subsequent character. Mannerheim is a historical figure, the commander of the Finnish army during the Second World War, and the president of Finland between 1944 and 1946. Juha Seppälä's novel radically turns upside down the image of Mannerheim as an esteemed personage in Finland's history. The largest section of the novel is written in the form of a memoir by the Marshal, and a very peculiar type of memoir it is. As quoted above, Mannerheim describes himself in a pejorative manner. It also turns out that on many historically important occasions he has been in a rather unexpected state of mind: desperately holding his diarrhoea, drunk out of his wit, or involved in amorous affairs.

It was not only the contents of the novel that surprised or even appalled many contemporary readers; the use of the first-person narrative voice designated to the Marshal himself also made the novel surprising as it seemed to be a confession. The reader seems to get everything "straight from the horse's mouth"– a saying fitting here especially well, as Mannerheim, a cavalry officer, admits in the novel to wanting to become a horse (*SH*, 45). This is just one of the revelations the novel offers. This play with the reader's expectations and the constant, deliberate failing makes *Suomen historia* fall outside some of the generic conventions of the historical novel. For example, Richard Maxwell states in *Encyclopedia of the Novel*, that the historical novel is "by definition referential, gesturing toward a world commonly understood to have existed" (Maxwell 1998, 545). Seppälä's novel does, in a way, gesture toward the reader's knowledge of a past world, but with a twist: the common understanding the reader holds is repeatedly contradicted.

Whereas the traditional historical novel in many cases was associated with the rise of the nation state, historical novels today are more inclined to question any cultural or ideological presumption. Seppälä's novel does this to Mannerheim, who was almost a mythical figure in Finnish history. Not only has the Finnish historical novel become more critical of the events of the past, it has also become increasingly aware of the problems involved in any historical writing, including the epistemological gap between past and present and the ideological implications of any historical account. The fictional reworking of historical material is central in the books of such prominent and award-winning authors as Kjell Westö, Leena Lander, Juha Seppälä and Lars Sund (see also, Hallila & Hägg 2007, 74). The popularity of the genre today is indisputable, and indicates that it has positive functions. These include revisiting some of the traumatic events in Finnish history. The 1918 civil war has been a particularly popular subject during the 21st century (see Varpio 2009), it was depicted in such contemporary novels as Frans Emil Sillanpää's *Hurskas kurjuus* (1919, *Meek Heritage* 1938), and continued by Väinö Linna's *Täällä Pohjantähden alla* (1959–1962, *Under the North Star* 2001–2003).

In this article, I will concentrate on two crucial features of Finnish postmodern historical fiction: the contradictions the story-world carries with historical presumptions and the use of multiple narrative modes and narrators. These are interconnected: epistemological questions are also questions of identity, since truth depends on the perspective of a subject. As Hutcheon (1999, 123) states, "[…]postmodern fiction does not aspire to tell the truth – as much as to question *whose* truth gets told". Postmodernism is deeply invested in probing the difference between the past as events and history as a representation of those events (see Hutcheon 1999, 122). In many cases it plays with different versions of history and assigns unexpected roles to historically familiar characters in an effort to multiply conceptions of both past and future (see Wesseling 1991, 193–194). In fiction, this diversity and self-awareness requires examining both story contents and narrative voices.

I will first take a closer look at *Suomen historia* and its relation to the more traditional historical representations. After that, I will turn to two other novels, which mark important turning points in Finnish historical fiction. Ralf Nordgren's *Det har aldrig hänt* (It Never Happened = *DH*) from 1977 already marked a change in the Finnish tradition of historical fiction. The novel investigates the question of narrative identity: the way the past influences and is used to affect the present. It has a character-narrator, who acts as a historian and studies the past. Elisabeth Wesseling (1991, 193) remarks on the difference between novels, that investigate "how the individual mind gathers, interprets, and assimilates historical meaning", and novels, that expose "the ways in which versions of history are used as instruments of power". *Det har aldrig hänt* incorporates both: the third person narrator in the time of writing the novel investigates the past and tries to write history, and the characters both in the past story-world and in the narrator's present are keenly invested in holding on to their versions of history. Although the novel precedes the designated time line for this collection, I feel it justified to analyse it here. The novel clearly is an important node in Finnish literary history; it is a starting point of Finnish postmodern historical fiction.

Besides Nordgren's self-reflexive, and in many ways metafictional novel, this article analyses Irja Rane's *Naurava neitsyt* (1996, "The Laughing Virgin" = *NN*), which in turn may be seen as an even more radical a statement about the uncertainty and subjectivity of any historical knowledge. Through three character-narrators located in two historical periods, the novel offers the reader access to the minds of these long-gone persons, but at the same time limits the perspective to them alone. Whereas in Nordgren's novel the reader may question the authorial narrator's version of the past, in Rane's novel the past seems to confront the reader as such, without mediating narrative levels. Although in *Suomen historia* the character-narrator seems to have access to the time of writing, in *Naurava neitsyt* the author creates the illusion of real past people speaking straight from their historical position. All three novels analysed in this article pose the reader questions about knowing and writing history, and the ideological implications necessarily involved.

Suomen historia on Finnish History

Suomen historia brings the postmodernist parodical practice to a head. It is also an important contribution to the overall, extensive discussion on the Marshal's person, which has been occurring recently. More recent amendments include a puppet animation by Katariina Lillqvist (*Uralin perhonen*, 2008), which takes homosexuality as a leading theme, and the novel *Marsalkka* (2010) by Hannu Raittila, which has several narrators and interviewers of the aging Mannerheim. Furthermore, a movie on a grand scale has been planned for some time by Renny Harlin. All of these recent artistic endeavors show Mannerheim's enduring importance to the Finnish self-image, which also makes his character a ready target for ridicule.

Seppälä's novel makes evident its parodic relationship to previous depictions of Finnish history in several ways. The title alone is an overstatement; it claims that the short novel comprises the history of Finland. It also points out the nationalistic tones often prominent in historical writing: naming and dividing the past into slices according to national boundaries. The title of the novel indicates the large subtext of Finnish historical writing, which is to be revised in the novel. Besides this paratextual signal of reversal, the novel's cover has an ekphrasis that contradicts what is to come. The ekhprasis describes perhaps the most well-known political painting in Finland, *Hyökkäys* (1899, The Attack) by Eetu Isto. *Hyökkäys* was painted during the time of Russification at the end of the 19th century. The painting, in which the Russian double headed eagle is tearing a law book from the maiden symbolizing Finland, became the symbol of protest against the actions of Tsar Nicholas II, who tried to overrule Finnish legislation. The maiden seems angry, even desperate, but heroically holds on to the law book. Against this background of a well-known nationalistic representation,

Suomen historia provides an alternative: it ridicules a historical character, who is commonly regarded as one of the backbones of Finnish independence and identity and a protector of the maiden of Finland. The novel makes Mannerheim's role ambiguous concerning both the maiden and the Russian eagle, as he is depicted as a womanizer and someone who is unconcerned about nationalistic ideals.

As already mentioned, Mannerheim acts as a narrator in the novel. The novel's narrative mode has two other interesting features. Firstly, Mannerheim the narrator is not restricted to the epistemological boundaries of his own time. On many occasions he sees the events from the temporal point of view that belongs to the age of the writing the novel. For example, in the text, Mannerheim mentions, that at that time no one knew about virtual pornography (*SH*, 31). Yet, this no one excludes himself, who died well before the phenomenon. Secondly, the section of the novel, in which Mannerheim is the narrator, begins as follows:

> Kaikki tietävät kuka minä olen. Minä olen minä. (*SH*, 30.)

> Everybody knows who I am. I am me.

This statement refers to the community as the basis of identity: Mannerheim is himself because of the common, shared image of him. The ambivalence inherited in the temporal positioning of Mannerheim, the narrator, makes this statement interesting: this "knowing" of Mannerheim may refer to what his contemporaries thought about him, or to the image maintained of him at the time of the writing of the novel. What is more, this opening statement plays a joke on the reader, as the narrator's identity has not yet been disclosed. Thus, the reader does not have a clue who this well-known person is.

The information that evidently makes the narrator a fictional representation of Mannerheim only builds up gradually. This is an important contradiction: The audience as a community with shared information and an image of the person is the acclaimed grounds for the marshal's identity. Still, this same audience is at the beginning left wondering who this "me" is. This includes a double trick: At the beginning of the text, the reader does not possess knowledge of the character, whom everybody knows. After getting enough clues to connect the character to Mannerheim, the reader is confronted with facts about him, which seem counterfactual. Mannerheim, a known historical character, is depicted through a mock-confessional narrative voice, and the reader constantly shifts between a previous image of the historical person and the story the narrator – allegedly the very same historical character – unfolds.

In historical fiction, historical characters referred to and depicted become fictionalized. This process, according to Dorrit Cohn (1999, 13–15), makes correspondence to real events and circumstances optional, but not mandatory. It is, however, crucial to the genre, that the reading process requires prior knowledge of these events. Even if Napoleon in *War and Peace* is not *the* Napoleon, the character certainly is associated with the historical person, and evaluated based on this knowledge. As Ann Rigney (2001, 19) has pointed out, historical fiction is characterized by the interplay between story elements that are historical and those that are invented. Seppälä's novel foregrounds this interplay, and also parodies the generic convention by making Mannerheim the character appear almost the opposite of how he is commonly portrayed in historical writing. This play with the reader's preconceptions is typical of postmodern historical fiction. As Linda Hutcheon (1999, 108) has concluded, postmodernity is concerned with the multiplicity of truths relative to specificity of culture. This further emphasizes the reader's role in relating a fictional representation of the past with prior knowledge of history.

With this short analysis of *Suomen historia,* I hope I have illustrated the character of the Finnish historical novel today. As a genre, the historical novel has recently undergone many changes. It more often serves the needs of the postmodern world that is marked by scepticism, doubt and diversity. Terry Eagleton (1996, 29) describes postmodernism and its relationship to modernism as follows: "[Postmodernism] does not come after modernism in the sense that positivism comes after idealism but in the sense that the recognition that the emperor has no clothes comes after gazing upon him". In the last twenty years, historical novels have gazed upon history, both as *res gestae* ("past, what happened") and as *rerum gestarum* ("historiography, a representation of what happened"). As exemplified by Maxwell's prior definition of the historical novel, the connection between the story-world and the past has often been emphasized when defining the genre. However, this has changed in the postmodern era as new kind of historical fiction has emerged, with a more complex relation to the past and history. In *Suomen historia* past events and historical writing become intermingled, as Mannerheim is both a character in the past story-world and a narrator with a retrospective point of view to the same story-world. Thus, he employs a temporal and epistemological double perspective on the depicted events.

Hutcheon (1999, 92–95) has coined the term historiographic metafiction to describe this new type of historical fiction. She, among others, regards the postmodern version of historical novel to concentrate on the epistemological problems involved in representing the past, and on the constructed nature of reality and history. Ansgar Nünning (2005, 216) defines the genre in *The Routledge Encyclopedia of Narrative Theory* as follows: "[...]historiographic metafiction deals not so much with historical events, personages, and facts as with the reconstruction of the past from the point of view of the present". Heightened self-awareness and self-reflexivity has marked historical novels all around the world during the last decades. During the 1980s such books as Umberto Eco's *Il nome della rosa* (1980, *The Name of the Rose*), Julian Barnes' *Flaubert's Parrot* (1984) and Orhan Pamuk's *Beyaz Kale* (1985, *White Castle*) began a new era in historical fiction. *The Name of the Rose* has an increased awareness of semiotics, signification and logical reasoning in the process of understanding the present as well as the past. It has partially adopted the form of the detective genre. This utilization of other genres is common in the postmodern historical novel. In Finland Kristina Carlson's

Maan ääreen (1999, "To the Edge of the World") is an example of the mixture between the historical novel and detective fiction. Pamuk's *White Castle* is intensely concerned with the question of identity: it has two main characters with different cultural backgrounds, who, nevertheless, find their identities almost identical and interchangeable. The postmodern historical novel often studies the effect of an individual or communal past on people. Barnes' *Flaubert's Parrot* has a narrator, who acts as the author of the novel, and openly investigates and contests the famous writer's life. It plays with the convention of drawing analogies between an author's life and work, and highlights the laborious, perhaps futile effort to know the past and write history.

Seppälä's novel *Suomen historia* exemplifies two crucial features of this new type of historical fiction called historiographic metafiction. Firstly, the novel uses previous artistic representations of a historical situation, such as the painting by Isto, as a frame; thus, it highlights its own textuality and the textuality of any historical representation. Secondly, the novel opposes common understanding of the historical events it depicts. Therefore, it is not only concerned with the past, but also with the representations and images of that past in the present, the construction of Finnish history.

History that Did Not Happen

Competing representations, contradictions and questions play such a central role in these newer historical novels that Nordgren's pioneering work, *Det har aldrig hänt* indicates a strong question, even denial in its very title. The thing that "never happened" is something that the novel's authorial narrator tries to determine, even though characters in both the past depicted and at the time of writing try to hide it. The novel illustrates the impact of ideological connections and choices on both individuals and groups.

Nünning's (2005, 216) quoted statement about historical metafiction and its disregard of past events and characters resembles Nordgren's title. Both operate through negation: the statement emphasizes what historical metafiction does *not* deal with. This working through negation and effacing is distinct to postmodernism (Wesseling 1991, 194). It is also symptomatic of the newer definitions of the historical novel, and illustrates that "post" builds on what precedes it and is, as Eagleton's quoted analogy suggests, a result of a new point of view. The negative formulation of Nünning's definition implies that historical novels even nowadays do have their relationship with the past events, even though this relationship is more complex and more openly discussed in historical novels. Postmodern historical novels do not try to ignore or hide ideological connections and impacts, but rather make the most of investigating them through a self-conscious narrative process. Monika Fludernik (1994, 93) has aptly maintained, that the self-reflexive metafictional element in postmodern historical novels does not mark a deviation from historiography proper, but rather an adaptation to new conceptualizations of both the novel and the historical.

It is important to note that denial of the past in the manner suggested in the title of Nordgren's novel requires historical knowledge as a background. References, even indirect, to known historical events, provide the reader with a frame of reference, which enables contesting and denying this frame–as already demonstrated in *Suomen historia*, which uses for example ekphrasis of Isto's painting to indicate a former representation. Brian McHale (1987, 100–102) discusses narrative self-erasure, in which the narrative denies events that it had earlier established and the rhetorical impacts of the technique. He notes that the denial of a previously told story element may not lead to a radical ontological uncertainty of the represented world in all cases: the instability in the narrative may be motivated by the narrator's character, for example. In historical fiction, the reader's prior knowledge of the depicted events may have a stabilizing effect on the world represented. With previous texts and images as an interpretative frame, the reader may well be persuaded to change his or her opinion of the historical events, but not easily be led to deny their occurrence altogether.

Det har aldrig hänt begins with a description of two men who ride along a frozen sea in the Åland islands in Finland. During the first three pages, the narrator discloses that the men are a Finnish farm hand and a Russian soldier, and that the latter has a red armband. From these clues, it is obvious that the story is set during the Finnish civil war in 1918. The war was fought in Finland shortly after independence from late January to mid-May 1918, between two forces: the forces of the socialists and worker's movement, commonly called the "Reds" and the forces of the non-socialist, conservative-led Senate, commonly called the "Whites". Those colours were used in armbands to indicate the group wo which individuals belonged. The Reds were supported by the Russian federation, while the Whites received military assistance from the German empire. Based on this very general historical knowledge, a native reader recognizes the historical events during which the story of *Det har aldrig hänt* takes place. The reader knows that the men described belong to the losing side of the Reds, which lost 27 000 people, out of which only about 5 000 were lost in battle; the rest were executed, killed in prison camps, or disappeared. For this reason, the future of the men described does not look very promising to the reader.

The novel begins right from the middle of the events, and the narrator offers the reader a glimpse into the world depicted with the following lines:

> Där är de!
> Över isen rider de. Hovarna kastar i jämn rytm snö i luften. Spåret drar mot nordväst. (*DH*, 5.)

> There they are!
> Over the ice they ride. Hooves whirl up snow at an even pace. The tracks lead to the northwest.

Here the story-world is disclosed like a scene, where the two men are visible as they journey across the ice. Later on in the story these two men are executed by the Whites, but before the reader learns about that, the narrative is taken over by the narrator and his efforts to learn what happens to the men: he goes through archives, interviews people and tries to construct a story with a coherent plot.

It soon becomes evident that the narrator is the only one who really wants to unravel the past. His preconception seems to be, that the men faced their deaths in the Åland Islands. This assumption does fit the historical period, in which the story is set, as the aftermath of the war was gloomy for the Reds who had lost. The narrator's problem is that characters in both past and present time try to deny this preconception and hold on to their preferred interpretation of the past. The surviving eyewitnesses claim to be unable to remember the past events, but also deny the alternatives offered by the narrator because of their subjective, partial understanding of the world now and then. This becomes obvious when one of the witnesses strongly denies the execution of the two Reds. The narrator explains ironically, that this is due to his brother being among the Whites involved (*DH*, 11). Similar explanations occur elsewhere in the text. The novel makes it very clear that everyone has his or her own reasons for holding a certain view of the past.

The narrator is occasionally able to visit the time of the story through the minds of the characters in the past. At times, the narrator has telepathic power to intrude upon the characters' minds, but these abilities do not provide the answers, either, as the characters in the past are just as unwilling to see the world around them as are the people in the time of writing to remember it. The characters repeatedly both think and say to each other: "vi ska vänta och se", ("we should wait and see"). On one occasion, Varg-Sluk, a prominent ship owner, is listening to his son conversing with some White soldiers:

> Bara han inte lånar dem pengar! tänker Varg-Sluk. Eller borde vi? Nej, inte ännu. Vi ska vänta och se, så ser vi sedan. (*DH*, 32)

> As long as he doesn't loan them money, Varg-Sluk thinks. Or should we? No, not yet. We'll wait and see, then we'll see.

Varg-Sluk is uncertain of the outcome of the war and thus cannot decide whether or not to help the Whites. In the midst of events, he cannot decide his position, because he is painfully aware of the consequences of a wrong choice. This "wait and see" attitude recurs in the novel. The characters plead ignorance of what is happening, and expect only the future to determine the nature and significance of the events. Thus, not only retrospective, but also contemporary perspective on the events fails to reach the truth about the past: both the past and the future remain unclear.

This uncertainty and openness of each moment is particular to historical metafiction (Wesseling 1991, 194). Narrative logic often organizes events into a causal chain, determined either by their origin or their outcome. Gary Saul Morson (1994, 6–14) uses the terms foreshadowing and backshadowing to designate this kind of history, which can be used to bolster one particular version of the past. On the contrary, sideshadowing, as defined by Morson, allows one to see alternatives: what could have happened in addition to what did happen. In *Det har aldrig hänt* the bewilderment of the characters creates a special kind of openness and hypotheticality. The events of the story become the target not only of the narrator's, but also the characters' interpretative efforts. However, the characters refuse really to try to understand the present, because they put such a strong emphasis on the future. In Morson's terms, they would really like to be able to foreshadow the present, to see the inevitable in what is to be. This urge for foreshadowing and its utter failure indicate its futility.

The significance of the future in the minds of the characters is demonstrated in the following quotation. Before the war reaches the Åland Islands, one of the inhabitants, named Blade, tries to make everyone openly declare their side in order for them to be able to go beyond that simple dichotomy, and interact as persons. Blade has made both red and white armbands, the symbols of the parties of the war, and he tries to make people choose one or other. No one will make a choice and take an armband, but a blind beggar says he might.

> – Jag skulle väl kunna ta en bindel jag. Men då jag är blind, så vet jag inte vilken jag ska välja, om det är min sak att ta. Tänk om jag får orätt bindel sen. Och det blir de andra som vinner. Hur går det då med mig. (*DH*, 23.)

> – I could take an armband, I suppose. But I'm blind. I don't know which one to choose, if I have to take one. What if I get a wrong one and it'll be the other ones who win. Then what's going to happen to me?

The blind beggar's problem, not knowing how to be on the winning side, seems to be shared by all the people in the village. With an obvious lack of knowledge of what is to happen, but determined to be on the winning side, the people cannot do anything – they are blinded by their cautiousness. The generations to come, for their part, are deeply affected by what they would rather believe instead of trying to determine what really happened. In a sense, they use backshadowing in a way that is very selective of the past events and are blinded by their conservatism.

Nünning (2005, 216) maintains that "[h]istoriographic metafiction reminds the reader that history [...] is accessible only as a narrative produced by human beings who remember, interpret, and represent events from a particular point of view". *Det har aldrig hänt* in a way pushes this even further, as the characters largely refuse to remember, interpret and represent events in both their present and their past. The novel indicates how both individuals and communities become impaired by their lack of a point of view. With this the novel encourages readers to take the past into consideration, to try to find out what exactly happened, even, and perhaps especially, in the case of events denied and historical accounts contested. The challenge for the reader is not to be or remain blind about the events of past and present, but to take a stand and to observe and evaluate the world from a chosen position.

History Alien and Known

Whereas Nordgren's novel has the authorial narrator with the mostly retrospective position concerning the past story-world, Irja Rane's *Naurava neitsyt* displays quite a different narrative strategy. The novel has three character narrators, and no overt retrospective point of view set at the time of the writing of the novel. Knowing and understanding past events changes as the novel lacks an explicit agent with a retrospective perspective. For a character narrator, the past is her life in the present or recent, personal past – presuming that the narrator does not have metaleptic abilities like Mannerheim does in Seppälä's *Suomen historia. Det har aldrig hänt* has a narrator with whom the reader shares the same temporal perspective, and is at least partly able to associate from, but *Naurava neitsyt* has no such frames or overt perspectives. It rather offers personal points of view of those who experience the past; this is a solution that quite radically points out the subjectivity of any understanding of history.

Rane's novel comprises three sections. The first is a monologue by a woman named Lydia, written down by a clerical officer. Lydia has been summoned to court, and is interrogated about events in her recent past. In the second section, a man named Bartolomeus writes, mostly to himself, a memoir about events in his own past. These two narratives have two temporal levels: the story-time in the characters' recent past and the discourse-time when Lydia and Bartolomeus record the events under scrutiny. The third and last part of the novel includes letters and diary entries, written by a man named Klein. The letters are addressed to his son in another town. The letters and entries mostly depict the same day or days right before it, so the temporal distance between the narrated and the act of narrating is very short. Both sections written down by their narrator openly problematize writing about reality and representing events.

Since first-person narrators in the historical novel cannot as characters communicate their present as history, the effort to convey history through such narration may require crossing epistemological limitations involved in character narration. These "unnatural" – in the sense of being alien to normal human beings – features of first-person narrators have raised growing interest among narratologists in recent years. Henrik Skov Nielsen has written an influential article about the mimetic and artificial side of first-person narration. Nielsen (2004, 137–138) sees features that break the mimetic, human-like appearance of character narrators as follows: knowledge not attainable by a normal person (including abundant detail and word-for-word dialogue written down after the fact), and situations, in which the narrator relates something already familiar to the receiver in the story-world. The former is a kind of epistemological metalepsis; the latter has been termed redundant telling by James Phelan (2001a). These qualities, the first one unattainable, the second alien to a real human being, are important tools for the first-person historical novel. Even if – perhaps just because – these techniques do not follow the rules of basic logic available to human beings, they help to build and maintain the reader's connection to the story-world as history.

Naurava neitsyt does use the techniques mentioned in a subtle way. Lydia does often recall and recount long dialogues as part of her testimony, and she claims to retell a story she heard another character tell word by word (see *NN*, 158–166). Redundant telling occurs when Lydia mentions something that the listeners in the story world, her judges, already know. For example, Lydia gives a long apologetic explanation about her passing out and what happened after that – even though the judges have been there the whole time to witness the very events she describes in detail. (*NN*, 55). Lydia's speech contains information about the past events familiar to those involved, but that could not be conveyed to the reader in other manner, since Lydia is the only narrator. Thus, the contents of Lydia's words are more directed to the reader than to the dramatized audience in the story-world.

However, this is not very obvious in the novel. In many cases, redundant telling is at least partly motivated through the communicative situation of the story-world. As Lydia in one case repeats what one of the judges has just said to her, this is due to her getting upset:

> Ettäkö Johannes olisi minuun juuri silloin muka oman hulluutensa manannut ja myrskyn avittamana suistanut minua syntiin ja kado-tuksen tielle? Ei, ei ja ei! (*NN*, 65.)

> Really? Johannes just then cursed me with his own insanity, and with the aid of the storm made me fall to sin and damnation, you say? No, no and no!

The third section of the novel with Klein's letters also includes word-for-word conversations, but they are few and quite brief. Additionally, the words and their meanings are extremely important in the story, which makes it easier to think the writer does or at least tries to recall them exactly.

Bartolomeus, who narrates the second section, is the most difficult – and in many ways the most interesting – subject to be defined either as a character experiencing the story-world or a narrator recounting it a little later. Even though *Naurava neitsyt* does not provide a doppelganger situation in the manner of Pamuk's *White Castle*, it does raise the same questions about a person's relation to his or her own past and the role of this past in the formation of identity today: the former Bartolomeus and the present Bartolomeus intermingle in many ways and are inalienable. Bartolomeus seems to be driven by the urge to come to terms with his past, but he still appears to feel alien to it. On many occasions, Bartolomeus ponders the question of memory, one of the most pressing ones discussed in recent historical novels. He often feels his memory to be fitful and coincidental (see *NN*, 241).

On many occasions, the process of telling seems to affect the story more than events in the past: Bartolomeus reflects on what he recalls and on the reasons for recollection. The next passage illustrates fluctuation between the experiencing self and the narrating self.

> Halusta käänsimmekin hevoset pinjojen, ei, mäntyjen varjoon. Puut olivat tiukkaoksaisia ja kiinteitä. Ne hajusivat väkevästi ja toisin paikoin niissä näki pihkanjuoksuttajain tekemiä haavoja. Kummaksemme monet astiat oli kuitenkin jätetty sinälleen, pihka kuorettunut ja muuttunut valkoisiksi pahkoiksi. Emme kiinnittäneet niihin mitään huomiota. (*NN*, 238.)

> With pleasure we turned our horses to the shades of the stone pines, no, pine trees. The trees had thick firm branches. They smelled intense, and you could see cuts made by resin collectors here and there. Much to our amazement, many bowls had been left lying there; the resin had developed a hard shell and turned into white gnarls. We did not pay any attention to them.

In the first sentence, Bartolomeus changes his recollection about the species of the trees. This highlights the moment of recollecting and remembering. The last two sentences seem to contradict each other: first, the group is amazed by the bowls of resin, then Bartolomeus states that they never paid any attention to them. This detail is surprising as the resin has no thematic meaning in the story; it never reappears. The passage is not aimed at disclosing something about the story but rather to characterize Bartolomeus as a groping, unreliable and self-correcting narrator . His mind and memory resemble those bowls of resin they have seeped from old cuts, but now hardened and encased in a shell.

With the three character narrators the reader is faced with the past seemingly as such, without having the opportunity to culturally associate with a given audience position. This alienates from the mimetic illusion of the story-world and leaves the reader uncertain of the timing and historical context. On the other hand, thematically this exemplifies the nature of past: it is alien to today, strange and unexplainable. Only at the end of the first section does the first overt indication of timing occur. In a short passage another narrator, Aeditca introduces herself as a reader in a monastery library, and says that she has written Lydia's story from the court records wishing it to be a cautionary education to the public (*NN*, 205). She states that the events took place many years after the Great Plague. This indicates that the story is located in Europe some time before the 1348–1351 Black Death. Rane's radical decision is to place Aeditca's short narrative, which helps to locate the story in time and place, at the end of this section. Before that, the reader has had to try to make the most out of indirect hints, like religious habits and the trade, and journeyman system, that pointed to

107

the time and place. The first two narratives in the novel lack information that would provide them with exact temporal and spatial information – information characteristic of historical fiction, but absent here. This changes the dynamics of reading, as the reader is not provided with a familiar frame of reference for the events.

Only the third narrative has more direct clues to enable the reader to guess the time and place. Quite early in the text, the narrator, who has already described unrest and military action, mentions that the blacksmith is mostly engaged in forging swastikas instead of the ornaments he used to make (*NN*, 335). A little later, the text refers to racial propaganda and adaptations of old mythology (*NN*, 340–343). Additionally, German cities like Berlin are mentioned. Thus, the story can be located to occur in Germany during the 1930s. None of the three sections includes known historical characters or specific events. The first two narratives thematically relate to battles over power between the church and secular leaders, and can be understood as battles between institutions and individuals, sexes, social classes, and ethnic groups. The third has a more specific context of the rise of national socialism.

Whereas historical novels typically activate intertextual subtexts and historical context right from the beginning – like *Det har aldrig hänt* with the red armbands – *Naurava neitsyt* works in the opposite way: only the last section indicates the historical context. The Second World War and the role of Germany in the war are subjects about which every reader has a preconception. *Naurava neitsyt* works to destabilize this preconceived image as the novel approaches the familiar era from the customary temporal direction. The first two sections lead the reader through mostly alien, hard to locate and contextualize territory, which may help the reader to perceive the familiar subject, national socialism, in a new way. Concealing information about the era the novel approaches works in a communicative way: it provides a new angle on a familiar subject or, in a way, it gives three new angles through the minds of the three narrators.

Naurava neitsyt builds its historical relevance towards the end. All three narrators occasionally overstep their roles as characters in order to better convey the story to the reader, to overcome the temporal gap between the reader and the story world – this is the reason why techniques like metaleptic information and redundant telling are employed (cf. Phelan 2001a). Bartolomeus thematises this as he discusses the gap between his former, experiencing self, and his present, writing self at the beginning of the text:

> Ehken vielä hetki sitten olin siinä luulossa, että kirjoitan historian
> niistä päivistä, joista moni ei tahdo enää mitään tietää ja joiden
> muistokaan ei enää ketään uteluta. Mutta kun nousin kalliolle
> ja tähystin, näin muutakin kuin Senessarin hiestyneet kasvot ja
> hänen tomun pilkuttaman vaippansa ja muulin, joka varmoin
> askelin mittoi tietä. Näin itseni kertomuksessa. Ja se mies oli tun-
> tematon ja outo, vaikka meillä on sama nimi, Bartolomeus, ja sa-

mat luut ja lihat, niin että hänen jalkaansa silloin iskenyt kivi yhä näkyy arpena pohkeeni reunassa. (*NN*, 211–212.)

Perhaps only a while ago I thought I am writing a history of those days, which many want to know nothing about, and even the memory of which makes nobody curious. But when I rose on the hill and looked out, I saw more than the sweaty face of Senessar and his dusty gown, and the mule passing down the road with steady steps. I saw myself in a narrative. And that man was unfamiliar and strange, although we share the same name, Bartolomeus, and the same bones and flesh, owing to which the stone that hit his leg then still is visible as a scar on the side of my calf.

In this extract, Bartolomeus the narrator sees his former self as unfamiliar, but also sees himself in a narrative. The form and existence of a narrative is already complete, even though the experiencing 'I' seems unfamiliar to the retrospective recaller.

The temporal positioning of the narrating Bartolomeus is unstable in the extract. First he contemplates writing about past events, but in the next passage he steps into the story world, rises on the hill and looks out, casts a direct gaze at the past as a character in that world. The ability of a character narrator to alternate between the points of view of a character and a narrator, to demonstrate changing focalization, has been regarded as a sign of self-reflexivity and metafiction. Phelan (2001b, 61–62) argues that a narrator conscious of the division between a previous and present 'I,' is most likely also conscious of his or her role as a narrator. This applies to Bartolomeus, who realizes the past world to appear to him as a narrative. Phelan, like many others, associates self-reflexive narrative with lowered mimetic illusion: as the act of producing the story by narrating becomes highlighted, the attention is directed more to the discourse than to the story.

However, I want to contest this assumption. Phelan (2007) has, in another article, demonstrated that narratorial unreliability may in some cases increase the bond between the narrator and the authorial audience. In an analogical manner, I claim that at least in historical fiction, this narratorial self-awareness and self-reflexivity may increase the plausibility and mimetic effect of the story depicted. As history is always something contemplated – *rerum gestarum* and not (solely) *res gestae* – the narrator of any historical writing is better to be conscious of his or her role. The same kind of intertextual awareness and referentiality that I claim is necessary for any reading of historical fiction, and that makes counterfactual historical representation possible, enables a narrator of historical fiction to increase the illusion of truly depicting the past by employing self-reflexive narrative modes. This self-reflexion arouses the intertextually motivated referential relationship between the story world and the past. Again, the reader has the power – and obligation – to draw conclusions and decide between representations and ideological interpretations of the past depicted.

Conclusion

Even though Finnish historical fiction has turned its attention to the ways of narrativising and reconstructing the past world, the genre has not lost its connection to history. As exemplified by Nünning's view on historiographic metafiction earlier in my paper, the emphasis on discourse is often assumed to diminish the illusion of the story world. However, I do not believe narrative communication is such a zero-sum game between the synthetic and the mimetic. At least this is not the case in historical fiction. Actually, with a narrative which emphasizes "how" in addition to "what", the reader is invited to take an interpretative position on a higher diegetic level, where he or she is encouraged to compare the contents of the given account of the past intertextually and contextually to his or her own world and understanding of the past.

Historiographic metafiction encourages reader engagement in imagining and evaluating the past, and in comparing competing historical accounts and representations. In this sense, all historical fiction is metafiction: the genre is self-reflexive and requires to be understood as a textual construction. This does not, however, make the genre lose its connection to the past through other textual constructions of that past. It does make the reader aware of the ideological implications always inherent in any reconstruction of the past. Parodic, metafictional and contesting historical narratives enrich our understanding of history as both events and representations.

The final version of this article was written during my stay at the Swedish Collegium for Advanced Study spring 2011. Many thanks for providing stimulating research environment.

References

Nordgren, Ralf 1977: *Det har aldrig hänt.* [= DH, It Never Happened.] Helsinki: Holger Schildts Förlag.

Rane, Irja 1996: *Naurava neitsyt.* [= NN, The Laughing Virgin.] Porvoo, Helsinki, Juva: WSOY.

Seppälä, Juha 1998: *Suomen historia.* [= SH, Finnish History.] Porvoo, Helsinki, Juva: WSOY.

Cohn, Dorrit 1999: *The Distinction of Fiction.* Baltimore: The Johns Hopkins University Press.

Eagleton, Terry 1996: *The Illusions of Postmodernism.* Oxford: Blackwell.

Fludernik, Monika 1994: History and Metafiction. Experientality, Causality, and Myth. In: Bernd Engler & Kurt Müller (eds.), *Historiographic Metafiction in Modern American and Canadian Literature.* Paderborn, München, Wien, Zürich: Ferdinand Schöningh.

Hallila, Mika & Samuli Hägg 2007: History and Historiography in Contemporary Finnish Novel. *Avain* 2007(4), 74–79.

Hutcheon, Linda 1988/1999: *A Poetics of Postmodernism. History, Theory, Fiction.* New York, London: Routledge.

Maxwell, Richard 1998: Historical Novel. In: Paul Schellinger (ed.), *Encyclopedia of the Novel I*. Chicago: Fitzroy Dearborn Publishers.

McHale, Brian 1987: *Postmodernist Fiction*. New York, London: Methuen.

Morson, Gary Saul 1994: *Narrative and Freedom. The Shadows of Time*. New Haven: Yale University Press.

Nielsen, Henrik Skov 2004: The Impersonal Voice in First-Person Narrative Fiction. *Narrative* 12(2) 2004, 133–150.

Nünning, Ansgar 2005: Historiographic Metafiction. In: David Herman, Manfred Jahn and Marie-Laure Ryan (eds.), *Routledge Encyclopedia of Narrative Theory*. London, New York: Routledge.

Phelan, James 2001a: Redundant Telling, Preserving the Mimetic, and the Functions of Character Narration. *Narrative* 9(2) 2001, 210–216.

Phelan, James 2001b: Why Narrators Can Be Focalizers – and Why It Matters. In: Willie van Peer & Seymour Chatman (eds.), *New Perspectives on Narrative Perspective*. Albany: State University of New York Press.

Phelan, James 2007: Estranging Unreliability, Bonding Unreliability, and the Ethics of *Lolita*. *Narrative* 15(3) 2007, 222–238.

Rigney, Ann 2001: *Imperfect Histories: The Elusive Past and the Legacy of Romantic Historicism*. Ithaca, London: Cornell University Press.

Varpio, Yrjö 2009: Vuosi 1918 kaunokirjallisuudessa. [Year 1918 Treated in Finnish Literature.] In: Pertti Haapala and Tuomas Hoppu (eds.), *Sisällissodan pikkujättiläinen*. [The WSOY Encyclopedia of the Finnish Civil War.] Helsinki: WSOY.

Wesseling, Elisabeth 1991: *Writing History as a Prophet. Postmodernist Innovations of the Historical Fiction*. Amsterdam: John Benjamins.

Outi Oja

From Autofictive Poetry to the New Romanticism

The Guises of Finnish Poetry in the 1990s and 2000s

In the early 1990s, Finland experienced the worst economic depression in its history. It had a deep effect on Finnish literature, too. Partly due to the collapse of the Finnish economy, the number of published poets fell radically in the first years of the decade. Since the publishing industry had too little energy and money to devote to the cultivation of poetry, there were even worries about the death of the genre in the air. Poets struggled to find a publisher and to justify their existence. For instance, an influential language school poet Helena Sinervo (b. 1961) has written about the bewilderment she encountered when being a first-time poet in 1994. The reason for her feelings lay in the fact that she was the only first-time poet debuting through a big publisher in Finland that year. (Sinervo 2006.) However, I claim in this article that the year 1994 does not represent a downhill, but a watershed in Finnish poetry, marking a clear end to the economic depression of the early 1990s.

In this article, my interest lies in the tendencies of Finnish poetry in the 1990s and 2000s. I will mainly concentrate on the poetry of the 1990s. Most of the poems in my analysis are self-reflective, i.e. metapoems, but my aim is not theoretical. Instead, I concentrate on the poetic speaker that takes a variety of different forms in a poem. These can be seen in three clear tendencies that I will deal with. First, contemporary Finnish poetry shows an increased interest in such genres as autofictive poetry and dramatic monologue. Second, it is assumed that the role of the poetry and subsequently the role of the poetic speaker have changed in the age of Digital culture. Third, I will concentrate on the rising interest in romantic poetry. In the 1990s, a clear tendency emerged in Finnish poetry, namely a turn toward oral poetry.

The poetry readings began as local movements in 1994 in Helsinki and Turku. Poets in these regions attracted more attention through their poetry readings. This literary activity in these two big cities helped revitalize Finnish poetry which thus entered a new phase. The number of small publishing companies increased towards the end of the decade. There were young, enthusiastic publishers (such as Sammakko, Enostone and Nihil Interit – each one of them founded at the end of the 1990s) wanting to concentrate on contemporary poetry. Moreover, new literary magazines such as *MotMot*, established in 1994 by Nuoren Voiman Liitto (= NVL, Young Power Association) and the biggest publishing house in Finland called WSOY)[1] and *Tuli & Savu* (Fire & Smoke, 1994–) were founded to attract new poetry readers and writers. As a result, young Finnish poets started publishing extensively in small literary magazines and with small presses. In all, the number of published poets continued to grow after the difficult years of the economic depression at the end of the century.

In the mid 1990s, Finnish poets took on a few different guises. According to Finnish poetry critics there were two strong and clear tendencies emerging. On the one hand, there were some active male poets from Turku, situated on the southwest coast of Finland. The Turku poets were considered to follow the tenets of the American Beat Generation in the footsteps of such writers as Jack Kerouac (1922–1969) and Allen Ginsberg (1926–1997). On the other hand, there were the Helsinki poets in the capital city region. They were thought to follow in the long tradition of Finnish and international modernism. The distinction between these two groups was made visible by contemporary poetry critics. However, in both cities – Helsinki and Turku – the poets seemed to put an emphasis on oral poeticity.

The Helsinki Poets were considered philosophical and academic. Of great importance was the *Nuori Voima* literary magazine (originally established and published by the NVL in 1908). The magazine gathered together some young poets who were greatly inspired by poetry. In the 1990s, the NVL wanted to devote more time to the cultivation of poetry. Some of its active members approached the publishing house WSOY and asked for some help in organizing a new poetry association (Koskelainen 1996, 132). As a result of this cooperation, the Elävien Runoilijoiden Klubi (the ERK = The Living Poets Society) was established in 1994. It aimed to introduce Finnish poetry and seek new poetry readers. In the 1990s, some of the most active members of the ERK included poets, critics, philosophers and researchers such as Sara Heinämaa, Silja Hiidenheimo, Jyrki Kiiskinen, Jukka Koskelainen, Tarja Roinila and Lauri Otonkoski. According to Jyrki Kiiskinen – a first-time poet in 1989 – the advent of the ERK in 1994 was very important for a great number of poets, since they were able to find some financial support for their poetry readings as well as magazine with the help of WSOY. (Kiiskinen 1996, 124.)

Along with the poet Jukka Koskelainen, Jyrki Kiiskinen (b. 1963) worked as editor in chief in the Nuori Voima literary magazine in 1991–1994. As Kiiskinen (1996) remembers, the ERK was established as a result of a number of popular poetry readings. He also ponders whether there was a connection between the ERK poets and French poststructuralists. Finally he concludes that the ERK poets were interested in discourse, power and language. In other words, they wanted to use poetry to examine the ways in which language operates. (Kiiskinen 1996, 118.)

The actual beginning of the ERK can be dated to about January 1994, when the first open poetry reading was held in the Ravintola Laulumiehet (Restaurant Singing Men), in the city centre of Helsinki. Media releases were directed towards the press on behalf of a new poetry association, and the poetry-reading was thus widely advertised. However, the success of the poetry reading came as a total surprise. The event turned out to be almost chaotic with hundreds of people following the show. Talented young poets presented some of their new poems along with older poets such as Arto Melleri (1956–2005) and Mirkka Rekola (b. 1931). They were introduced by Lauri Otonkoski (b. 1959) who had published his first collection of verse in 1990. (Säntti 1996, 135.) The poetry reading was a real success, the ERK signing on 800 new members in one night. In Säntti's opinion, the ERK introduced the idea of poetry as public performance, indicating that poetry is not always to be taken primarily as written literature. Further, the cooperation between the ERK and the large publisher WSOY seemed to flourish in the field of Finnish poetry. (Säntti 1996, 143.)

On June 16, 1994, an interesting event occurred in Turku. Some young male poets had gathered together in Restaurant Hunter's Inn in the centre of Turku in order to read their poetry. The reading was organized by five local poets – Markus Jääskeläinen (b. 1969), Tapani Kinnunen (b. 1962), Ilkka Koponen (1973–1998), Timo Lappalainen (b. 1959) and Tommi Parkko (b. 1969) – as an independent event of the first Down By the Laituri festival (the Quayside festival, see Stenbäck 2001.) They were by no means a homogeneous group, but they shared an interest in poetry reading. It can be claimed that they introduced the idea of poetry as public performance in Turku. Poetry readings in different bars and literature festivals gained big popularity in Turku in the late 1990s and 2000s.[2]

According to Finnish poetry critics, the Turku Poets sought to determine their writing through the American Beat Tradition and the semi-autobiographical works of Charles Bukowski (1920–1994). Interestingly, they were sometimes named "*bukojunkkarit*" – the concept stems from Bukowski's name and the knife-fighters (in Finnish "puukkojunkkarit", "häjyt") from the Southern Ostrobothnia region of Finland in the 19th century (Oksanen 2007).[3] The name "bukojunkkarit" however is used in quite an ironical way by the male poets in Turku – by using this name they possibly wanted to point out how they have strength to stand up to the high-modernist values of art. Poets such as Kari Aartoma (b. 1958), Esa Hirvonen (b. 1969), Marjo Isopahkala (b. 1974), Tapani Kinnunen (b. 1962), Seppo Lahtinen (b. 1967), Henry Lehtonen (b. 1978) and Mika Terho (b. 1968) are usually considered the best known examples of the Turku Poets. All of them started their career in the 1990s or in the 2000s. As the list indicates, Marjo Isopahkala is the only woman poet associated with the group.

Central elements of the writing of the Turku Poets include descriptions of alcohol and drug use, an interest in the life of the poet in all its aspects. They explore the issue of writing a poem or the role of the performing or writing poet within the poem itself, and thus their poetry is highly metapoetic. A great number of the Turku Poets write explicitly about sexuality, too. One of the best examples in this respect is Tapani Kinnunen and his third book of verse called *Show Time* that appeared in 1998. *Show Time* consists of poems that can easily be understood as pornography, as women are described solely as objects of male desire and most poems contain descriptions of sexual intercourse. In addition, the Turku Poets are keen on presenting suburban life. It is then understandable that some contemporary critics have identified them with the Turku Underground Poets of the 1970s. Older Turku Underground authors such as Markku Into (b. 1945), Jarkko Laine (1947–2006) and M. A. Numminen (b. 1940) have been considered the literary father-figures for the younger poets in Turku.

A Generation without a Manifesto

In 1995, young romantic poet Panu Tuomi (b. 1968) claimed in his essay titled "Sukupolvi vailla manifestia" (A generation without a manifesto) that the wellspring of new Finnish poetry might be found in subjectivity and individuality (Tuomi 1995, 43). Along with Tuomi, a young poet Johanna Venho (b. 1971) emphasizes subjectivity, individuality and personality as sources of inspiration, too. As Venho indicates, in Finnish poetry in the 1990s, each writer is able to possess the state of being an individual writer separately from other poets' goals and poetics. No homogeneous groups exist, only a shared interest in subjectivity. As Venho rightly concludes, we should understand that Finnish contemporary poets are individuals. (Venho 1995, 49.)

Johanna Venho's and Panu Tuomi's arguments suggest there is a turn toward individual aesthetics in Finnish poetry in the 1990s. However, I argue that there identifiable tenets are emerging. The first tenet might be seen in the increasing amount of autofictive poetry, the genre strongly favored by the Turku Poets. In my article I begin with this genre, by taking the poetry of Tapani Kinnunen as well as his figure as a poet as my starting point. Second, I claim that in the 1990s interest in dramatic monologue increased strongly in Finnish poetry. Especially young women poets saw this genre useful for the purposes of social critique and overtly feminist politics. In the analysis of dramatic monologue my main focus lies on the poetry of Merja Virolainen.

In the 1990s, Finnish poets and critics took up the issue of writing poetry in the age of Digital culture. There was wide concern about the survival of poetry in an age when new technologies are constantly introduced into all areas of media. One of the active poets considering this theme was Helena Sinervo. By analyzing her poetry, I indicate how Sinervo's concept of "imagery overload" works as a key to reading her works. In the last part of the article I concentrate on the meditative mode in contemporary Finnish poetry. The last section of the text is devoted to the analysis of Tomi Kontio's (b. 1966) romantic poetry.

Autofictive Poetry in Turku

> "Welcome Tapani Kinnunen", the TV says
> and I feel warmly
> welcomed.
> This is a room for two,
> paid by Lounais-Suomen kirjailijat.
> The literature festival in Kotka
> begins very well.
> A room for two is enough
> for me, egoist, big
> prick. I open
> the first beer today.
> (*PK*, 14.)[4]

Tapani Kinnunen's (b. 1962) ironic poem appeared in 2004 in his book of poems *Pyhä kankkunen* (*PK* = Holy Hangover). The confessional poem lurks interestingly between autobiography and fiction: a poet called Tapani Kinnunen has written a poem about a poet called Tapani Kinnunen arriving at a literature festival in Kotka, a small harbor town on the Gulf of Finland in southern Finland. The overt use of the poet's name in a poem indicates that the theme of the poem is the life of a real poet in all its aspects. The countercultural life of the poet Kinnunen seems to be dedicated to boozing and visiting literature festivals.

Tapani Kinnunen's confessional poetry reflects a large range of influences from the poetry of the Beat Generation and the American confessional poet Charles Bukowski. The connection is clear if one compares the poetics of Kinnunen to that of Bukowski. The American Beat Generation galvanized media interest through their poetry readings.[5] Also Kinnunen has attracted readers' attention through his peculiar poetry readings. His performance can well be compared to that of Allen Ginsberg. When Ginsberg read "Howl", he performed it more like an orgiastic chant than a traditional poem (Beach 2003, 190). One of Kinnunen's trademarks is that he reads his poetry wearing a pair of women's tights on his head.

There are numerous signs in Kinnunen's poem that encourage conflation of poet and speaker. The first sign is found immediately in the title of the poem that refers directly to the poet himself. Kinnunen's poem can be defined as an example of autofictive poetry. Autofiction is a term that refers to fictionalized autobiography. The term was coined by French author Serge Doubrovsky in 1977. In autofictive works an author openly tells about his / her life in the third person – fiction is applied in the service of a search for self (Koivisto 2005, 16).[6] A growing interest in autofiction is part of a larger phenomenon in Finnish literature. More specifically, the increase in autobiographical and self-revelatory writing has attracted the attention of scholars, critics, and readers during the decades of the 1990s and 2000s (Kirstinä 2005; Koivisto 2004 and 2005; Ojajärvi 2006, 10–12). The rise in self-revelatory writing can be witnessed in our contemporary prose as well as in poetry.

The Turku Poets – Tapani Kinnunen here as an example – write poems that are presented in the first-person with little distance between the speaker and the poet. What is more, the texts contain many autobiographical elements. The paratexts in the collections written by the Turku Poets also refer to confessional moments. They often contain forewords or afterwords that deal with some documentary and confessional moments of the life of the poet. A book in verse may contain a diary written by the poet in addition to poems. For instance, Kinnunen's book in verse *Alaskan runot* (The Poems from Alaska, 2001) contains a documentary text that sheds light on the poetry performance trip to Estonia made by a group of Turku Poets. Further, male poets have typically written forewords to the collections of their colleagues. For example, Kinnunen's collection entitled *Show Time* opens with a foreword written by Markku Into, the Turku Underground poet who debuted in the 1970s. Kinnunen himself has for his part written forewords to the collections of his male colleagues.

In his essay on poetics, Tapani Kinnunen writes about his relationship to confessional literature. He admits that a great part of his poetry is based on the truth and on his own experience (Kinnunen 2007, 35). However, one needs to doubt Kinnunen's words, because his third collection of poems is entitled *Show Time* (1998), referring directly to posing and acting. One sign of this overt narcissism is that Kinnunen openly mentions his own name many times in his oeuvre – thus indicating that his collections of poems belong to the field of autofiction. One poem in *Show Time* (1998, 49) is titled "Kinnunen". In *Alaskan runot* there is a poem about a violent fight between "Tapani" and a boxer, a director's boy. *Pyhä kankkunen* includes a poem written in the form of a radio interview (Kinnunen 2004, 18–19), in which the poet Kinnunen gives an interview about his work as a poet for a local radio station. Moreover, in one text Kinnunen fights with his publisher in order to get his manuscript accepted (Kinnunen 2004, 26). These autofictive poems give a somewhat unfavorable impression of the poet Kinnunen: his behavior seems to be characterized by masculine aggression.

Book publisher and poet Seppo Lahtinen (b. 1967) published his first book of poems *Hammas* (*H = A Tooth*) in 1998. The speaker of the collection travels around the world in the spirit of the American Beat Generation and is closely linked to the poet himself. In one poem, a travel companion asks if the speaker really is "Urpo Lahtinen's son" (Lahtinen 1998, 52), referring to the scandalous magazine publisher Urpo Lahtinen (1931–1994). The above mentioned quotation shows how poetic I is directly associated with the poet himself. – In Lahtinen's *Hammas*, there is a poem entitled "Pane pallot Cocon suuhun" (Put the balls into Coco's mouth, 1998) that takes the figure of the performing poet Tapani Kinnunen as a focus of the text:

Yes, he reads his book and wears women's tights on his head.
Yes, he is the theatrical Flower of Evil:
Leatherhead Fuck
jumps three meters onto the bar stool,
constantly defying intellectuality and death, presses
the breast of the club hostess, falls down and hits his head on the
parquet, a yelled sentence breaks suddenly, but continues:
"Love affairs never end!"

Academic agro music follows in the show,
an iron kantele, and an electric lyre.
A sexy Finlandia Prize candidate reads her short stories.

Having boozed our wages, we depart.
(*T*, 10.)[7]

The speaker in Lahtinen's poem sits in the bar. He answers a question on what Kinnunen's poetry performance is like. The speaker has already witnessed Kinnunen's performance before, as he assures his auditor with the words "yes". "Yes", Tapani Kinnunen, also called "Fuck", really wears women's tights on his head during poetry readings. The second line gives an impression that Kinnunen probably stands somewhere near the speaker and the questioner.

The poem contains an allusion to the poem entitled "Constantly Risking Absurdity" (appeared in the collection titled *These Are My Rivers*, 1955) by the American Beat poet Lawrence Ferlinghetti (b. 1919). In Ferlinghetti's metapoem, a performing male poet is described: "[…] he performs / above the heads / of his audience / the poet like an acrobat" (Ferlinghetti 1993, 96).[8] Kinnunen's performance is closely connected to the figure of the male poet in Ferlinghetti's poem. Moreover, the allusion directly indicates how one of the Turku Poets is actively associated with the rebellious American Beat Generation. The poem also points out how the Turku Poets usually treat women as objects. In the poem by Lahtinen, Kinnunen presses "the breast of the club hostess" and the Finlandia Prize candidate is solely seen as an object when described as "sexy".

The poem refers to Tapani Kinnunen's nickname "Fuck". "The theatrical Flower of Evil", on the other hand, is connected to Charles Baudelaire and his breaking collection *Les fleurs du mal* (1857). "The Flower of Evil" refers to Kinnunen in that he published his first two collections of poems at his own expense. In spite of this, on the front page of the collections there is the name of the publisher, "Flower of Evil" (Pahan kukka), mentioned. It can thus be argued that Kinnunen himself is this Flower of Evil.[9] He probably wants to be as scandalous and rebellious as his French predecessor. In Kinnunen's poetry, the speaker often celebrates his literary father-figures. The poem "Isältä pojalle" (From Father to Son) starts with a long litany of names: "Villon, Rabelais… / the story must go on, / Baudelaire, Artaud…

/ so the story goes, / Dylan Thomas, Bukowski… / fuck, give me a beer / fast!" (Kinnunen 1996, 11).[10] This poem is a representative example of namedropping, a technique widely used by the Turku Poets.

The namedropping technique indicates how the Turku Poets' poetry shares much with American Beat literature. For instance, in his most famous poem "Howl" Allen Ginsberg openly writes about his Beat friends, such as Herbert Huncke (1915–1996), William S. Burroughs (1914–1997), and Neil Cassady (1926–1968). The intertextual net is formed when Jack Kerouac refers to the happenings described in "Howl" in his book *The Town and the City* (1950); moreover, John Clellon Holmes (1926–1988) and William S. Burroughs have written their own interpretations of the same poem in their works of art (Stephenson 1990, 53). Namedropping works as a strategy with which the American Beat Poets show how they should be taken as a community rather than a set of individuals.

Namedropping is so important a strategy that Kinnunen has dealt with it in his poems. His collection of poems entitled *Englantilainen keittiö* (The English Kitchen, 2007) includes a poem called "Huittinen". The poem describes how the Turku Poets arrive home from a poetry reading. The speaker travels together with "Jysky, Santtu, Ville" (Kinnunen 2007, 10), referring to the real-life poets J. K. Ihalainen, Santtu Puukka, and Ville Hytönen. In the car, Santtu suddenly asks the speaker of the poem: "Have you already / written many / poems about me?" (Kinnunen 2007, 10).[11] The textual strategy often used by the Turku Poets is so familiar to "Santtu" that he poses a question about it. At the same time, the poem refers to itself: Santtu's question becomes a part of a poem when his name finally appears in Kinnunen's poem.

The functions of namedropping and autofictive traits in lyrics are many. The Turku Poets employ them in order to make a division between us ("The Turku Poets") and the others. The Turku Poets share the same kind of aesthetics. Moreover, the father-figures – Baudelaire, Villon, Thomas, Bukowski, the Underground Poets of Turku – are also considered a part of this homosocial group. Male poets thus define their identity by its relationship with other male identities. Consequently, poetry written by women authors of the period is largely overlooked by the Turku Poets. Where the American Beat Generation challenged the dominant New Critical mode, the Turku Poets write against the Helsinki Poets, too. It seems that the self is assumed to have a powerful role mediating, judging and producing meaning.

All the above mentioned poems indicate how the poetry written by the Turku Poets illustrate a speaking voice closely linked to the poet himself / herself. Therefore, the happenings described in the poem cannot be distinguished from the real-life poet. It seems to a reader that the Turku Poets write a lyric of experience in their own voices. There are no signals that the speaker should be distinguished from the poem; on the contrary, it seems obvious that the poet should be conflated with the speaker. This is a part of those metalyric strategies that the Turku Poets cultivate. They seem to gaze inward: a magnifying mirror returns to them their own image.

119

Women Poets and Polemical Dramatic Monologues

"Sometimes I would like to write about men / in the same way as men write about women / that / a river winds its way through the valley / and I remembered those sparkling nights / her passion that tasted of a trench" (Katajavuori 1994, 56).[12] These lines are written by Riina Katajavuori (b. 1968) in her second book of verse *Kuka puhuu* (*KP* = Who is talking, 1994). The female speaker of Katajavuori's poem proves to be a rebellious author, ironically describing how she aims to imitate the style of the male poets who have underestimated women or taken them only as objects of their desire. Full of defiance, she wants to re-write the old stories from a new point of view: "I write with my left hand / the old melodies [...] again" (*KP*, 56).[13] By writing parodistically on what it is to be a female poet, Katajavuori challenges the canon – she helps the reader understand what is seen as the marginalization of women's and women authors' experience typical of the works in the male-authored canon.

Eino Santanen and Saila Susiluoto consider Riina Katajavuori and the poet Merja Virolainen (b. 1962) pioneers in the field of Finnish poetry in the 1990s. Katajavuori and Virolainen were already exploring the issue of being a woman and a girl and writing as a woman at the beginning of the decade. From the mid 1990s onwards, this theme of womanhood became dominant in the Finnish poetry written by young female authors. Katajavuori and Virolainen were soon followed in the 1990s by such important women poets as Pauliina Haasjoki (b. 1976), Kristiina Lähde (b. 1961), Tittamari Marttinen (b. 1968), and Johanna Venho (b. 1971). Moreover, their poetry has influenced such first-time poets in the 2000s as Vilja-Tuulia Huotarinen (b. 1977), Sanna Karlström (b. 1975), Juuli Niemi (b. 1981) and Kristiina Wallin (b. 1971). (Santanen and Susiluoto 2006, 12–13.) Although Santanen and Susiluoto – contemporary poets themselves – want to put emphasis on Katajavuori's and Virolainen's role as forerunners, their poetry must also be seen against the longer tradition of Finnish verse. All of the above-mentioned women poets are indebted to such modernist poets as Aale Tynni (1913–1997) and Maila Pylkkönen (1931–1986) who wanted to give a voice to women by writing dramatic monologues – a genre suitable for dramatizing an individual's destiny.

Especially young women poets like Riina Katajavuori, Tittamari Marttinen, and Merja Virolainen have considered dramatic monologue to be useful for the purposes of social critique and overtly feminist politics. With this genre a poet is able to give a voice to those whom history has forgotten or silenced. The genre dates back to the 19th century and the period of Victorian poetry. Dramatic mask or persona might be a strategy for self-protection, as Glennis Byron has suggested. As she puts it, "[...] speaking in the voice of a dramatized 'I' is a way of insisting that the voice is not to be identified with her own, that her [poet's] work is art, not simply an outpouring of personal feeling" (Byron 2003, 47).

Riina Katajavuori wrote dramatic monologues in the 1990s, and especially in the 2000s; the best example of this being her fifth book of verse called

Kerttu ja Hannu (Gretel and Hansel, 2007). The title of the collection refers directly to a famous German fairy tale recorded by the Brothers Grimm and published in 1812. As the title of the collection suggests, the role of Gretel is underlined by Katajavuori. Nevertheless, the most interesting dramatic monologues are the ones where the speaker is a "wicked witch" living in a cottage built of gingerbread and cakes. In the original tale by the Brothers Grimm, the witch attacks Hansel and Gretel to eat them. Katajavuori instead gives her a voice in the monologue of her own and sheds new light on the personal history of the terrifying women characters. She turns out to be a victim of difficult conditions herself.

Tittamari Marttinen started her career as a poet in 1991. Her poetry collections *Tuhkamorsian* (Ash Bride, 1993) and *Käärmesormus* (Snake Ring, 2001) are solely dramatic monologues. In *Tuhkamorsian*, Marttinen concentrates on the biographies of some women martyrs who lived in Hellenistic Greece. They were killed for maintaining their religious beliefs, and Marttinen highlights their mental strength, sympathizes with them. As a poet Marttinen works like a Hellenistic editor. She writes down the life stories of women martyrs in order to give a voice to religious women whom history has silenced.[14] The dramatic monologues in *Käärmesormus* are situated in late medieval times, in the 13th century. They shed light on the life of a fictive woman called Beata of Lyon, an inhabitant of Burgundy.

My main focus is on the poetry of Merja Virolainen who made her debut with her collection of poems *Hellyyttäsi taitat gardenian* (HTG = Because of Your Tenderness You Break a Gardenia, 1990). Virolainen writes dramatic monologues in order to dramatize women's (and also women poets') role in society. The speakers of her dramatic monologues are usually taken from history or from older poetry. For instance, her first book of verse contains two sections of dramatic monologues that are indebted to Homer's *Odyssey*. In these poems, Virolainen gives a voice to silenced female characters in the epic. Where *The Odyssey* has its focus on its male hero Odysseus and his long journey home after the fall of Troy, Virolainen centers on the women in the story. These women have had no possibilities to open their mouth in Homer's work. One of the speakers of Virolainen's dramatic monologues is Penelope, who in the absence of her husband must deal with men competing for her hand in marriage. Ridiculous as it seems, in *The Odyssey* Penelope waits for her husband for ten years, although she assumes Odysseus to be dead. In Virolainen's version, Penelope openly tells about her dissatisfaction with Odysseus.

In Virolainen's debut collection of poems, she gives a voice to a well-known late medieval author Christine de Pizan (1363–c. 1430)[15], often regarded as France's "first professional woman of letters" (Quilligan 1991, 1). De Pizan is sometimes even considered a proto-feminist, since she strongly fought against misogyny and male-dominated culture in her oeuvre.[16] The first dramatic monologue dealing with the life of Christine de Pizan is set at the execution place. The scene is paradoxical if we think about the real-life Christine and her destiny: being a highly regarded writer, she died of natural causes.[17] On the contrary, Virolainen's poem introduces to us Christine de

Pizan before an executioner's axe. She takes the opportunity to give her last speech before the execution:

> Hey, you prick on the balcony
> are you still able to do it?
> 'Course you can't, take a swig,
> let the eagle into your woman's pussy!
>
> Here I am, a stumpy little woman, a rotten hernia,
> Only a pussyful of wind blowing down the middle.
> My heart married a roller,
> I was only a little girl
> when I died with open arms, without honour!
> Now I can only offer the lips
> of my privates and my face.[18]
> (*HGT*, 35.)

In her long dramatic monologues featuring Christine de Pizan, Virolainen makes use of rhymes (e.g. "naukka" – "haukka" / "a swig – "an eagle"), meter and *apocopes*. This technique is very atypical of Finnish contemporary poetry.[19] However, it is understandable at least in the context of Virolainen's debut collection of verse: with the help of this technique she imitates Renaissance poetry and writes pastiches.

The poem is a typical dramatic monologue because it consists of an auditor whose interventions and responses are implied by the speaker's – Christine de Pizan's – words. In other words, interplay between speaker and auditor is clearly made visible in this genre (Byron 2003, 9). When Christine starts her monologue by rudely saying "Hey, you prick on the balcony", she is clearly trying to get into contact with her audience. Consequently, the existence of the auditors is evident in Christine's exclamations and questions. The exclamations are directed to a group of men, because Christine directs her ironical speech to "a dickhead" or later in the poem to "Gentlemen". Her speech is full of strong irony that derives from the presence of double-voiced discourse. On the one hand, she shouts insults to her listeners; on the other hand, she seems to be polite.

Christine presents herself as having a bad reputation as a woman. To her audience she says that she is "a stumpy little woman", and "a rotten hernia". Moreover, she ironically claims that she is an unchaste woman having lost her virginity as a little girl. Consequently, she does not fear anything. She can thus present a grotesque and fearless monologue in the manner of François Villon (c. 1431–1463), but from a woman's point of view. Christine seems to be a carnivalesque satirist, criticizing "the Gentlemen". The social hierarchy is turned upside down – those at the very top are now being criticized.

The quotation is taken from a four-page poem entitled "Christine de Pisan". Two series of poems in the collection are named after this famous woman of letters. The speaker of the poem has taken the mask of the real-life Christine de Pisan herself. They resemble each other closely. First, they both speak out against a male-dominated culture. Second, they are brave and quick-tongued enough to challenge what is seen as the marginalization of women's experience typical of the male-authored canon. As Rosalind Brown-Grant rightly concludes, besides being the first professional woman of letters Christine de Pizan "achieved eminence in her own time but also because modern scholars have hailed her as the first woman to attack the medieval tradition of clerkly misogyny for its portrayal of the female sex as intrinsically sinful and immoral" (Brown-Grant 1999/2003, 2).

In the dramatic monologues in Virolainen's debut collection in verse, it is Christine de Pizan who primarily is given a voice. However, in the poem entitled "Pyövelin opissa" (The Teachings of the Executioner, Virolainen 1990, 39–43), the speaker is the executioner, wanting to break down Christine's resistance and the opinions she has presented in the poem titled "Christine de Pizan".

"Pyövelin opissa" is a long dramatic monologue, consisting of twelve stanzas. The speaker of the poem is an executioner, directing his rude words to Christine. The poem can be interpreted as an answer to Christine's dramatic monologue given at the execution place. The executioner seems to be rude as Christine, calling her "whore" ("lunttu") and "mule" ("muuli") (see *HTG*, 39–42). He takes the poetess as a sexual object, describing her as having a churn (used as an image of the vagina), although she at the same time is told to write verse. The second stanza indicates how the executioner is totally confused in front of Christine. Although he has wounded Christine's honor in the first stanza, he tries to take his words back in the second by asking for forgiveness. He demands Christine stop her writing. According to the executioner, Christine as woman (called donna, thus referring to women's role as muse) must be quiet. Poetry writing is meant for men – "the troubadours". The dramatic monologue spoken by a male figure thus indicates how Virolainen puts strong emphasis on the role of the women poets in society.

Virolainen's poems interestingly show why dramatic monologue is usually considered as simultaneously drawing upon and reacting against the primary poetic kinds, lyric, dramatic and narrative. Although Virolainen writes dramatic monologues from medieval society with Christine de Pizan, she still calls forth the contemporary context. On the one hand, the poem is a grotesque description about the role of the female poet in the medieval age; on the other hand, it raises the question about the role of female authors today. These two voices are brought together in Virolainen's dramatic monologues making her poetry strongly political.

Poetry is in Crisis – Media Effects on Finnish poetry in the 1990s and 2000s

A great number of the poetry essays in the 1990s focused on the role of poetry in the age of Digital culture. The poets and critics began to come to terms with the changes in visual culture. In the 1990s and 2000s, many poets and critics discussed extensively how poetry is able to survive if new technologies are constantly introduced into all areas of media. If visual culture becomes even more dominant than it is today, will poetry be pushed to the extreme margins of our literature and culture? These themes were especially raised for discussion by such active poets as Risto Ahti (b. 1943), Juhani Ahvenjärvi (b. 1965), Jyrki Kiiskinen, Jukka Koskelainen, Helena Sinervo, and Panu Tuomi.

In 1994, Jukka Koskelainen pondered on the status of poetry in the age of mass media. As a poet he was worried about the ways in which mass media affects people. In his opinion, mass media – hectic and fast as it is – weakens the individual's capacity to concentrate on one thing. In the information society we are believed to exist as digital citizens, in other words, constantly fed with information. As Koskelainen states, hectic mass media is not a suitable arena for poetry. However, digital citizens need poetry, because it influences our behavior; with the help of poetry the individual might still be capable of finding the bedrock of her existence, to meditate. (Koskelainen 1994, 74–78.) Koskelainen's opinion was widely shared by many of his colleagues in the 1990s and 2000s.

One of the poets writing about the crisis of poetry was Juhani Ahvenjärvi (b. 1965). His debut collection of absurd humor titled *Hölkkä* (A Jog) was published in 1992. Ahvenjärvi considers the problems of poetry in a time of mass media especially in his third volume of poems *Kahvin hyvyydestä* (On the Goodness of Coffee, 1998). Interestingly the collection is not a typical book of poems: the volume contains two series of poems, an essay entitled "Kahvin hyvyydestä kahvin syvyyteen" (From the Goodness of Coffee to the Depth of Coffee), and the poet's own interpretations of the poems that appeared in his second volume of poems *Viivoitettu uni* (Lined Sleep, 1996). Ahvenjärvi understands poetry as the most visual of all art forms. However, he is convinced that contemporary poetry has not found suitable ways of writing symbols and images. Therefore he wants to find new, non-symbolic ways of writing poetry. (Ahvenjärvi 1998, 8–9.)

In his essay "Hysterian hedelmistä" (On the Fruits of Hysteria, 1998), Ahvenjärvi deals with poetic imagery that has turned out to be hysterical in a time influenced by mass media. The concept of a hysterical image is a key to Ahvenjärvi's poetics. As Ahvenjärvi puts it, an image is not able to captivate the world in the Information and Digital Age. Reading so called postmodern poets resulted in his being in a hysterical situation – trying to interpret images that take sudden turns. He recalls that he was unable to make any contact with them. (Ahvenjärvi 1998, 121.) He concludes then, that the reason for these problems lies in the visual overload people encounter in contemporary culture.

In the Finnish poetry of the 1990s, there are some poets who rely on imagery that takes sudden turns. Jyrki Kiiskinen and Helena Sinervo are good examples of this. The first collection of poems by Kiiskinen appeared in 1989, representing poems written in concise and acute form. However, his fourth book in verse *Kun elän* (When I Live, 1999) is somewhat different, also in that it stems from Kiiskinen's own experience. Consisting of long poems, the collection seeks towards a more prose-like form, although the lines usually contain only two or three words. The central metaphor is a car. The poetic I has been in a car crash. As a result, he needs to ponder who was at fault as well as the reasons for his survival. After the crash, the poetic I understands that he needs to put more effort into his relationship with his son, so that the son would not become too distant. Kiiskinen's poems take a great number of sudden and witty turns, as if the reader were travelling by car and watching the ever-changing scenery from its window. The imagery of roads and driving is constantly mixed with internal visions and insights.

The speaker of Helena Sinervo's poem from her collection *Oodeja korvalle* (Odes to an ear, 2003) thanks the reader for concentrating on the poem, "although she is flooded with messages that come from other channels" (Sinervo 2003, 9).[20] Together with Ahvenjärvi and Koskelainen, Sinervo has taken up the status of poetry in the age of mass media. In her essay titled "Voiko runoutta uudistaa" (Is it possible to reconceptualize poetry? 2002), she writes about the problematic role of the poetic image (Sinervo makes use of the terms "montage", and "punktum") as the world moves into the Digital and Information Age. The presence of too much information causes a poet as well as a reader a certain kind of sensory overload that Sinervo calls "imagery overload" (in Finnish "kuvatulva"). According to Sinervo, imagery overload is a very difficult problem for a poet, because reading and writing poetry requires sustained concentration. Conversely, the Digital and Information Age is full of information flow, creating a world in which people are required to read pictures and texts too rapidly. Therefore, they are not capable of reading poetry – a slow medium – anymore. (Sinervo 2002.)

An understanding of Sinervo's concept of imagery overload works as a key to reading her poetry. She published her first collection of poems *Lukemattomiin* (*L* = Untold) in 1994. It reflects a range of influences from the poetry of Eeva-Liisa Manner (1921–1995) and Pentti Saarikoski (1937–1983) – two strong modern poets who started their career in the 1940s and 1950s. Sinervo's poetry is obviously on the threshold of a new era. On the one hand, she makes use of images that are not so slippery, but behave as clear representations of things. This can be witnessed in the poems titled "Linnutko sinut söivät?" (Did the birds eat you up?), and "Lapsi on talo jota vanhemmat asuvat" (A child is a house that parents inhabit). On the other hand, there are a great number of poems in which Sinervo's writing can be read as an experiment in stream-of-consciousness technique. Many of the later poems are written in the footsteps of Saarikoski and his trilogy of poems entitled *Tiarnia* (1977–1983)[21].

A good example of sudden turns in and speed of composition is a three-page poem "Sido lanka oviripaan" (Tie a thread around the door handle). In the poem, different frames of reference and registers merge into each other. Moreover, the poem becomes a spacious and temporal experience.

Tie a thread around the door handle and let the ball unwind,
      there are endless halls and corridors
   rooms that float in the fog
cabins where passengers yell
      louder than the ship, when I sail
   from port and the eras change,
     wharfs, pilots, terminals,
Come talk with the dead, in the libraries
   men and women talk
      about their own births, how even it doesn't end,
expressions, gestures, timbres, pauses, stammers,
   We move through musical chambers, there
     a quartet practices, there is soprano
    and pianist, dining rooms,
     long tables, hum of voices,
and hum of feet under tables
   or on the dance floor, the entire night
     slow pieces have been played, come and dance, [...]
(*L*, 9–10.)[22]

The title of the poem contains an allusion to the famous myth of Ariadne, Theseus and Minotaur, with a reference to thread and thus to Ariadne. The Minotaur appears in many other poems of Sinervo's collection. It is also important to note that Ariadne's thread works as a thread that connects the heterogeneous series of poems together. Moreover, Ariadne's thread can be interpreted as a symbol that describes how postmodern poetry needs to be solved using all available routes. The symbol suggests that reading poetry can be compared to walking in a labyrinth that hides its meaning.

The poem starts as an invocation directed to the audience. The speaker (equated with Ariadne) orders the person addressed, reader (equated with Theseus), to tie a thread around the door handle so that they do not get lost in the labyrinth that symbolizes a work of art. Soon the reader understands what is meant with the imagery that takes fast and sudden turns. There is a verbal and emotional energy in the speed of the composition: different frames of reference are surprisingly mixed in the lines.

The labyrinth is full of life and energetic movement: "there are endless halls and corridors". Moreover, the labyrinth contains weird "rooms that float in the fog" and "cabins where passengers yell". The labyrinth seems to be associated with a ship that after leaving the harbor sails on the big sea of creation. The poetic speaker asks if her audience is ready for conversations "with the dead, / at the libraries". This refers to the situation where people can find information everywhere. The speaker wants to invite you to the dance. First, this invitation works as an allusion to Saarikoski's *Tiarnia* trilogy, as does the typography of the poem and the connection to labyrinth which is a central figure in Saarikoski's late oeuvre. Second, the invitation shows how the poetic speaker believes in cooperation between individuals. Language and art are not created without the help of other people.

The quotation indicates how Sinervo endeavors to give a multifaceted picture of the events in her poems. This multifaceted picture is given not only through the use of imagery but in the ways Sinervo makes use of grammatical forms in her first collection of poems. She often violates the rules of agreement for person: "We walks and bickers, and feet grinds" (Sinervo 1994, 51).[23] Finnish language has a particularly great amount of agreement. All regular verbs in Finnish agree in all the singular and plural form of the present indicative by adding different suffixes to the end of the verb stem. In the above mentioned quotation, Sinervo for instance uses the third-person singular form of the present indicative "kävelee" ("he / she walks"), but instead of using the pronoun "hän" ("he" / "she") with this verb as it should be, she uses the first-person plural "me" ("we"). As a result, the reader can interpret the sentence in different ways: it remains unclear whether the poetic I is talking about her own subjective feelings or whether her descriptions of events are experienced by more than one person.

Sinervo's poetry shows how Finnish poetry acquired postmodern tendencies in the 1990s. The use of imagery that contains fast turns is something that goes against modern poetics. However, the tenet is not a new one in Finnish poetry. Finnish avant-garde poets (e. g. Kari Aronpuro b. 1940, Väinö Kirstinä 1936–2007, Pentti Saarikoski 1937–1983) in the 1960s were already using the same strategies. In their poems, they provided a variety of perspectives to the voices and happenings in the streets.

Lyric as Mysticism and Meditation

One of the clearest features of Finnish lyric poetry during the 1990s and 2000s is the poetry which is highly interested in the ways of contemplation and meditation. I am using here the term "meditative" in the way Christopher Beach (2003) does in his *Introduction to Twentieth-Century American Poetry*. As he puts it, "meditative" in its most general sense indicates "a state of prolonged or concentrated contemplation in which the poet engages with ideas, objects in the natural world, the self, or some combination of these" (Beach 2003, 173).

In the Yearbook *MotMot* in 1994, first-time poet Panu Tuomi writes how a poet must always trust to chance – it is the poet's lifeblood. According to Tuomi, post-structuralism – as a rejection of the Cartesian subject – was overly concerned with the role of language. The problem with post-structuralism is that it leads to a too clinic situation: words suffer if a poet is too much concerned with words and varied surfaces instead of symbolic depth and thought (Tuomi 1994). The meditative mode of lyric appeared in Finnish poetry in the 1990s as a counterblow to post-structuralist thought. In the 1990s, there happened to be many Finnish poets who were interested either in the esoteric, mystic beliefs or in traditional Christian thought. Among these poets are especially Tomi Kontio, Markku Paasonen, Panu Tuomi and Maritta Lintunen.

Tomi Kontio (b. 1966) is considered a suburban poet and generally recognized as one of our greatest contemporary poets. Since starting his career in 1993 with his work *Tanssisalitaivaan alla* (Under the Ballroom Sky), he has published five volumes of poems as well as collections of short stories, novels and children's books. His books of poems are full of autotextual elements: the same imagery is found in every collection. Romantic images of the suburbs of Helsinki, figures taken from the infinite space and revisions of the old myths are combined together. Further, the tone of his poetry is often melancholic – the poetic I is not able to heal his heart. However, he is still sometimes able to feel a bit of irony. Kontio's poetry can be understood as the primary line of a late symbolistic poetry in Finland. In this respect, Kontio is indebted to such important pioneers of Finnish poetry as Eino Leino (1878–1926) and Otto Manninen (1872–1950).

Where Kontio's debut collection of poems consists of heterogeneous themes, his third collection in verse *Taivaan latvassa* (*TL* = At the Crown of the Sky, 1998) seems to be a solid composition in that the focus of the poems is on the relationship between the poetic I and you. The reader easily interprets the poems as descriptions of an ended love affair. The speaker has not got over it, thus thinking about her all the time. On the one hand, the distance between the speaker and you seems to be infinite, as the speaker tells about you being a star in the sky; on the other hand, you seems to be so near that the speaker can nearly touch her.

A good example of the problematic relationship between the speaker and you is a poem "Every mark on your body I knew by heart". It sheds light on their affair, and moreover, it explains how an ended love affair might trigger off the creation of a work of art:

> Every mark on your body I knew by heart,
> every star, every letter,
> in their light my movements turned into shadows
> and all my deeds into the darkness of the world.
> Pegasus departed from the nightstand to liberate Andromeda
> and left an imprint of his flight on the sky.
> I will stamp you on a rock
> and the name of that rock is time.
> Now that your light has disappeared from my room
> and the wind has released its hold from the window sill,
> I don't remember or know you anymore,
> but the letters do and that universe
> into which you've been written,
> that shadow, that lining of the poet's cape.
> (*TL*, 20.)[24]

The poem works as an example of the play of repetitive lines – of language focused upon itself. The speaker of the poem is inspired by grief and suffering – he has turned to you by describing his inner feelings about their past relationship. He seems to be in a resigned mood: already in the first lines of the poem the speaker seems to be just repeating the word "every", thus revealing his deep grief and suffering.

The poem is based on a figure of speech called *prosopopoeia*, in which an absent or imaginary person (in this poem "you") is represented. More specifically, *prosopopoeia* is used as a metapoetic vehicle, pointing out that the person addressed becomes a muse of the speaker. The poetic you means a source of writing, when the speaker tells how he knows "every mark on your body". The wind as a metaphor is very important in this context, since the image of wind has often been interpreted as a metaphor symbolizing inspiration. For instance, the Romantic poets of the nineteenth century have privileged the image of the "correspondent breeze" (Abrams 1975, 37–54).[25] In all, it seems that the absence of the addressed you is a source of inspiration, because the speaker strongly claims: "I will stamp you on a rock / and the name of that rock is time". "Ars longa, vita brevis", the poem wants to tell. Although the speaker is never able to touch his object of longing, he wants to create a piece of art, representing his eternal longing.

The same theme of eternal longing is present in the following untitled poem:

> Every snowflake draws its own name
> not in the sky or on the ground, but here, on paper.
> Every snowflake, even this one
> in this poor neighborhood of mine, is outlined
> not on the churchyard's severe soil
> or the frosty moors but right here
> on this paper where I will sit you down
> and myself right next to you.
>
> Not a thing stirs, how could it,
> because even the remotest star is just as close as the hand
> my temple is leaning on, the light-years
> belong to the wrong cosmology, the one
> that aspires to separate us.
>
> In the palm of my hand, I have just as many
> universes as there are stars in the sky,
> as many infinite points, images.
>
> Crows are circling the top of a birch tree
> like graphics engraved on a cloud.
> They're not flying, they're breathing just like you
> in a poor neighborhood under a poor poet's arm
> always at the same point.
> (*TL*, 25.)[26]

The poem attracts its reader's attention with the repetition of pronouns in the first and second stanzas. Already in the first lines of the poem, the speaker tells about "this paper", putting the emphasis on the very act of writing. As the reader of Kontio's poem understands, the poetic speaker is writing this poem at the window. Therefore, the speaker is conflated with the figure of the poet. Moreover, the role of the reader is being underlined, too. The possible interplay between the reader and the speaker is created in the end lines of the first stanza when the speaker says: "I will sit you down / and myself right next to you". The interest in the very act of writing in a poem is a clear signal of self-reflexive poetry (Hollsten 2004, 23). Further, the poem is an example of expanded spaces. The time described in the poem is compared to eternity.

The speaker of the poem makes use of negations in the first and second stanzas in order to confirm the reader. For instance the following quotation is full of them: "Every snowflake draws [...] / not in the sky or on the ground, but here, on paper [...]/ not on the churchyard's severe soil / or the frosty moors but right here / on this paper". With the help of repetitions and negations, a contemplative mood is achieved. The poem can be interpreted against the tradition of the Graveyard Poetry of the 18th century, because it makes use of images – churchyard and the frosty moors – that are typical of the pre-Romantic English Graveyard poetry.[27] These two poems indicate how Kontio's poetry writing is an artistic exploration where everything is open to comparison. His poetics is based on the understanding of correspondences. The speaker's inner world is compared to a solar system. Moreover, the solar system is reflected back to the speaker's inner world.

The idea of correspondences in the footsteps of Emanuel Swedenborg and Charles Baudelaire is very important if we are to understand Kontio's poetry. The speaker of Kontio's prose poem says: "I walk along Purchase Road and put a piece of the Milky Way in my pocket" (Kontio 1998, 54)[28]. He wants to indicate how there is a correspondence between the visible, physical world and the divine world. What seems to be far ("Milky Way") can be found near ("in my pocket"). In this respect, Kontio's poems bear a seed of mysticism. The correspondence between the physical world (everyday routines of the speaker) and the spiritual (represented by heaven and all the figures connected with it) is described with the help of mythology. Moreover, the poet is able to travel between these worlds with his Pegasus.

Conclusion

In the 1990s and 2000s, Finnish poetry was a vivid playground of individual poets. Despite worries about the "death of poetry" in a time of economic depression in the early 1990s, there were strong poets writing personal diction. Where the Turku Poets wrote autofictive poetry, putting emphasis on the biographical facts of the poet himself, there were a great number of female poets who wanted to write dramatic monologues. As genres, autofictive poetry and dramatic monologues are somewhat opposite: where the former deals openly with the life of real-life poets, the latter is written by poets in the voice of characters separate from their own. Helena

Sinervo's avant-garde poetry on the other hand seems to work as a critique of mass media. It illustrates to us sudden turns in imagery. The last tendency shown in this article was illustrated via poetry written by Tomi Kontio. This tendency is clearly romantic and has evolved in the footsteps of such authors as Charles Baudelaire.

Although I have concentrated on these four streams in the Finnish poetry of the 1990s and 2000s, there are still a few tendencies that I have not dealt with in this article. In the early 2000s, there were many young and talented poets who started writing prose poems. The use of computers and the internet in publishing and in what is being called "digital poetry" or "flarf poetry" was also extremely favorable in the 2000s. As these two tendencies were in the early stages of their development in the first years of the 2000s, it is still too early to evaluate their long-term significance.

Notes

1   *MotMot* was an important yearbook, consisting of critiques, essays and new poetry written by unpublished writers. It appeared 1996–2006. From 2007 onwards the annual poetry issue of *Nuori Voima* literary magazine has replaced the yearbook.

2   Thanks to the increased interest in poetry readings in the mid 1990s, poetry slam competitions were introduced to audiences in 1999. In August 1999, the first poetry slam competition was organized in a small town called Uusikaarlepyy, located in a Swedish-speaking region of Finland. The slam was held in Swedish. The first Finnish poetry slam took place in Kuopio on the 24th April, 2000.

3   The knife-fighters were big troublemakers at weddings and big parties in the 19th century in the Southern Ostrobothnia region. Fights among them often resulted in homicides. Moreover, they were difficult to prosecute because people feared to testify against them.

4   "Tervetuloa Tapani Kinnunen", seisoo / TV-apparaatissa, ja tunnen / itseni terve-tulleeksi. / Tämä on kahden hengen huone, / jonka Lounais-Suomen kirjailijat / maksaa. Kirjailijapäivät Kotkassa / alkavat osaltani hyvin. / Kahden hengen huone riittää / minulle, egoistille, suurelle / mulkvistille. Korkkaan päivän / ensimmäisen kaljan. (Kinnunen 2004, 14.) All the translations are mine unless otherwise stated.

5   The biggest success was the famous Six Gallery reading in San Francisco that brought together East Coast writers of the Beat Generation.

6   Päivi Koivisto (2004, 2005) has written about the role of autofiction in Finnish literature. In her articles, she concentrates especially on the autofictive oeuvres of the following authors: Pentti Holappa, Kari Hotakainen, Anna-Leena Härkönen, Hannu Mäkelä, Peter Sandström, Anja Snellman (previously known as Kauranen) and Tuomas Vimma. Nevertheless, she does not broaden the scope of her articles into the field of lyrics.

7   Kyllä, hän lukee kirjaansa sukkahousut päässään. / Kyllä, hän on se teatraalinen Pahan Kukka: / Nahkapäärunoilija Fuck / hyppää kolmesta metristä baarijakkaralle, / alati uhmaten älyllisyyttä ja kuolemaa, kouraisee / klubiemännän rintaa, kaatuu ja lyö päänsä parkettiin, / huudettu lause katkeaa hetkeksi, jatkuu: / "Rakkaussuhteet eivät koskaan pääty!" // Seuraa akateemista agromusiikkia, / rautakanteletta ja sähkölyyraa. / Seksikäs Finlandia-ehdokas lukee novellejaan. // Hörpättyämme lausuntapalkkiomme poistumme alueelta. / (Lahtinen 1998, 10.)

8   The Turku Underground poet Markku Into has translated Ferlinghetti's collection *These Are My Rivers* into Finnish in 2002.

131

9   In his documentary book *90-luvun kuvat* (2000, The Pictures of the 1990s), Mika Terho has called Tapani Kinnunen "the Flower of Evil" (Terho 2000, 37).

10 "Villon, Rabelais… / tarinan on jatkuttava, / Baudelaire, Artaud… / näin se menee, / Dylan Thomas, Bukowski… / vittu, kalja tänne / ja äkkiä" (Kinnunen 1996, 11).

11 "Oletko jo / kirjoittanut monta / runoa minusta?" (Kinnunen 2007, 10).

12 "Tahtoisin joskus kirjoittaa miehistä sillä / tavoin kuin miehet kirjoittavat naisista / että / joki kiemurteli uomassaan / ja minä muistin nuo helmeilevät yöt, /hänen juoksuhaudalta maistuvan halunsa" (Katajavuori 1994, 56).

13 "[…] vasemmalla kädellä / vanhat sävelmät […] uudestaan!" (Katajavuori 1994, 56).

14 Voice is given for instance to Margaret The Virgin (also known as Margaret of Antioch, celebrated as a saint by the Roman Catholic and Anglican Churches), Christian martyr Felicitas of Rome (c. 101–165) and Saint Catherine of Alexandria (c. 282–305, also known as Saint Catherine of the Wheel and The Great Martyr Saint Catherine) – all of them were condemned to death because of their religious beliefs. In focusing upon women martyrs' lives, Marttinen gives them a possibility to speak about the reasons behind their deaths.

15 De Pizan's name is sometimes written in the form of Christine de Pisan. Virolainen uses the latter.

16 In the beginning of the 15th century, she published her works entitled *Le Livre de la Cité des Dames* (*The Book of the City of Ladies*, 1404–1405) and *Livre des trois vertus* (*The Book of the Three Virtues*, 1405). The former is an allegorical description of a symbolic city in which women are appreciated.

17 The death of the real-life Christine de Pizan is also taken into consideration by the author: Virolainen has added a motto at the start of the series of dramatic poems that deal with Christine de Pizan. The motto is as follows: "Christine de Pizan. France, the beginning of the 15th century. According to the historical evidence, the poetess was never murdered." (Virolainen 1990, 33.)

18 Hei, kyrpä siellä parvella, / liekös kyvyt vielä tallella? / Kosk' ei ole, ota naukka, / muijas pilluun menee haukka! // Tässä teille pikku tappi, mätä tyrä, / keskelt' kulkee pillun verran tuulta! / Sydämeni nai jo jyrä, / pikkutyttö olin kaikin puolin / kun avosylin, kunniatta kuolin! / Nyt on enää antaa huulta / sekä ylä- että alapäästä. […] (Virolainen 1990, 35.)

19 In the 1990s, rhymes were very not common in Finnish poetry. Ilpo Tiihonen (b. 1950) is often considered an atypical poet of his own era, because he has often made use of rhymes and meter in his poetry in the 1990s and 2000s (see Dahl 1999). In addition to Tiihonen and Virolainen, there are a number of contemporary children's poetry authors who favor rhymes (e. g. Jukka Itkonen and Hannele Huovi).

20 "[…] vaikka tulva riuhtoo mukaan muille kanaville" (Sinervo 2003, 9).

21 Saarikoski's *Tiarnia* trilogy has been translated into English by Anselm Hollo in 2003. *The Trilogy* is comprised of three separate volumes of poems: *Tanssilattia vuorella* (*The Dance Floor on the Mountain*, 1977), *Tanssiinkutsu* (*Invitation to the Dance*, 1980) and *Hämärän tanssit* (*The Dark One's Dances*, 1983).

22 Sido lanka oviripaan ja anna kerän juosta, / saleja ja käytäviä on loputtomasti / sumussa ajelehtivia huoneita / hyttejä joissa matkustajat huutavat / laivaa kantavammin, kun irrotan / satamasta ja aikakaudet vaihtuvat, / laiturit, luotsit, terminaalit, / tule keskustelemaan kuolleitten kanssa, / kirjastoissa / miehet ja naiset keskustelevat / omasta syntymästään, miten sekään ei lopu,/ ilmeet, eleet, äänenvärit, katkot, änkytykset, / kuljetaan musiikkihuoneitten läpi, tuolla / kvartetti harjoittelee, tuolla sopraano / ja pianisti, ruokasaleja, / pitkät pöydät, puheensorinat / ja jalkojen puheet pöytien alla / tai tanssilattialla, koko ilta / on soitettu hitaita, tule tanssimaan,[…] (Sinervo 1994, 9–10.)

23 "Me kävelee ja kinastele ja jalat ratisee" (Sinervo 1994, 51).

24 Jokaisen ruumiisi merkin osasin ulkoa, / jokaisen tähden, kirjaimen, / jonka valossa liikkeeni muuttuivat varjoiksi / ja kaikki tekoni maailman pimeydeksi. / Pegasus lähti yöpöydältä vapauttamaan Andromedaa / ja jätti taivaalle lentonsa kuvan. / Minä lyön sinut kiveen / ja sen kiven nimi on aika. / Nyt kun valosi on kadonnut huoneestani / ja tuuli hellittänyt otteensa ikkunalaudasta, / en enää muista enkä tunne sinua, / mutta kirjaimet tuntevat ja se avaruus / johon sinut on kirjoitettu / se varjo, se runoilijan viitan vuori. (Kontio 1998, 20.) All the English versions of Kontio's poems in my article have been translated by Sarka Hantula. The translations are available in the Internet at the site entitled "Sähköiset säkeet" (Electric Verses).

25 For instance Percy Bysshe Shelley refers to inspiration as "some invisible influence, like an inconstant wind" (Shelley 2002, 35). In his famous "Ode to the West Wind", the speaker describes the power of the wind in inspiration. William Wordsworth starts his biographical poem "The Prelude" with the lines: "Oh there is blessing in this gentle breeze, / That blows from the green fields and from the clouds / And from the sky; it beats against my cheek" (Wordsworth 1983, 430–431).

26 Jokainen lumihiutale piirtää oman nimensä / ei taivaaseen eikä maahan, vaan tähän paperille. / Jokainen lumihiutale, tämäkin / tässä köyhässä lähiössäni, piirtyy / ei kirkkomaan ankaraan multaan / tai kuuraisille nummille vaan juuri tähän / tälle paperille johon sinutkin laitan istumaan / ja itseni sinun viereesi. // Ei mikään liiku, miten voisikaan, / sillä kaukaisinkin tähti on yhtä lähellä kuin käteni, / jota nojaan ohimoani vasten, valovuodet / kuuluvat väärään kosmologiaan, siihen / joka haluaisi erottaa meidät. // Minulla on kämmenelläni yhtä monta / maailmankaikkeutta kuin taivaalla on tähtiä / yhtä monta ääretöntä pistettä, kuvaa. // Varikset kiertävät koivunlatvaa / kuin pilveen kaiverrettua grafiikkaa. / Eivät ne lennä, ne hengittävät kuten sinäkin / köyhässä lähiössä köyhän runoilijan kainalossa, / aina samassa pisteessä. (Kontio 1998, 25.)

27 Kontio's poem resembles Thomas Gray's celebrated "Elegy Written in a Country Churchyard" (1751) in its themes and imagery. Gray (1716–1771) was included in the Graveyard poets. In the "Elegy", the poetic speaker ponders the destinies of the poor rustics buried in the churchyard. The tone of the speaker is tinged with melancholy, because he knows his destiny in advance. Both poems – Kontio's and Gray's – illustrate the same theme, *memento mori*. An individual must always be aware of his own death, meditate on death.

28 "Kävelen Ostostiellä ja panen taskuuni / palasen Linnunrataa" (Kontio 1998, 54).

References

Ferlinghetti, Lawrence 1993: *These Are My Rivers. New & Selected Poems 1955–1993*. 6th Edition. New York: New Direction Books.

Katajavuori, Riina 1993: *Kuka puhuu*. [Who is Talking.] Helsinki: Otava.

Kinnunen, Tapani 1996: *Tupakoiva munkki*. [A Smoking Monk.] Turku: Pahan Kukka.

Kinnunen, Tapani 1998: *Show Time*. [Show Time.] Turku: Sammakko.

Kinnunen, Tapani 2004: *Pyhä kankkunen*. [Holy Hangover.] Turku: Savukeidas.

Kontio, Tomi 1998: *Taivaan latvassa*. [At the Crown of the Sky.] Helsinki: Tammi.

Lahtinen, Seppo 1998: *Hammas*. [A Tooth.] Vantaa: Nihil Interit.

Shelley, Percy Bysshe 2002: *Shelley's Poetry and Prose. A Norton Critical Edition*. Ed. Donald H. Reiman and Neil Fraistat. 2nd ed. New York: Norton.

Sinervo, Helena 1994: *Lukemattomiin*. [Countless.] Helsinki: Tammi.

Virolainen, Merja 1990: *Hellyyttäsi taitat gardenian*. [Because of Your Tenderness You Break a Gardenia.] Helsinki: WSOY.

Wordsworth, William 1983: *Poems, in Two Volumes, and Other Poems: 1800–1807*. Ed. Jared Curtis. Ithaca, New York: Cornell University Press.

Abrams, M. H. 1975/1957: The Correspondent Breeze: A Romantic Metaphor. In: M. H. Abrams (ed.), *English Romantic Poets: Modern Essays in Criticism*. 2nd edition. Oxford: Oxford University Press, 27–54.

Ahvenjärvi, Juhani 1997: Kahvin hyvyydestä kahvin syvyyteen. [From the Goodness of Coffee to the Depth of Coffee.] In: Juhani Ahvenjärvi (ed.), *Kahvin hyvyydestä*. [On the Goodness of Coffee.] Tampere: Sanasato.

Ahvenjärvi, Juhani 1998: Hysterian hedelmistä. [About the Fruits of Hystery]. In: Juhani Ahvenjärvi and Panu Tuomi (eds.), *MotMot. Elävien Runoilijoiden Klubin vuosikirja 1998*. [MotMot. The Yearbook of the Living Poets Society in 1998.] Helsinki: WSOY, 7–13.

Beach, Christopher 2003: *The Cambridge Introduction to Twentieth-Century American Poetry*. Cambridge and New York: University Press.

Brown-Grant, Rosalind 1999/2003: *Christine de Pizan and the Moral Defence of Women. Reading Beyond Gender*. Cambridge Studies in Medieval Literature. Cambridge: Cambridge UP.

Byron, Glennis 2003: *Dramatic Monologue*. London and New York: Routledge.

Dahl, Rita 1999: Rimmaavia runolauseita. [Rhymed poem sentences.] The text can be found athttp://www.unikankare.net/kirjoitukset/rt_rimmaavia_runolauseita_010999.html. Quoted in 1.10.2008.

Hollsten, Anna 2004: *Ei kattoa, ei seiniä. Näkökulmia Bo Carpelanin kirjallisuuskäsitykseen*. [No roof, no walls. Aspects of Bo Carpelan's poetics.] Helsinki: SKS.

Kiiskinen, Jyrki 1996: Viimeinen voitelu – Nuoren Voiman Liitto vuosina 1991–1994. [Extreme Unction.] In: Silja Hiidenheimo (ed.), *Ikaroksen perilliset. NVL:n 75-vuotisjuhlakirja*. [The Children of Icarus. The 75th Yearbook of NVL.] Helsinki: WSOY, 117–118.

Kirstinä, Leena 2005: Kristina Carlsonin *Maan ääreen* lajisekoitelmana. [Kristina Carlson's *Maan ääreen* as a mixture of genres.] In: Yrjö Heinonen, Leena Kirstinä, and Urpo Kovala (eds.), *Ilmaisun murroksia vuosituhannen vaihteen suomalaisessa kulttuurissa*. [The Ruptures of Expression in the Finnish Culture in 1990s and 2000s.] Helsinki: SKS, 21–44.

Koivisto, Päivi 2004: Anja Kauranen-Snellmanin omaelämäkerralliset romaanit autofiktioina. [The Autobiographical works by Anja Kauranen-Snellman as autofiction.] In: Tuomo Lahdelma, Risto Niemi-Pynttäri, Outi Oja, and Keijo Virtanen (eds.), *Laji, tekijä, instituutio*. [Genre, Author, and Institution.] Helsinki: SKS, 11–31.

Koivisto, Päivi 2005: Minähän se olen! Miten elämästä tulee fiktiota Pirkko Saision romaanissa *Pienin yhteinen jaettava*. [It is me! How Life Becomes Fiction in Pirkko Saisio's novel Pienin yhteinen jaettava.] In: Pirjo Lyytikäinen, Jyrki Nummi, and Päivi Koivisto (eds.), *Lajit yli rajojen. Suomalaisen kirjallisuuden lajeja*. [Genres across the boundaries. On the genres in Finnish literature.] Helsinki: SKS, 117–205.

Koskelainen, Jukka 1996: Nuoren Voiman Liitto 1991–1994: Esseen ekonomiaa. [Young Power Association in 1991–1994: The Economy of essay.] In: Silja Hiidenheimo (ed.), *Ikaroksen perilliset. NVL:n 75-vuotisjuhlakirja*. [The Children of Icarus. The 75th Yearbook of NVL.] Helsinki: WSOY.

Ojajärvi, Jussi 2006: *Supermarketin valossa. Kapitalismi, subjekti ja minuus Mari Mörön romaanissa Kiltin yön lahjat ja Juha Seppälän novellissa "Supermarket"*. [In the Light of the Supermarket. Capitalism, the Subject and the Self in Mari Mörö's *Good-Night Gifts* and Juha Seppälä's "Supermarket".] Helsinki: SKS.

Oksanen, Atte 2007: Kokeilkaa minua, nymfomaanit! Performatiivinen maskuliinisuus turkulaisilla miesrunoilijoilla. [Try me, nymphos! Performative masculinity in the poetry by Turku poets.] *Naistutkimus* 2/2007, 31–42.

Quilligan, Maureen 1991: *The Allegory of Female Authority. Christine de Pizan's Cité des dames.* Ithaca and London: Cornell University Press.

Santanen, Eino and Saila Susiluoto 2006: Alkusoittoa. [Prelude.] In: Eino Santanen and Saila Susiluoto (eds.), *Uusi ääni. Uuden runouden antologia.* [New voice. The Anthology of New Poetry.] Helsinki: Otava, 9–17.

Sinervo, Helena 2006: Kuvan ja sanan kynnyksellä – Sukupolveni runous. [At the Threshold of Image and Word – The Poetry of my Generation.] *Parnasso* 4/2006, 28–31.

Stenbäck, Irma 2001: Turun kapakoissa soi runous eikä rokki. [The Pubs in Turku are full of Poetry, not Rock'n Roll.] *Helsingin Sanomat* 19.10.2001.

Stephenson, Gregory 1990: *The Daybreak Boys. Essays on the Literature of the Beat Generation.* Carbondale and Edwardsville: Southern Illinois University Press.

Säntti, Maria 1996: Elävät runoilijat. [Living Poets.] In: Silja Hiidenheimo (ed.), *Ikaroksen perilliset. NVL:n 75-vuotisjuhlakirja.* [The Children of Icarus. The 75th Yearbook of NVL.] Helsinki: WSOY.

Terho, Mika 2000: *90-luvun kuvat.* [Pictures from the 1990s.] Turku: Sammakko.

Tuomi, Panu 1995: Sukupolvi vailla manifestia. [Generation Without a Manifesto.] In: Riina Katajavuori and Helena Sinervo (eds.), *Elävien Runoilijoiden Klubin Vuosikirja MotMot 1995.* [*MotMot.* The Yearbook of the Living Poets Society in 1995.] Helsinki: WSOY, 43–48.

Venho, Johanna 1995: Runous ja individualismi. [Poetry and Individualism.] In: Riina Katajavuori and Helena Sinervo (eds.), *Elävien Runoilijoiden Klubin Vuosikirja MotMot 1995.* [*MotMot.* The Yearbook of the Living Poets Society in 1995.] Helsinki: WSOY, 49–57.

Päivi Heikkilä-Halttunen

Idyllic Childhood, Jagged Youth

Finnish Books for Children and Young People Meet the World

When we speak of the development of contemporary Finnish literature for children and young people, it is warranted to consider two significant eras of transition. The first took place after the wars and the 1950s, when children and young people's literature became independent and was established as a genre in its own right alongside adult literature. These years produced many works of children's literature that became instant classics, maintaining their endearing status to this day (see Heikkilä-Halttunen 2000, 510–517, Heikkilä-Halttunen 2001, 34–41). The second crucial period began in the 1980s, when a dramatic increase in number of new books for children and young people was set in motion. It continues still. At the same time, the diversity of children's and young person's literary topics grew and fewer subjects were considered taboo. The number of books published in Finland for children and young people has tripled in just 25 years. Over one thousand children's and young people's books were published in 1996, a rate that has since expanded to over 1,500 titles annually. As a matter of fact, more literature is published in Finland today for children and young people than for adults! Only one-fifth of this amount originates in Finland, however. The legacy of the Anglo-Saxons leads the market, as over half of the books for children and young people in Finland today are translated from English.

In the 1980s, young people's literature became filled with angst and problem-focused realism in an effort to gain greater recognition from the higher echelons of literary circles. The status of young people's novels rose briefly in the eyes of the bookish elite in the 1990s, when their authors began to break the conventions of the straight-forward narrative with experiments into metafiction and reflectivity. At the same time, the last vestiges of Finnish cultural homogeneity had dissipated. The reading preferences of avid young readers fragmented even further, and over the last ten years, British and American fantasy works in particular produced entirely new cultures of devotees.

More Books, less Attention

Contemporary Finnish authors of books for children and young people follow these international trends, but a few of the most gifted also develop innovative new adaptations that better suit the Finnish reading culture. These culture-specific adaptations are attracting more and more interest abroad. Worldwide interest in Finnish literature for children and young people can be attributable in part to PISA testing results. PISA student aptitude assessments are organized annually by the OECD, and for several years running now, Finnish 15-year-old school children have placed among the top in skills testing in the natural sciences, mathematics and reading.

In Finland today, reading increasingly competes with the other leisure time activities of children and young people. In 2009 Pirkko Saarinen and Mikko Korkiakangas carried out a cross-sectional study examining young people's reading behaviour for a span of nearly fifty years, entitled *Lukemaan vai tietokoneelle? Nuorten lukemisharrastuksen muuttuminen 1960-luvulta 2000-luvulle* (Reading vs. the computer – changes in young people's reading habits from the 1960s to the 2000s). Contrary to what some might expect, the amount of reading and the popularity of reading as a pastime did not wane at the turn of the century – at least not in equal proportion to the increase in the diversity of media available. For example, online publications have yet to displace traditional newspapers as young people's media of choice. The study found that the teen years were often the make-or-break threshold for young boys: over half of the 14 and 15-year-old male study participants reported reading nothing at all on a weekly basis. They found reading slow and cumbersome, requiring too much effort to be of interest to them in their free time.

This decline of reading as an intrinsic value, along with the growing competition to capture the interest of the readers, is reflected in the domestic marketing of children's and young person's literature. Finnish production is forced to compete against engrossing translated series like J. K. Rowling's *Harry Potter* books (available in Finnish from 1998 to 2008) and Stephenie Meyer's *Twilight* series (translated into Finnish 2006–2008). Series like these sparked a global mega-hype phenomenon that has now become the prototype for marketing similar media-friendly series of Finnish literature for children and young people. Over 60 per cent of the titles produced by the three largest publishing houses in Finland (WSOY, Otava and Tammi) for children and young people centred around familiar characters from earlier books or clearly functioned as the introduction of a new book series.

At the same time that the number of new titles in children's and young people's literature has skyrocketed, however, the general interest of the media has subsided. Careful, professional reviews of new titles appear less frequently in the mainstream media, leaving the observation and assessment of genre development to special interest periodicals and publications of institutions specialized in the literature, culture and wellbeing of children. These days it is apparent that literature for children and young people is considered more newsworthy by virtue of its awards, sales success and movie and theatre adaptations. Authors of children's and young person's literature now rarely attain the status of celebrity (see Heikkilä-Halttunen, 2010).

All for one and one for all! Solidarity in Young Person's Literature from Finland

Scarcely any taboos remained in terms of subject matter as children's and young people's literature entered the twenty-first century. Topic selection now extended from stories detailing the utter abandonment of its child heroes to descriptions of the downfall of our society. The most interesting title in autumn 2009 was a children's novel by Mari Kujanpää & Aino-Maija Metsola entitled *Minä ja Muro* (Muro and I.) It depicts the life of a nine-year-old girl who is completely ostracized at school and whose parents are devoid of empathy and neglect her daily care. Upon its publication, the book won the most prestigious and financially-significant prize in Finland for children's and young people's literature, the Finlandia Junior. At the time, many felt it should be necessary reading for anyone working in child welfare and protection services. In opposition to this award-winning topic, however, it is clear that a sense of community in young people's literature is now a trendy theme. In current storylines, an eclectic mix of activities forges the teens into a close-knit team and teaches them the important playing rules of cooperation. No one is left behind among friends; a theme in direct conflict with today's news about escalating harassment in Finnish schools.

Translated into Swedish in 1985, Danish in 1988 and German in 1989, Anna-Leena Härkönen's *Häräntappoase* (A weapon for killing bulls) was a pivotal work that revolutionized Finnish literature for young people when published in 1984, in much the same way that the Finnish translation of J. D. Salinger's *The Catcher in the Rye* (1951) did when it was published in 1961. Salinger's masterpiece sparked a new generation of male authors in Finland to pen works describing the nuance-rich transformation of sensitive boys into manhood and their search for identity (examples include Uolevi Nojonen and Asko Martinheimo).

Although Härkönen's novel was released as adult literature, young people were quick to claim it as their own. Its status as a classic is now undisputable: the book has been reissued several times and dramatized for both television and the theatre. But *Häräntappoase* received a cool response from the critics at first. Reviews fixated on the novel's baffling crossover between the supposedly separate genres of adult and young people's literature into "no-man's land". On the one hand, the fact that the novel's departure from the conventional juvenile literature format was seen as a good thing; on the other, the touching description of the uncertain world of puberty was seen as a negative epithet. This kind of dissonant reception is indicative of the literary elite's need to maintain a division between young person's literature and so-called "proper" literature intended for an adult audience.

Härkönen's pioneering book quickly inspired similar works featuring unprecedentedly free descriptions of sexual exploration and romance between young people. As an assessment of sexual taboos, Tuija Lehtinen's stories about a group of drifting dilettante boys were in particular groundbreaking (e.g. 1989's *Siivet varpaiden välissä* (Wings between our toes, translated into Swedish and Danish in 1992). The boys of Lehtinen's novels consider themselves coarse and thoroughly street-smart, but when they finally come into close contact with girls, their confusion is evident.

On a textual level, the experimental work of Riitta Jalonen also opened many new doors. Her 1990 novel *Enkeliyöt* (Night of Angels) was the Finnish winner of a Nordic young person's literature competition and tells the story of a young girl named Vilja whose diary entries are weaved into the storyline. With her writing, our heroine finds an outlet for dealing with the trauma of her mother's mental instability. In accordance with the genre's classic formula, she is made whole in the end with the help of an understanding boyfriend and is finally able to take responsibility for her own wellbeing and approaching adulthood. The novel has been translated into Swedish, Norwegian, Danish and German.

Self-expression as a partition of growth and fortification of self-understanding is on display in Hannele Huovi's 1994 novel *Tuliraja* (Border of Fire), in which a 15-year-old boy named Janne unravels the history of his dementia-afflicted grandmother, and in the process discovers his own identity. *Tuliraja* tells a coming-of-age story about the struggle between life and death, our right to our memories, and obligations that transcend generations – all with an intensity never seen before in Finnish literature for young people. Her novel preceded the increasingly fevered discussion about the right of elderly people to age in dignity currently underway in Finland. Books for young people in Finland that picture an egalitarian relationship between the old and young tend to focus without exception on the close communications between a boy and his grandparent. The elderly person is not only an important confidant and source of stability through the crises of youth, but also the only dependable adult in the child's immediate life, as the young person's parents tend to be preoccupied with their own harried life. Hannele Huovi's *Tuliraja* has been translated into Danish, Estonian and German.

The sparsely populated countryside of Finland has always provided an opportune backdrop for young people's realist tales. The wilderness surroundings inevitably function as a source of comfort to youth in the throes of growing pains. In line with the cliché, the young hero (or heroine) flees into the tranquillity of the forest to ponder the uniqueness of his existence and ascertain his place in the universe. The therapeutic significance of the forest has been a recurring theme in young people's literature of Finland until the early 2000s, with the many novels of Marja-Leena Lempinen, a native of Eastern Finland, a good example of this motif. Siri Kolu's 2008 debut, *Metsänpimeä* (The Darkness of the Forest), however, breaks off with this time-honoured forest-idolatry tradition. In her novel, a girl of 17 attends a literature-emphasis high school, where she is captivated by mystic descriptions of the forest as found in Aino Kallas' 1928 novel *Sudenmorsian (The Wolf's Bride)*. She and her friends found a secret society, for which the forest represents primitive passions. Little do they know that this worship of the forest will eventually have tragic consequences.

A noteworthy vanguard in her depiction of the abandoned milieu of Northern Finland and living conditions for growing teens, author Anna-Liisa Haakana's 1980 novel *Ykä yksinäinen* (Ykä the Lonely One), translated into Norwegian in 1983, Danish in 1985 and Swedish in 1990, tells the story of a young boy growing up in Finnish Lapland who, for lack of same-age friends, withdraws into himself and the study of the local nature. After forming a friendship with a boy and then losing him to cancer, Ykä begins to see the relative nature of his problems. Despite the death in the story, Haakana's novel is an optimistic portrayal of growing up and becoming an adult (see Haakana 2009, 848).

Young people that derivate from the mainstream in some way or another are clearly gaining ground in Finnish literature for young people. Homosexuality was presented timidly already in the juvenile books of the late 1980s, but only in supporting characters and described virtually without fail in a somewhat orthodox fashion. Contemporary young people's literature, in contrast, handles the onset of sexual identification naturally, without tension, even as presented in the first person perspective of the main character. An intriguing related phenomenon in recent years has been the total disappearance of the so-called nuclear family from young people's literature. Enthusiasm to be politically and socially correct has evolved to the extent that parents of the same sex in reconstituted families are on their way to becoming the cliché mannerism of most new juvenile book series!

Finnish authors of young people's literature still collectively respect the intrinsic value of youth, even as the books endings are increasing left open and subject to many different interpretations. A significant narrative experiment, Marja-Leena Tiainen's *Rakas Mikael* (Dear Mikael), written in 1999, translated into Danish and Swedish in 2001 and Lithuanian in 2008, details the observations of a teenage boy who has died in a car crash as he tracks the later stages of his girlfriend's pregnancy.

Terhi Rannela's *Taivaan tuuliin* (Carried off by the wind), released in 2007 and translated into German in 2011, was published just before a school shooting incident in Jokela, Finland, in which an 18-year-old student shot and killed eight people and himself. Rannela adeptly illustrates the skilful manipulation of the human mind. The typical development arc of juvenile literature is extended even further here, as the reader follows our heroine Aura's growth via a series of flashbacks from 10 years of age to early adulthood. Her mother's accidental death, the persecution of her classmates at school, and her father's inability to assume responsibility for the care of his daughter combine to cloud Aura's grasp of reality. She falls for an angry young man she encounters who teaches her to admire the direct militant methods of German terrorist Ulrike Meinhof. Never before had the polar extremes of the teen years – malevolence and vulnerability – been so palpably explored in Finnish juvenile literature. In the book's open-ended finish, Aura attends an Independence Day celebration at her old school with a ticking bomb hidden in her rucksack.

For whatever reason, women have historically dominated the field of young people's literature. Most authors of young people's literature are women and the majority of their books centre around the experiences of young women. The struggle for Finnish independence, subsequent civil war, and the social stratification that resulted have not inspired stories about the recent history of Finland in juvenile literature to the extent seen in other countries. In this respect, Hannele Huovi's 1988 novel *Vladimirin kirja* (Vladimir's book), with its historic Slavic setting, is an exception. Translated into Danish in 1993 and German in 1994, the novel's ambitious execution and experimental literary devices is admirable still today. Huovi favours the use of embedded narrative: in the novel, Prince Vladimir relates his life story to his son Miiron. Vladimir grows up as a lowly orphan until he hears that he has royal roots and sets off to find his family. Vladimir is endearingly human in all of his actions, and as such functions as a universal character that readers can easily identify with. Hannele Huovi's work is typified by its combination of folklore and history, supported by an overtone of benevolence and admiration for the wonders of life (see Rättyä 2009, 205–210).

Another epoch in the revival of contemporary juvenile literature was Hannele Huovi's first novel for young people, released in 1986 and titled *Madonna*, (translated into Swedish and Danish in 1988), in which the identity of a teenage girl becomes distorted by her pathological weight loss from *anorexia nervosa*. Huovi did not choose the path of problem-centred realism that was popular at the time, preferring instead to draw analogous lyrical material about the mother/daughter relationship from the Finnish national epic, the *Kalevala*. She chooses an excerpt from the epic's final poem about Marjatta, who eats a cowberry while tending her sheep and becomes pregnant. Her son later becomes the great hero Väinämöinen's heir. Several novels for young people were written about anorexia on 1990s, and Kira Poutanen's 2001 novel *Ihana meri* (Beautiful Sea) joins Huovi's as most conveyable. Based on the author's own experience, it won the Finlandia Junior prize in 2001 and has been translated in Danish (2002), Latvian (2007) and Hungarian (2009).

Kari Hotakainen, a writer more known for his work for an adult audience, has also dabbed into writing for children and young people. His work has consistently shaken the understanding of what is considered appropriate for literature intended for certain age groups. His 1999 collection of stories, *Näytän hyvältä ilman paitaa* (I look good without a shirt) translated into German in 2003, caricatures youth without restrain and disarmingly turns the clichés associated with the current generation on their head. The best short stories of the collection include "Koukku" (Addicted), about a "dealer" of assorted candies, coffee and Italian ice cream, "Suomen etä-isät värikuvina" (Finland's absent Dads, in colour), a defence of children of divorced parents that succinctly illustrates the changing structure of the family, and "Pizzeria 2037", a Somali business owner's racist musings on young Finns told in a charming, humorous light. Young people have flocked to Hotakainen's books and numerous schools now include his work as elective reading. Tuula Kallioniemi's 1999 novel *Lanka palaa* (The string burns), describes the ensuing events after a confirmation camp has to be cancelled due to youth hooliganism. The novel, which can also be read as separate stories, did not gain much attention when it was published in Finland, but went on to sell an incredible 18,000 editions in German (*Die Lunte brennt*, 2003) and has joined many library collections in German-speaking countries.

Traditionally, or until the early 2000s at any rate, any moralizing presented in Finnish literature for young people was cautious and reserved as a rule – at least when compared to the more strident stands taken in contemporary translated literature. The most pointed books in this respect have addressed such issues as ecology (see Kuivasmäki 2006), the displacement of young people, and sexual identity. The turn of the century saw the publication of the first novels to see racism from the perspective of a young Finnish male, like Marja-Leena Tiainen's 2002 work, *Pikkuskini* (Little skinhead), translated into Danish in 2003. Tiainen expands on the story of Alex, a victim of racism, in a trilogy (2006–2008) that gives immigrants a human face. Residents of a fictitious country in which human rights are trampled; Alex's father and brother are accused of terrorism and jailed. Alex is sent to a children's' shelter, but escapes and lives on the streets. After a series of events, Alex ends up at a Finnish immigrant centre. Tiainen invested much of her time in research for the book, interviewing immigrant children at reception centres in Eastern Finland. Unaffected, natural descriptions of multiculturism like hers are only slowly gaining ground in the Finnish genre, however.

Realist Finnish literature for young people has shown itself to be a culturally-bound genre with little export potential. Before 2000, translations were commissioned by fellow Nordic countries exclusively, with only an occasional showing in Germany. On the whole, the distinctive fantasy writing of Swedish-speaking Finnish authors Tove Jansson and Irmelin Sandman Lilius is better recognized in Scandinavia, Great Britain, continental Europe, and Japan than the Swedish-speaking Finnish authors are appreciated in their home country. Part of the explanation could be that both writers were tied closely to the Anglo-Saxon fantasy tradition, which was relatively unknown in Finland in the 1940s, 50s and 60s when their work debuted. Tove Jansson's *Moomin* books have achieved world-class status and Jansson's insurmountable position as the most translated Finnish author of children's literature has gone a long way towards easing the export prospects of new Finnish literature for children and young people beyond European borders as well.

As the popularity of fantasy literature grows, the volume of interest from foreign publishers in Finnish fantasy has soared. The "magic realism" and "urban fantasy" of Seita Parkkola's books for young people have surpassed the publishing threshold in the USA, a traditionally difficult place to market Finnish literature. Her 2006 novel entitled *Viima* (*The School of Possibilities*) was published in the spring of 2010 in the USA and translation rights to her 2009 novel *Usva* (*Mist*) were recently secured in Hungary and the USA. *The School of Possibilities* is one of the most successful Finnish books for young people in recent years abroad, with translation rights sold to publishers in Sweden, Denmark, Hungary, France, Italy and Germany.

The events in *The School of Possibilities* take place in an imaginary community in which insubordinate children are sent off to a questionable institution. The adults are either cruel and calculating, or powerless to dissent against the single-minded authorities. The young hero meets a self-sufficient girl, India, who lives together with other defiant children in an abandoned Factory. India is a fascinating blend of dismal Goth girl and mischievous Little My from Jansson's *Moomin* books. Seita Parkkola's novel talks straight about young people's rebellion against adult oppression. A supplementary storyline describes parental divorce and the problems caused by the conflict between children of a blended family.

The main character of *Usva* is a thirteen-year-old girl unnaturally tall for her age. Usva resists growing older; she sees her thirteenth birthday as a lamentable rite of passage, one step closer to being an adult:

> The world changes when you turn thirteen. You are expelled from the land of children, just like Adam and Eve were driven out from the Garden of Eden.

Seita Parkkola paints a harrowing picture of a deteriorating world with a vivid intensity that trumps even the ideal-averse and dystopic landscapes of young person's literature from Sweden. She visualizes the mindscape of young people brutally, but in a way that speaks to the reader. Her ability to speak to her teen audience is no doubt partially explained by her alternate profession as a literary art trainer for children and young people. This work provides her with a direct line to the complex world of contemporary youth – with its tender spots, tensions, fears and coping mechanisms. Important to the overall art form of Parkkola's books are Jani Ikonen's graphic illustrations that underscore the decadent, romanticist feel of her work even further.

Visions of the North in Picture Books

Finnish picture books for children first gained international exposure in the 1980s. Raija Siekkinen's *Herra kuningas* (*Mr. King*) of 1986 was a milestone, with illustrator Hannu Taina winning the 1987 Grand prix award at the illustration biennial in Bratislava. This award remains the most significant achievement to date in terms of international recognition in the field of Finnish picture book illustration. The book was translated into English, German and Swedish in 1987.

Children's picture books by Mauri Kunnas have been translated into 28 languages and published in 31 countries outside of Finland. The most exotic recent translations have been into Chinese and Faroese. Picture books by Kunnas have surpassed the English-language publishing threshold via either his Finnish publishing house Otava or its equivalents in the USA or the UK. Examples include *Suomalainen tonttukirja* (*The Book of Finnish Elves*),

Koiramäen lapset kaupungissa (*The Doghill Kids Go to Town*), *Koirien Kalevala* (*The Canine Kalevala*), *Kuningas Artturin ritarit* (*The Tails Of King Arthur And The Knights Of The Round Table*), *Seitsemän koiraveljestä* (*The Seven Dog Brothers*), *Robin Hood* and *Viikingit tulevat* (*The Vikings Are Coming!*). The trademark Kunnas characters are humanlike dogs – with cats as their adversaries – who undertake adventures reminiscent of those found in the Finnish national epic Kalevala, the legend of the British king Arthur, or the sagas of the ancient Vikings. Several of Mauri Kunnas's books are justifiably cross-classified as instructional, as they enrich their readers' knowledge of such topics as the Finnish peasant tradition, the national heritage and literary history (see Heiskanen 2003, 54–58; www.maurikunnas.net).

Finnish nature, holiday traditions and winter wonderlands have without exception intrigued foreign audiences. This tradition has been fortified by Mauri Kunnas picture books with a Christmas theme like *Joulupukki* (*Santa Claus*), *Joulupukki ja noitarumpu* (*Santa Claus and the Magic Drum*) and *12 lahjaa joulupukille* (*Twelve Gifts for Santa Claus*), and books from Pekka Vuori on the Finnish Christmas folk heritage, *Korvatunturi: Tarinoita Joulupukin valtakunnasta* (*Korvatunturi: Tales from the land of Santa Claus*) published in 1999 and translated in English (1999), Japanese (2001) and Hungarian (2007), and 2008's *Korvatunturin keitto kuplii...: sarjakuvia Joulupukin valtakunnasta* (*Santa's pot is bubbling, Comics from the Land of Santa Claus*), translated into English in the same year.

Another series of books that has seen international success are the picture books for small children from Kristiina Louhi. In her illustrated *Aino* (1984–1996) and *Tomppa* series, (1993 –present), Louhi has engendered a universal familiarity and family-centred lifestyle that has undoubtedly promoted the global embrace of her work. The adventurous and energetic toddler Aino and the curious baby Tomppa make a common connection, regardless of cultural differences or child-rearing principles.

At times, the ethos or sexual/political orientation of a picture book can be subject to censure during the translation process. This was the case with Louhi's book *Aino ja Pakkasen poika* from the Aino-series. For the 1987 English translation *Annie and the new baby* in Great Britain, the illustration of a naked baby boy for the cover was judged inappropriate and a new cover illustration was commissioned for the English version that featured the baby in trousers.

In 2004, Anne Peltola's picture book for young children, *Pom pom*, successfully reached the semi-finals of a Nordic picture book competition arranged by the Finnish publishing house WSOY. Published in America under the name *Boing Boing* in 2009, it is a good representative of the "retro" trend which gained ground in Finland at the turn of the 21st century. The illustrations are characterized by collages and the visual look of the 50s and 60s, typified by a strong language of form, contrasting colours and a uniform colour surface.

At its best, Finnish illustrated literature has taken brand new language areas by storm. In 2005 the Finnish Literature Exchange FILI began a campaign called 'From Muumilaakso to Austraasia', promoting the export of Finnish literature for children and young people. One of the pilot projects was the introduction of system for the export of picture books, aimed at foreign publishers and funded by Finland's Ministry of Education and Culture. Now an established process, the system has to date supported the export of Finnish picture books to Denmark, Russia, Lithuania and Great Britain. Starting in the early 2000s FILI also devoted its resources to a push in the Asian markets, with children's literature from Finland attracting great interest at the Tokyo Book Fairs in 2007 and 2009 and at Peking in 2009.

Talented translators of literature for children and young people that actively follow the development of the genre often contribute important grassroots level work in the marketing of domestic titles abroad. The breakthrough of a certain writer in the Russian, Japanese or Chinese market, for example, can often be attributable to a single, motivated translator's efforts. Finland is slowly transitioning to the Anglo-American practice – already in use to some extent in Sweden – of employing literary agents professionally specialized in the sale of translation rights to international publishers. A large new joint project was recently set in motion between a Chinese publisher and a Finnish literary agent, with publication contracts in the works for the *Tammenterho* picture book series and the *Vesta-Linnea* series of books by Tove Appelgren and Salla Savolainen. In the same fashion, the *Siiri* book series from Tiina Nopola and Mervi Lindman will soon be introduced in Korea.

The *Vesta-Linnea* series from Tove Appelgren and Salla Savolainen, with its first instalment published in 2001, is a good example of the way in which Finnish picture books honestly and constructively describe the emotional settings of young families. Series topics cover everything from children's rebellion, troubles falling asleep, and longing for a family pet to sibling rivalry. It also is a fine illustration of how a book series can serve the picture book narrative well. The bohemian blended family portrayed in the books becomes more and more familiar to the reader with each new instalment. The duel authors also demonstrate their proficiency in their combined efforts to alternatively draw the focus to either the text or illustration as the story arch develops. Nothing is redundant, as Appelgren leaves plenty of room for Savolainen's illustrations to explain and fill in the story. The lessening of taboos in children's illustrated literature is attested to in the last book of the series, 2008's *Vesta-Linnea mieli mustana* (Vesta-Linnea's dark thoughts), illustrated by Salla Savolainen, in which Vesta-Linnea becomes fed up with the innocent acts of her younger siblings and runs off to hide in the lakeshore reeds, where she broodingly plans her own funeral.

Finnish illustrators (e.g. Markus Majaluoma, Mervi Lindman, Salla Savolainen and Christel Rönns) are now working on more and more projects with Nordic authors, mainly from Sweden and Denmark. Recognition of illustrated literature from Finland has spread, due in part to the practice of pan-Nordic publication of picture books in the last few years. The *Vesta-Linnea* series is a case in point, with publication quickly spreading to Sweden, Denmark and Norway, followed by sales of the entire series recently to China and Pakistan as well. The serial form has been recognized as having a good coattail effect in the picture book market: if a publisher shows interest in one book from the series, future series instalments are easier to sell. This has been true for Tiina Nopola's *Siiri* books, first released in 2002, which now boast readers in Germany, Russia and Sweden. For its part, Mervi Lindman's *Memmuli* picture book series began in 2005 started its Nordic conquest in Denmark.

The British publishing house WingedChariot has published the last instalment of Riitta Jalonen and Kristiina Louhi's *Tyttö* (*Girl*) picture book series of 2004–2006, *Minä, äiti ja tunturihärkki* (*Tundra mouse mountain: an arctic journey*, 2006) and has expressed an interest in publishing the first two books of the series in the near future. A German publisher has also shown interest in the trilogy and negotiations are taking place in the USA, Japan, Korea, Taiwan and China.

The first book of the series from Jalonen and Louhi, 2004's *Tyttö ja naakkapuu* (*Girl and the Jackdaw tree*), won the Finlandia Junior prize for literature in the year it was published. It tells the story of a 10-year-old girl's remorse following her father's sudden death. Throughout the three books of the series, the girl's relationship with her mother and herself goes through several stages and takes on new forms – the recovery process is slow. Riitta Jalonen does not underestimate her young readers, writing worldly text imbued with feeling, and sharpened even further by the vivid chalk images of Kristiina Louhi (see Jalonen & Louhi 2009, 378–379). It is of interest that Jalonen's subtle yet charged narrative, coupled with Louhi's stylized illustration, has found such an eager audience in Asia, where the culture of illustration and tones is dramatically different than that of the Nordic countries. In China, *Tyttö ja naakkapuu* has been welcomed enthusiastically: a Chinese publisher has even commissioned a preface for the book from one of the country's most esteemed education experts to shed light on the book's humanistic themes and virtuosic treatment of a difficult subject. The impression that the book has made has also gathered an exceptional amount of attention throughout China.

The fine-tuned Finnish tradition of literary illustration may be admired abroad, but the dialogue between the text and the pictures and respect for the child as the reader and interpreter is equally important. Both are major considerations in the decision to translate a work.

Some Finnish writers of children's literature have built up a loyal fan base in particular linguistic areas. For instance, Hannu Mäkelä's & Jukka Parkkinen's children's books in the *Herra Huu* (1973-present, *Mr. Boo*) and *Korppi* (Raven) series (1978–1985), have gained favour in the Slavic language regions of Russia, Latvia, the Czech Republic and Bulgaria as well as in Hungary. The success of Hannu Mäkelä's children's books in Russia can largely be explained by his friendship with one of the preeminent writers of children's literature in the country, Eduard Uspenski, and yet, many other Finnish picture books in the wake of *Herra Huu* have sparked interest there in the 2000s by virtue of their slanting humour and absurd situations. These newcomers include Markus Majaluoma's *Isä* (Dad) picture book series (from

2002), Tiina Nopola's *Siiri* series and Salla Savolainen's *Vesta-Linnea* series, all of which are not afraid to poke fun, even at the adults!

Children's Lyricism. Romping Rhymes and Nature's Wonders

Finnish children's poetry has freed itself in increments from the yoke of obligatory tuition that accompanied it until the war years. Beginning in the early 2000s, one could even declare a boom in children's lyricism, when thematic collections bursting with illustration suddenly propagated exponentially. Unfortunately, a merry nonsense language playing upon the various meanings of the words is notoriously difficult to translate. As a case in point, only a few poems from Finland's grand old lady of children's lyricism, Kirsi Kunnas, have been translated into English at all (see Kunnas 1991, Kunnas 1992, Kunnas 2004). Recognized in Finland with an honourable title in 2009, Kunnas is the paragon that every new author making a debut in children's lyricism is compared to – whether they like it or not (see Kirstinä 2005, 179; Kirstinä 2009, 87–93). Her benchmark is openly apparent at times, but at the same time it artistically functions as the source a new creative influence in contemporary children's poetry like that from such writers as Johanna Venho and Laura Ruohonen, to name just two. Originally a writer of adult verse, Johanna Venho drew from ancient vocal-harmonic lullabies and songs of soothing for her first collection of children's poetry, 2006's *Puolukkavarvas* (Lingonberry toe), illustrated by Anne Peltola. Venho calls the babe by the names of the birds and plants, linking the child's growth to its place in nature and the changing of the seasons.

The French poet and writer of children's literature and professor of Finno-Ugric languages Jean-Luc Moreau has translated Venho's poems from the *Puolukkavarvas* collection freely into French (*Poèmes pour mon Bébé*, 2009). Stella Parland's Swedish translation *Smaskens damaskens* of Laura Ruohonen's poem collection *Allakka pullakka* (2004, Almanac flapjack, illustrated by Erika Kallasmaa, was likewise released in autumn 2010. The translator is to be commended for her excellent work translating the wild verbal acrobats of the original work.

Easy-to-read Children's Books

The Finnish market for easy-to-read literature catering to children learning to read was founded in the 1980s. Growing research on the development of reading skills has encouraged publishers to take a more intensified interest in books of this kind; virtually every general publisher of children's literature in Finland now has a series of easy-to-read books with generous illustrations. Designed to improve reading skills and strengthen reading habits incrementally, these books have steadily gained a more humorous emphasis, in a trend that began in the 1990s. The popularity of Tuula

Kallioniemi's books about the Tossavainen family, published in Finnish from 1994 to 1996, in German from 1997, and in Estonian since 1999, and Timo Parvela's *Ella* series, first appearing in Finnish in 1995, Swedish in 2004, German in 2007 and Russian in 2008, is largely based on their hefty dose of situational comedy and beguiling dialogue (see Ekroos 2006, 267–269; Parvela 2006, 270–278). The *Ella* series was first introduced in Germany as a serial feature in a daily paper, but will soon be adapted as part of the school reading curriculum.

Publishers today are clearly investing in the marketing of a few book series that are targeted at young chain readers, with an unprecedented volume of books being published. Illustrative of this example are the two wildly successful book series by the sister writing team of Sinikka and Tiina Nopola, *Heinähattu ja Vilttitossu* (Hayflower and Quiltshoe) from 1989 and *Risto Räppääjä* (Ricky Rapper) from 1997, whose adaptations have gained a wider audience in the form of animated features, plays, musical adaptations and films (see Ahola 2000, 10–11; Nopola & Nopola 2009, 640; 684). The adventures of the clever sisters Hayflower and Quiltshoe have spread to Sweden, Japan, Hungary, and Lithuania, and children in Bulgaria and Sweden now can read about Ricky Rapper.

The Ricky Rapper series is a modern twist on the classic orphan theme of children's literature, as Ricky's mom works abroad and the boy lives permanently with his aunt Serena. The series also typifies deconstruction of the traditional children's literature hero myths, as Ricky is shy and self-conscious in his everyday life, but together with his best friend Nelly Butterfly, he becomes caught up in many exciting adventures.

Much of Ricky Rapper's success can be attributed to its wacky, caricatured illustrations, the work of Aino Havukainen and Sami Toivonen. The husband and wife team's own picture book series about *Tatu and Patu*, with the first book appearing in 2003, has also attracted interest abroad. Tatu and Patu are brothers from the town of Oddsville and are accustomed to doing things in a less-than-normal way. The books are a sort of modern day Laurel and Hardy, complete with the wonder, abandonment and absurd humour that accompany the age-old genre. The lush, detailed and joke-filled computer-aided animation has unmistakeably drawn inspiration– as has Mauri Kunnas, for that matter – from the work of American children's author and illustrator Richard Scarry. The 2007 book *Tatun ja Patun Suomi* (*This is Finland,* 2007), written to celebrate the 90th year of Finnish independence, serves as an effective tongue-in-cheek introduction to the true nature of the Finns. The rights to the *Tatu and Patu* books have been sold in 13 languages to date, including France and Germany, which are generally considered challenging markets for Finnish children's literature. China is the latest country to secure publishing rights and join the *Tatu and Patu* world conquest (see Ekroos 2008, 38–46; Havukainen & Toivonen 2009, 177).

Folklore Boom Revives the Kalevala

Finnish folklore provides a wealth of material to enchant readers of every age. The fantasy literature boom brought on by J. K. Rowling's *Harry Potter* books has inspired Finnish writers of literature for children and young people to draw more progressively on the Finnish national mythology in recent years. Special mention must go to the real renaissance man of children's literature in Finland today, Timo Parvela, for his *Sammon vartijat* (Keepers of the Sampo) trilogy of 2007–2009. The story's impetus sprang from the author's desire to write an enticing, action-packed adventure for Finnish boys, whose infrequent reading habits were a continual source of worry. The trilogy continues the saga of the Finland's national epic, the Kalevala, in our modern day. The transition from the everyday into adventure occurs when the story's main character, Ahti, falls into a trance while playing an electronic version of the Finnish traditional stringed instrument, the kantele. As he plays, the principle of his school is swallowed up into a hole in the ground. The story mimics the opening scenes of the Kalevala, when the wise old sage Väinömöinen, sings and plays his kantele in order to sink his opponent Joukohainen in the swamp. In Parvela's trilogy, the fifth-grade boys then embark on a quest to recover the scattered fragments of the magic Sampo mill and find their missing fathers. In Parvela's modern adaptation, the Sampo is portrayed as Finland's number one export, i.e. a global mobile phone manufacturer, and the nasty witch of the north, the Pohjan Akka Louhi, as a power-hungry CEO.

Suomen lasten Kalevala (The Children's Kalevala), related in prose by Kirsti Mäkinen and illustrated by Pirkko-Liisa Surojegin, was no less than an act of Finnish national and cultural heritage preservation upon its publication in 2002. The book was published in English in 2009 under the title *The Kalevala: Tales of Magic and Adventure* by a Canadian publishing house known as Simply Read Books. The most exotic translation for children on record of stories from the Finnish national epic is without a doubt Martti Haavio's 1966 prose rendition of *Kalevalan tarinat* (*Stories from the Kalevala*) with illustrations by Alexander Lindeberg, which was translated into Arabic in 2005. It was the very first children's book from Finland to be translated into Arabic, and has since branched out from the local children's cultural centre in Abu Dhabi to every school in the United Arab Emirates.

A Safe Mix of Freedom and Responsibility

In terms of the numbers of titles being produced and the diversity of work available, literature for children and young people in Finland is now decidedly in the midst of a time of plenty. While children's literature still finds its equilibrium safely in the idyll of hearth and home, the humour of easy-to-read series in particular is stretching traditional boundaries in a welcome way. In apposition, Finnish literature for young people is ever more deluged with assorted extremes and experimentation. The youth that we meet there may be raw and wounded, but portrayed with empathy all the same.

References

Ahola, Suvi 2000: Sinikka Nopola and Tiina Nopola: Writing together is hard work. In: Suvi Ahola (ed.), *Finnish books for young readers: a selection of relevant books from the 1990s*. Helsinki: Finnish Literature Information Centre 2000, 10–11.

Ekroos, Anna-Leena 2006: Classroom capers. Interview of Timo Parvela. *Books from Finland* 4/2006, 267–269.

Ekroos, Anna-Leena 2008: Tough cookies. Interview of Aino Havukainen and Sami Toivonen. Transl. Owen Witesman. *Books from Finland* 1/2008, 38–46.

Haakana, Anna-Liisa 2009: My One-legged Friend and Me. Article by Laura Kyllönen. In: Julia Eccleshare (ed.), *1001 children's books you must read before you grow up*. New York: Universe.

Havukainen, Aino & Toivonen, Sami 2009: Tatu and Patu in Helsinki. In: Julia Eccleshare (ed.), *1001 children's books you must read before you grow up*. New York: Universe.

Heikkilä-Halttunen, Päivi 2000: An interloper in charge of the house: the institutionalisation and canonisation of Finnish children's literature in the 1940s and 1950s. Transl. Virginia Mattila. [Summary for thesis.] In: Heikkilä-Halttunen, Päivi 2000: *Kuokkavieraasta oman talon haltijaksi. Suomalaisen lasten- ja nuortenkirjallisuuden institutionalisoituminen ja kanonisoituminen 1940–1950-luvulla*. Helsinki 2000: SKS, 510–517.

Heikkilä-Halttunen, Päivi 2001: Der ergiebigen Jahre der Kinder- und Jugendliteratur. [A Productive Year for Children's and Young People's Literature.] In: *Jahrbuch für finnisch-deutsche Literaturbeziehungen*. Nr. 33. Herausgegeben von Hans Fromm, Maria-Liisa Nevala und Ingrid Schellbach-Kopra. Helsinki: Die Deutsche Bibliothek, 34–41.

Heikkilä-Halttunen, Päivi 2010: Who for? On new books for children and young people. *Books from Finland* 29 January 2010. http://www.booksfromfinland.fi/categories/non-fiction/articles. Referenced 18.5.2012.

Heiskanen, Seppo 2003: Canine capers. Mauri Kunnas' canine makeover of a literary classic. *Books from Finland* 1/2003, 54–58.

Husk Porridge and Space Bunnies: Finnish Books for Children and Young People 2006: Ed. Janna Kantola, transl. David Hackston. Helsinki: Ministry for Foreign Affairs/ Finnish Literature Information Centre.

Kirstinä, Leena 2005: Classic Finnish writers. Kirsi Kunnas: Earth, Tree, Wind. *Books from Finland* 3/2005, 179.

Kirstinä, Leena 2009: How did Kirsi Kunnas renew Finnish children's poetry. In: Barbara Drillsma-Milgrom & Leena Kirstinä (eds.), *Metamorphoses in Children's Literature and Culture*. Turku: Enostone, 87–93.

Kuivasmäki, Riitta 2006: Finnish children's literature from the ecological point of view. In: *The Second World Children's Literature Convention: the 8th Asia children's literature convention in Seoul organized by the Korea Children's Literature Society, 21–25 August 2006*. Seuol: Asia Children's Literature Society, 23–25.

Kunnas, Kirsi 1991: English translations of Kirsi Kunnas poems from 1956's *Tiitiäisen satupuu*. [Tumpkins wonder tree.] Transl. and ed. Herbert Lomas. Newcastle: Bloodaxe Books, 170–175.

Kunnas, Kirsi 1992: More Tumpkin tales. English translations from 1991's *Tiitiäisen pippurimylly*. [The Tumpkins Peppermill.] Transl. Herbert Lomas. *Books from Finland* 2/1992, 75–78.

Kunnas, Kirsi 2005: Animal Crackers. Poems for children and adults. Children's lyrics from the 2004 anthology *Tapahtui Tiitiäisen maassa*. [*It happened in Tumpkin's Land.*] Transl. by Herbert Lomas. *Books from Finland* 3/2005, 180–185.

Kyllönen, Laura 2009: The Girl and the Jackdaw Tree. In: Julia Eccleshare (ed.), *1001 children's books you must read before you grow up*. New York: Universe, 378–379.

Kyllönen, Laura 2009: Hayflower and Quiltshoe. In: Julia Eccleshare (ed.), *1001 children's books you must read before you grow up*. *New York: Universe,* 640.

Kyllönen, Laura 2009: Rupert the Rapper and Aunt Deep Freeze. In: Julia Eccleshare (ed.), *1001 children's books you must read before you grow up*. New York: Universe 2009, 684.

Parvela, Timo 2006: In a class of their own. Extracts from the 2006 children's book from Tammi Publishing *Ella: Varokaa lapsia!* [*Ella: Look out for children!*] Transl. Lola Rogers. *Books from Finland* 4/2006.

Rättyä, Kaisu 2009: Border of Life. The theme of death in Hannele Huovi's novels. In: Barbara Drillsma-Milgrom & Leena Kirstinä (eds.), *Metamorphoses in Children's Literature and Culture*. Turku: Enostone, 205–210.

http://www.maurikunnas.net. Referenced 18.5.2012.

Further Reading

Finnish Children's and Youth Books VI (1987–1992). Eds. Vuokko Blinnikka et al., transl. Eva Buchwald. The Finnish section of IBBY 1992.

Finnish Children's and Youth Books VII (1993–1998). Eds. Vuokko Blinnikka et al., transl. John Pickering. The Finnish section of IBBY 1998.

Finnish Children's and Youth Books VIII (1999–2001). Eds Maija Karjalainen et al., transl. Kieron Norris & Laura Pitkonen. The Finnish Section of IBBY 2002.

Finnish Children's and Youth Books IX (2002–2003). Eds. Kaarina Kolu et al., transl. Kieron Norris & Laura Pitkonen. The Finnish Section of IBBY 2004.

Finnish Picture Books and Illustrations for Children. Eds. Kaarina Kolu et al., transl. Kieron Norris & Laura Pitkonen. The Finnish Section of IBBY 2005.

Finnish Children's and Youth Books X (2004–2005). Eds. Kaarina Kolu et al., transl. Kieron Norris & Laura Pitkonen. The Finnish Section of IBBY 2006.

Finnish Children's and Youth books XI (2006–2008). Eds. Kaarina Kolu et al., trans. Kieron Norris & Laura Pitkonen. The Finnish Section of IBBY 2008.

Heikkilä-Halttunen, Päivi 2000: Finnish children and young people's literature: A time of growth and renewal. In: Suvi Ahola (ed.), *Finnish books for young readers: a selection of relevant books from the 1990s*. Helsinki: Finnish Literature Information Centre, 2–3.

Jussi Ojajärvi

Capitalism in the Family

On Realistic Involvement after the Neoliberal Turn

The Ethos of Realistic Involvement

In recent Finnish novels, the context of the neoliberal turn in global and local politics (see Harvey 2005; Julkunen 2000) and the resulting "society of competitiveness" (Heiskala & Luhtakallio 2006) have given rise to a wide thematic field. Many novels have focused on the development of capitalism and its effects on socio-cultural practices and identity formation.

Some key texts share the 'post-industrialisation' of production as the background of their social milieu: *Bronks* by Kari Hotakainen (1993) is a cultural history of capitalist modernisation and the marginalisation of the workers, who belong to an outdated phase of Western industrial society; *Pamisoksen purkaus* by Hannu Raittila (2005) begins as a story of the depression of the 1990s and evolves into a representation of society in which the sense of reality is vanishing due to the production of the 'spectacle' (marketing, images, media); the latter theme is also used by Juha Seppälä in *Paholaisen haarukka* (2008). In fiction situated in the near future, there has often been a dystopian tone (*Ocean City* by Kauko Röyhkä, 1999; *Unelmakuolema* by Leena Krohn, 2004; *Karsintavaihe* by Maarit Verronen, 2008). These dystopian novels, as well as *Martina Dagers längtan* by Henrika Ringbom (1998) or the works of Arto Salminen (e.g. *Varasto*, 1998; *Kalavale*, 2005), clearly represent the question of alienation as topical. Consumption has appeared as a recurrent motif in recent literature and as one key theme in novels such as the two considered further in this article: *Drakarna over Helsingfors* by Kjell Westö (1996) and *Kiltin yön lahjat* by Mari Mörö (1998). The neoliberalist language and thinking, in which the social appears as a market place and the individual as *homo oeconomicus*, has been ironically remarked upon (*Pyydys* by Jyrki Tuulari, 1998; *Kunnian mies* by Tommi Melender, 2007; see Ojajärvi 2008). One of the objects of critical representation in literature has been the 'brand' (image and fame produced and seen in terms of capital) as a media phenomenon and as the cultural logic of neoliberalist agenda (*Klassikko* by Hotakainen, 1997; *Mansikoita marraskuussa* by Pirjo Hassinen, 2000; *Lang* by Westö, 2002). Moreover, around the year 2000, several Finnish writers – especially Arto Salminen, Reko Lundán and Hanna Marjut Marttila – took class difference under serious scrutiny.[1]

Could these texts be described as 'social' or 'sociological' novels? They centre around the pressures and effects of social, economic and environmental conditions on characters and events. The reader may also find a strong sense of the shortcomings of society. Whether these novels have – as some definitions of the 'sociological novel' imply – a didactic purpose, a clear thesis or some radical solution to point out is a complex issue.[2] In any case, the novels address the expansion of the hold of money and capital; they are social novels in the sense that they are literary reactions to the global and local context, in which there is a growing tension between commodification and other modes of the social.

However, it would be insatisfactory to name these novels only 'social'. Firstly, their social view does not exclude the personal. Secondly, this double-view is the essence of 'realism', as Raymond Williams (1958, 22) once reminded:

> [Realism] offers a valuing creation of a whole way of life, a society, that is larger than any of the individuals composing it, and at the same time valuing creations of human beings, who while belonging to and affected by and helping to define this way of life, are also, in their own terms, absolute ends in themselves.

Williams's definition of the "method" of the realistic novel – or what I will call *the ethos of realistic involvement*[3] – is obviously an ideal type of definition.[4] Yet it is a useful thematic conception in considering the tone of many Finnish novels written in the context of neoliberal capitalism during the last two decades: those texts situate in a loose genre of 'realistic novel' in the precise sense that while trying to grasp the social whole, they reflect upon society through character figurations and subjectivities constructed as a part of that society.

Let us also note that by privileging this kind of ethos as the essence of realism, Williams makes room for the account according to which there is no reason to define and delimit the concept of realism in terms of a certain periodic agreement on the forms by which the mimetic relation between the text and its social context is constructed (see Peltonen 2008; Williams 1977a, 216–220; Williams 1989, 230, 233; also Ojajärvi 2006, 35–36). In other words, 'realistic involvement' does not presuppose any simple 'realistic form' (for instance, the one with omniscient narrator). As Bertolt Brecht (1974, 53) wrote:

> Whether a work is realistic or not cannot be determined merely by checking whether or not it is like existing works which are said to be realistic, or were realistic in their time. In each case, one must compare the depiction of life in a work of art with the life that is being depicted (instead of comparing it with another depiction).

Williams's conception of realism seems to adopt Brecht's repudiation of Georg Lukács's preference for traditional aesthetic of realism, though simultaneously Williams's account is related to the Lukácsian stance on the importance of considering the social whole ('totality') in relation to the subjectivity of characters.[5]

In his own time, thinking about the English novel, Williams saw that a division had occurred in the realistic tradition. On the one hand, he saw the 'social' novel with two main genres; the social documentary, and the dystopian future story. In the latter, which he also called the 'social formula', a pattern taken from contemporary society is represented and heightened in another time and place. On the other hand, there was the 'personal' novel concentrating on selected personal relationships or offering (as a 'personal formula') a highly personalized landscape. (Williams 1958.) Roughly speaking, we could draw some kind of analogy between the 'personal' tendency and the emerging post-war modernism in Finnish literature. However, considering the features of the former development, the analogy does not seem so clear at all. Although the genre of social documentary emerged during the 1960s (Zilliacus 1999), the dystopian tradition remained very narrow, and the realistic novel with a rather Williamsian societal and emancipatory emphasis[6] did not lose its touch for a long time. It was perhaps not until the 1980s and the heyday of postmodernism that a remarkable number of Finnish writers problematised the shared ethos of depicting a common reality, or sections *of* that reality, and when the progressive realistic tendency of the Finnish novel – relying on the modern view that all people should and could become recognised as members of society (cf. Ruohonen 1999, 270) – got its most paradigmatic contraries. In some aspects of the 'blank fiction' (Annesley 1998) of Rosa Liksom's collection *Yhden yön pysäkki* (1985, transl. in the compilation *One Night Stands*, 1993), in the rather cynical postmodernism of Markku Eskelinen's *Nonstop* (1988), and in many of the writings of the so called "School of Evil" the common trust in the progressive project of modernity was replaced with a spatial present and a body of isolated individual focalisations.

However, since the 1980s, a new kind of realistic involvement seems to have emerged. The 1990s and the beginning of the new century produced a great deal of literature with a critically realistic concern, which more or less openly questions the effects of capitalism – basically, an economic system consisting of capital, production, class divisions, the market, consumption, and a tendency to reify – on society and on the life worlds and identity practices of individual subjects.[7] Amongst the impulses of this questioning, there is a particularly Finnish one: the exceptionally deep economic depression in Finland during the first half of the 1990s, due to the financial deregulation in the 1980s and the dramatic decline of the Soviet trade. From 1991 to 1994, unemployment more than quadrupled, and many people were left in serious debt. The depression, as well as the comparatively neoliberal economic and social policy, adopted partially as a response to it, left many lasting traces in Finnish society, income distribution, welfare, media culture, and mentalities. A significant number of ideological binary oppositions, between individuality and the nurturing state, were constructed in political discourse. The Scandinavian welfare model was not totally abandoned, yet what has been stressed as the main objective of the state and the good citizens since the depression, has not been social justice, but competitiveness (Heiskala & Luhtakallio 2006).

On a more general level, the global neoliberalism (which had a strong hold at least until autumn 2008, when the latest recession began) can be conceptualised as an intensive period of 'commodification'. Commodification is an economic and also a political process, as neoliberalism goes to show. The concept owes a lot to Marx and the first volume of *Capital* (1867). I use the term to designate the subjection of social reality to the commodity form, the essence of which is the seller-buyer relationship of the market and the surplus-value logic of capital accumulation. If social reality is increasingly seen in the light of these two factors, there is good reason to speak of 'commodification'.

It is in these local and global contexts where the different kinds of realistic involvement have recently been found topical. The texts mentioned in the beginning are a vital sign of literary thematicization of capitalism as not only an economic circumstance, but also as a certain kind of rationality that has social and cultural effects on subjectivity. In these novels, realistic involvement appears as a node of many literary modes and traditions. The dystopian mode, which Williams (1958) called the 'social formula', has been quite commonly adopted, and – since Hotakainen's 1993 novel *Bronks* – quite clearly with an implicit or explicit tendency to question the commodification of social realities and subjective life worlds. A re-articulation of the highly "personal" (if not somewhat atomistic) formulas of modernism and postmodernism has also emerged in relation to the mapping of contemporary society. For instance, during the first half of the 1990s, the so called "School of Evil" writers of the 1980s began to relate societal background more clearly into their texts (Leiwo 2002; on some novels of the 1980s, see Sassi 2009). The post- or late modernist fragmented and metafictional modes of narration have also been adopted in thematicizing the societal span resulting in the neoliberal era (*Routavuosi* by Juha Seppälä, 2004) or the 'society of the spectacle' (*Pamisoksen purkaus* by Raittila; *Paholaisen haarukka* by Seppälä). Indeed, the neoliberal era has been addressed by literary thematicization and counter-culture (see Ojajärvi 2006).

Correspondingly, Mervi Kantokorpi notes that "the most obvious commonly shared background" for the literature that currently critically analyses society is the depression of the 1990s. Admittedly, the task it has taken is demanding, for there is not one common culture or experience about which to tell, and the socio-economic mechanisms in question – Kantokorpi mentions market liberalism, the virtualization of the economy, and the media – are global and not just local. Yet Kantokorpi concludes that in the recent Finnish prose we find plenty of such critical societal thematicization, which had previously been thought to have disappeared. (Kantokorpi 2007, 323–324; cf. Ojajärvi 2006, 272–304.)

A Look at the Family as a Look at the Social Construction of Reality

For Raymond Williams (1958), the critical power of realistic literature lies not in any particular narrative form, but in the recognition of the dialectics of the 'social' and 'personal' dimensions of reality. Williams sees realistic literature as a way of studying the historical construction of reality. Leaving aside the obvious background of Marxist literary theory, I want to make a short comparison and note that his notion of realism seems to be a literary equivalent of the sociology of knowledge that was formulated some years later by Peter L. Berger and Thomas Luckmann in their book *The Social Construction of Reality* (1966).

According to Berger and Luckmann, reality is constantly constituted in a cyclic social process. Human subjects 'externalise' their subjectivities in their actions and interactions. They continually construct the social world, which then becomes a set of 'objectivations,' including symbolic systems, artefacts, social and political institutions; even 'reifications,' i.e. social products that are no longer treated as social ones, but as things above them. 'Internalisation' (ideal-typically speaking) completes and re-starts the cycle. Most clearly, although not at all exclusively, internalisation concerns children and the usual site of primary socialisation; the family. Children internalise the ideas and ways of their culture in socialisation. They acquire skills that enable them to participate in meaningful interaction with other people; to respond to the reality that was there before them; to re-construct that reality, more or less. (Berger & Luckmann 1984; Burr 2005, 185–187.)

I would like to argue that it is useful to consider Williams's notion of realistic literary representation as analogical to the dialectics pointed out in the model by Berger and Luckmann: realistic novel focuses on the social construction of both society and subjectivity.[8] The main thing to add would be that in Williams we find a more obvious critique of capitalist reproduction of class relations. Accordingly, there is clearly a commitment to the ideas of emancipation and solidarity; in his Marxist view, the kind of 'structure of feeling' (Williams 1977b) that the realistic novel should produce, in one way or another, is the experience of individual human beings as ends in themselves (Williams 1958, 22).

With Berger's and Luckmann's dialectical model in mind, it is interesting to notice that in the 1990s, when the Finnish novel kind of re-discovered its realistic potential for the thematicization of capitalism, one of the central milieus was the family, the site of primary socialisation. By showing how capitalism may intertwine with family life, literature's realistic interest in the relation of the personal and the social critically brought together such dimensions of modern reality, which are commonly (ideologically, to be sure) regarded as if they were not internally related. In everyday discussions, family life is often seen as if it was only an intimate sphere of life, and the economic rationality of society a matter outside the intimate. However, due to the intensive neoliberal commodification during the last decades, this common assumption obviously does not hold true. (See Hochschild 2003.) What is more, it is questionable if it ever did. According to Louis Althusser (1971), family has served (along with church, school, media etc.) as an 'ideological state apparatus' constantly reproducing the social relations that capitalist production needs. Marxists have argued that in capitalism the family has functioned as a source of gendered, hierarchical, privatised and exclusionary models of sharing, thus offering a core model and institution for the accumulation and transfer of private property (see Hardt & Negri 2009, 160–161). In what follows, I am not trying to track down these ideological functions in their full array, as I am not focusing so much on 'the family in capitalism' than on 'capitalism in the family'.[9] Yet perhaps already these remarks have made clear, why the articulation of capitalism and the family may, indeed, be a remarkable area of interest of realistic involvement.

I focus briefly on two novels which include the motif of 'capitalism in the family': Kjell Westö's *Drakarna över Helsingfors* (Kites above Helsinki, not transl. into English),[10] and Mari Mörö's *Kiltin yön lahjat* (Good-Night Gifts, not transl.).[11] They are both highly lauded novels of the late 1990s. The former is the story of an upper-middle-class family, spanning many decades. One of the interpretative keys to the novel is its intertextual allusion to Marx's famous prediction of the modern capitalist era as a force due to which all formerly "solid" structures – including institutionalised social practices such as familial relations – are subject to dramatic change.[12] The latter novel tells the story of the relationship of a six-year-old girl to her lower-working-class mother, and it represents a situation in which market practices constitute a replacement for love and care, as I will show by close reading of the novel's *leitmotif*.

In these novels, a glimpse into the life of a family functions exemplarily as Williams's "realistic method": as a view into the social construction of reality and subjectivity. They articulate the societal to the familial. As Margaret and Michael Rustin (2002) mention in their book on drama, psychoanalysis and society, this combination has always been a subject matter of Western drama (not to mention the Western novel). Central tensions of society have been represented in the form of family crisis. In regard to Finnish literature, the gender divisions of society depicted in women's literature are the most obvious example. Many times in these family representations the contradictions of capitalism have also been present. This is the line of Minna Canth's *Työmiehen vaimo* (1885) and Maria Jotuni's *Kultainen vasikka* (1918). In the prose of the Swedish-speaking Finns, too, there is a small tradition of relating family conflicts to the tensions of capitalism. Making this articulation in *Drakarna över Helsingfors*, Westö is actually the heir of Christer Kihlman.

Capitalism in the Bexar Family

> The bourgeoisie has torn away from the family its sentimental veil, and turned the family relation into a pure money relation. (Marx & Engels, *The Communist Manifesto*.)

In *Drakarna över Helsingfors* identity is ascribed with multiple meanings. The relationship between capitalism and identity is one of its main concerns. While describing post-war Finland from the 1960s to the middle of the 1990s, the text frequently refers to the expansion of capitalist consumer society: a background hum to the story is composed of commodification. At first, the signs of it are almost unnoticeable in the text. In the beginning of the 1960s Henrik, the father of the Bexar family, decides:

> In the autumn I will buy a car. I guess it will be a Ford, a trustworthy vehicle.
> There's no room for more children in this apartment. We need something larger.
> And a TV shall we have. (*DÖH*, 20; *LHY*, 23.)[13]

The sixties was the decade when middle-class consumer practices became rapidly more common in Finland. Henrik's thoughts refer to this context: the pursuit of consumer wealth, coupled with the older identity model of hard work and reasonable saving, is becoming a new norm (cf. Mäenpää 2004, 287–292). To buy a car, a larger apartment, and a television represents happiness and, more accurately, the happiness of the family. As a matter of fact, Henrik seems to understand his consumption as care. At this point, the consumer desires are directed at acquisitions with a relatively long-term use value, which is an attitude significantly different from what sociologist Zygmunt Bauman (2008, 85) calls the present-day 'consumerist cultural syndrome' of aiming at instant self-satisfaction. In brief, Henrik lives in a society where consumption has not yet turned into 'consumerism' (cf. Bauman 2008, 28). Social bonds with a long-term perspective still direct the logic of consumption.

Nevertheless, Henrik is attracted by an emergent ideology of consumer capitalism; in Althusserian terms he is 'interpellated' by an emergent social system, which proposes that the prerequisites for family happiness lie in consumption. The prerequisite for consumption, in turn, is obviously money. To earn money and happiness for his family, Henrik works a lot. Henrik is a young, petit-bourgeois father of his time. In working hard to consume for his family he employs a 'productivist' life programme (see Bauman 2008, 85), which holds together different impulses, such as impulses to consume, desires like Henrik's unfulfilled dreams of a German girl,[14] and proclivities for hard work. The unfortunate but regrettably logical result is his estrangement and distance, as he loses the thing he works for: soon he has no time for his family. His son Riku (Rickard) notes some years later:

> At Ritokalliontie, Riku understands that time is a scarcity. [...]
>
> The truth is: Henrik does not have any more time. On numerous Sunday mornings, he wakes up early and has entrenched himself behind the massive wooden door of his study when Riku gets up from his bed, which resembles a sea of ice-hockey cards and [Donald Duck comics].
>
> And as many are the Sunday mornings Henrik is travelling. (*DÖH*, 63–64; *LHY*, 74.)

Along with his labour power, Henrik has sold his time. Even at home he is obliged to construct an isolated castle of work.[15] Riku, in turn, is just beginning his consumer odyssey on the sea[16] of commodities. The scene transverses the experience of proximity in another of Riku's memories, in which he and Henrik are driving together, and Riku feels safe and close to Henrik. A common factor in the two memories is the presence of the market. It is present even in the earlier memory: at that time, Riku is learning to read, and the very first word he reads while driving the streets of Helsinki with his father is "A-J-A-T-A-R"; an articulation of the market and time is represented here, for Ajatar is a *shop* with a name that refers to a (female) time carrier or, metaphorically, to living the era intensively.[17] There is a thematic tension between Riku's two memories of his father, and it refers to the commodification of time and to the deepening cycle of alienation.

Of course this phase of capitalism has an influence on mothers as well. The gendered division of labour, where 'the angel in the house' provides a protecting home, the springboard from which the entrepreneurial male takes part in the competitive market place, has been a familiar premise of capitalism since the 18th century and Adam Smith's *Theory of the Moral Sentiments* (see Wheeler 1999, 10). In Westö's novel this social role, or subject position, is related to the exhaustion or depression of Riku's mother. When Henrik has begun to travel a lot and has finally become the "Long-Distance Henrik", Riku's mother begins to peel potatoes in a telling way: "Slowly, slowly she peels, like she was asleep." She cannot keep up; the dinner is delayed "from five until half past, and until six, and finally until six thirty." (*DÖH*, 155; *LHY*, 183.)[18]

Thus, we find the Bexar nuclear family beginning to fall apart:

> Everything has become a little chilly, Riku notes for sure. He looks at Henrik and Benita and finds two people longing to be somewhere else, though not knowing exactly *where*.
>
> Yet he pushes the feeling aside. Since, what are family dinners needed for, when one is young and owns the whole town, when one has Rolls, Davy's and American Steak House, and generous pocket money? (*DÖH*, 155; *LHY*, 183.)

The social bonds of the family erode and, as the narrator ironically notes, the relationship between young Riku and his parents is mediated by money. Riku's teenage subjectivity becomes increasingly dependent on consumption and less on intrapsychic identifications with his parents (cf. Richards 1984, 134). It almost seems as if, for Riku, hard cash can displace the family bond.

159

These scenes depict social erosion and commodification as going hand in hand. What is more, this parallelism is heavily emphasised at the end of the first part of the novel.

Subjectivity into Air

During the turn of the 1970s into the 1980s, the family is seriously falling apart: the parents divorce, Riku's brother disappears, and even the dog dies. Riku thinks about some beautiful words:

> For years I had been mocking the ideas of Dani and Benno, the hippies and the like, as well as those of the communists. But now I had read a long article in the Rolling Stone, called "Facing Life's Uncertainties", and there I had found some words that seemed beautiful to me.
>
> The ironic part was that I, who had no idea of their origin, wanted to have them engraved on Jimbo's headstone:
>
> **All that is solid melts into air, Jimbo baby** (*DÖH*, 176–177; *LHY*, 208; original emphasis.)

The origin that the young Riku does not know about is *The Communist Manifesto* by Marx and Engels in 1848:

> Constant revolutionising of production, uninterrupted disturbance of all social conditions, everlasting uncertainty and agitation distinguish the bourgeois epoch from all earlier ones. All fixed, fast-frozen relations, with their train of ancient and venerable prejudices and opinions, are swept away, all new-formed ones become antiquated before they can ossify. All that is solid melts into air [...] (Marx & Engels 1969, Chapter 1.)

By an allusion to this intertext, Marx's dramatisation of capitalism is brought into the textual play and reconstructed as a thematic element of the novel. Young Riku finds the words beautiful at the very moment he recognises the fragility of the social world around him. Then, as nothing else seems to offer regularity to rely on, at least uncertainty itself seems reliable to him. In his interpretation of his situation, "life's uncertainty" and the modern, capitalist experience of everything around melting into air, becomes a fact that could be (paradoxical as it is) engraved in stone.

Furthermore, these events are a prologue to the full-blown consumerism of the 1980s. The 'capitalism in the family' motif opens up into a larger thematic; namely the historical development in which capitalist practices of the socio-economic context, and the individual subject's sense of 'self', overlap and intertwine with each other. This articulation is represented very clearly in the novel's picture of the economic boom decade. During the 1980s, many of Riku's generation become so-called yuppies, with a great interest in money and conspicuous consumption as a means of attaining social status. In the real-life Finnish context, those attitudes were strongly encouraged by the liberation of the financial market and the flow of easy credit during the second half of the eighties. The yuppies identify human action and sociality with the market; indeed, one of Riku's peers sees also art in terms of the market, for he is a cynical interpreter of Pierre Bourdieu's (1984) distinction theory.

> *Capitalism has become the natural human condition in all areas of life.*
>
> *Through it, we intuitively regulate our relations to our fellow creatures, using the means and structures characteristic to it in order to understand and manage our life.*
>
> *And, moreover, as we collect symbolic capital by just existing and being productive, so should we also have the freedom to use this natural condition in art in the best possible way.* (DÖH, 274; LHY, 321.)

Under the terms of this 'end of history', i.e. the naturalisation of liberal capitalism, the self is also understood as a commodity. Riku later notes: "We were the first to realise: *the trade mark is all that matters.* We wanted to be stars. We wanted to be winners." (*DÖH*, 438; *LHY*, 516.) The self is constructed as a saleable brand and social relations are seen as competitive; as the accumulation of status/fame/capital. The tendency of late capitalist commodification (see Jameson 1999, 35–36, 269) or full-blown consumerism (Bauman 2008) is the transformation of all objects *and* the consumer subjects, as well, into commodities in the market. Thus, the cynical distinctionist may proclaim: "*Capitalism has become the natural human condition in all areas of life.*" (*DÖH*, 274; *LHY,* 321.) With such characters, the booming eighties is thematicized as a decade of emergent neoliberal ideology (although, at that time, it was not commonly known by that name). It gains a strong hold on the ways in which the new generation sees social reality and humanity. Of course, they forget "[t]hat with winning and defeat, it is a zero-sum game. That not everyone can be a winner." (*DÖH*, 438; *LHY*, 516.)

In his book *All That Is Solid Melts Into Air. The Experience of Modernity*, Marshall Berman (1988, orig. 1982) depicts this kind of ideological turn as a liable problem in capitalism. In his reading of Marx – specifically the very part of Marx's writing that is the intertext of Westö's novel –, Berman, perhaps surprisingly for those unfamiliar with Marx's texts, argues that capitalism creates human possibilities. It fosters "new and endlessly renewed" modes of human activity. (Berman 1988, 93.) However, this occurs within class and commodity restrictions, and the severe problem Berman notes is that capitalism simultaneously destroys the possibilities it creates. It restricts and distorts humanity:

> Those traits, impulses and talents that the market can use are rushed (often prematurely) into development and squeezed desperately till there is nothing left; everything else within us, everything nonmarketable, gets draconically repressed, or withers away for lack of use, or never has a chance to come to life at all. (Berman 1988, 96.)

Marx knew this; let us just recall his concept of commodity fetishism.[19] On the other hand, Marx was quite optimistic, or even fetishistic, argues Berman (1988, e.g. 96, 127), about the idea of development, and particularly the full development of individuality. Marx proclaimed that the ultimate result of the process of 'all things solid melting into air' would be the subject "at last compelled to face with sober senses his real conditions of life, and his relations with his kind."[20] That was to say that when the capitalists strip down the old halos, they accidentally encourage modern subjectivity, enable the individuals to see their positions, their social relations, and even the possibility of emancipation. Thus the historical dialectic would, Marx hoped, open up a space for the socialist synthesis, in which the possibility of individual development for all would be tightly related to the idea of solidarity. (See Berman 1998, 95–98, 103–105.) Yet to the extent that subjective dispositions to empathy and (on a larger scale) to solidarity actually presuppose certain *solid* ground in the social environment, such as reliable human care during childhood,[21] there may be a troublesome paradox at the core of Marx's vision of modernity, according to which it is precisely "all that is solid" (including the family) that is dismantled and turned into a "pure money relation".[22] According to Berman (1998, 110), it is not hard to imagine alternate endings to the dialectic, endings less beautiful than Marx's:

> Indeed, the sort of individualism that scorns and fears connections with other people as threats to the self's integrity, and the sort of collectivism that seeks to submerge the self in a social role, may be more appealing than the Marxian synthesis, because they are intellectually and emotionally so much easier.

I would suggest that these affective tendencies in capitalist modernity are 'in the air' in *Drakarna över Helsingfors* ("Kites over Helsinki"). That is to say, they can be found in the text's thematics. The prototypically neoliberal competitiveness of the 1980s embodies the cynical, defensive individualism Berman refers to. Simultaneously, the "brand" self is a self that submerges in the social role as a commodity in the market.

The Swedish word *drake*, 'kite', of the title of the novel is Westö's romanticist metaphor for dreams. It signifies the 'air' of modernity in the latter half of the 20th century which, when compared to the more black-and-white picture that the novel gives of the pre-1950s Finland, seems to offer a relatively good wind and space for the dreams and identities of the (middle-class) characters. However, another meaning of *drake* is 'dragon', and importantly, the events also thematicize the more dragonish faces of modernity, or to be more precise, of capitalism.

Here we should also note that the double-sidedness of modernity depicted in Westö's novel is related to the tension between capitalist instrumentalisation and its romanticist counter-tendency (see Löwy & Sayre 2001). A character whose life is most tragically caught in-between those poles is Riku's rebellious brother, Daniel. As a teenager, Daniel has fallen in love with rock music and regards it, with a truly romantic devotion, as an artistic area of authenticity. However, at the turn of the 1990s, Daniel feels lonely, outdated and betrayed by the culture industry:

> *Uncle Dan says: Everything you love is treated like waste. [...] For everything has been branded with the Best Before stamp. Everything you love has that stamp. And after that date, your love is sold in a clearance sale. That's how the world is. That's how the conditions of love are... do you get it, if one is good in remembering but lives in a world that throws away and forgets everything and everyone and urges all people to do the same, then good memory is a burden and one becomes sad like this... [...] Thank you for using LIFE and HUMANITY. [...] Please dispose carefully of used LIFE and HUMANITY containers. (DÖH, 301–302; LHY, 354; some parts originally in English.)*

The final part of the novel depicts the depression years. It is dominated by the death – a possible suicide – of Daniel, and makes Riku and Henrik look back. Commodification of life and humanity is raised as a problem in their conversation, too. Henrik talks about the ad-men he has encountered at the company meeting:

> Dynamic. Quick of mind and tongue, I must admit. Yet I don't know... they said that as a CEO I should think in the style of the nineties... [...] 'One must be at the fore', said one of them. 'The brand is everything', added another. Then they picked up a pile of diagrams. Monitoring research. My desk was soon covered with papers. Studies from Finland and Sweden. From the USA and England. From France and Spain and the Benelux countries. Teenage habits mapped out in every detail. Rival subcultures analysed. Potential customer segments defined. And it was not just the consumer habits, you see, in a sense it was the whole life, behavioural models, desires, dreams, fears, hates. Quite simply everything. And I thought... or actually, I didn't think much of anything. Suddenly everything just felt so thoroughly manipulated that... I started to sweat and felt sick. I mean, is it really like that nowadays? (*DÖH*, 437; *LHY*, 514–515.)

In these and other final events, *Drakarna över Helsingfors* also re-turns to the idea of family and to the chain of generations; not just of Henrik and Riku but also of Riku's grandmother and his son – one of the representatives of this chain being a caterpillar toy, resembling a kite. The family appears as a fragile haven of love and care in a heartless world. This is a re-articulation of the family's societal position, often abused ideologically by liberal and neoliberal ideology, which treat it unproblematically as a buffer zone to capitalist rationality and as a remarkable producer of such un- or de-commodified social relations as trust (cf. Hobsbawm 1999, 31–33; Ojajärvi 2006, 116–118; Ziehe 1991, 21). In the novel, the return to the family signifies hope for an authentic source of identity and for an area that would not be reducible to the commodity logic of selling and buying. Yet as the novel has shown, under the sway of commodification in capitalist modernity, the family may not, as such, be a sustainable or progressive counterpart for "life's uncertainties". To put it in a dialectical way (see Jameson 1979; 2002, 271–290), in the novel's return to the family there are both ideological symptomatics (for solidarity appears mainly as a matter of intimate bourgeois family life) and utopian implications (for this *is* nevertheless a part of the novel's dreaming of a life beyond commodification).

In neither case should we evade the awareness that no family is an island. Keeping that in mind, I will turn to another novel with the 'capitalism in the family' motif as the crux of its realistic involvement.

Good-Night Commodities

> Oh now I must tell you what a good-night gift is.
> It's what you get 'cos you're alone. (*KYL*, 166.)

Mari Mörö's *Kiltin yön lahjat* was published 1998, when the late waves of the depression were still felt by many in the middle and lower classes. Many signs of the neoliberal times – concerning the labour market, the widening division between the rich and the poor, etc. – are indicated in the suburban, working-class social milieu of the text. During the long weekend, the six-year-old girl Siia is left on her own with some "good-night gifts" given by her single-parenting mother Miima, who has gone out, seemingly not to come back for a long time. Siia is alone, and then looked after by a middle-aged man, Viikki, who is visiting the neighbour Pöyhönen after a period working in Russia. Miima is a central figure through her absence. How we understand her absence is the crucial question in the interpretation of the novel. Does the text represent simply a story of a child missing her parent, or do its thematic elements offer us a microscopic view into societal conditions? Indeed, does the text situate the story in the context of a family, or of a certain kind of society?

To begin with, we may note that via Viikki, any moralistic interpretations of the character Miima ('bad mother', as it might seem) are precluded in the text. In his dream, half awake, Viikki recalls what his uncle once said: "There are no worthless people, you know, only worthless situations". (*KYL*, 138.) This resembles a phrase in the film *Stray Dog* by Akira Kurosawa (1949): "There are no bad people, only bad circumstances".

What are the circumstances in this case? In my interpretation, I argue that Siia's relationship to her mother is deeply entwined in the practices of the market. This can be shown simply by analysing the *leitmotif* of the text – the good-night gifts.[23] When Miima is gone, Siia misses her:

> Miima said that she has so many things to do and that she goes straight to the studio. [...] I think studio is a fine word. A little like radio but softer. I will still get to go there many times. Miima came from the bath and I watched her dry her hair with a towel and put on her make up in front of the mirror. After the moisturiser she used the concealer cream and then the powder and the blush. I got an old lipstick to play with and a cracked eye shadow palette. Miima took me in her arms and said that I could have them as good-night gifts. She asked if the drawer was full already. When I go to sleep alone I always get something or at least when Miima comes home I get it. Love is smiley. (*KYL*, 71.)

164

I guess Raymond Williams would like the fact that Mörö's text treats Siia with empathy, as an end in herself. In Siia's narration, the text captures the tone of a child cherishing the image of her beloved yet absent caretaker. In terms of psychoanalytic object relation theory, the inner object is kept alive, while the outer is absent. Even the place to which Miima has gone, the "studio", a euphemism for a strip tease bar, is given an oral life by Siia, as she tastes and holds the word in her mouth ("I think studio is a fine word"). However, despite the intimate personal tone of Siia's narration, we should simultaneously consider the societal discourses veiled in it. Once again, in a realistic text the personal does not exclude the social.

The "good-night gifts" are gendered signs of a consumer society – old goodies – and Siia receives them as compensation for her mother's absence. Yet these are not "gifts" in a genuine sense. A genuine gift would be given without the urge for an immediate gift of return (Bourdieu 1998, 115). Siia, for her part, has to pay for the gifts by being nice while Miima is away. Thus, we may ask whether the good-night gifts are a kind of salary that Siia receives in selling the labour of being a nice child and sleeping alone? Looking at other instances of the *leitmotif*, this seems to be the case. When Viikki takes the position of a caretaker, he describes:

> I hustled her back to bed. Promised her a tenner, if she would fall asleep like a good girl. I went to the bedside and wrapped her up in the blanket so that she looked like a mummy. I said that it was a bedtime wrap, not to be unwrapped until the morning.
> – Hush hush the little duck, bird is making an omelette Quack.
> – Will you put that tenner under my pillow?
> I took a coin from my pocket. Siia was shivering and grinding her teeth. (*KYL*, 146.)

Siia regards the ten marks that Viikki promises her if she falls asleep with import. Thus, the text draws a parallel between this good-night "gift" of money, and a wage. Viikki's nursery rhyme (orig. "Aa aa allin lasta, lintu tekee munakasta") stealthily darkens this thematic crystallisation with a disconsolate shade: sleep well; the caretaker will eat its child. Accordingly, slumbering Siia shudders in her dream as if she was threatened.[24]

Earlier on, Siia has asked for a "tenner". Viikki's narration:

> Siia was playing in the bath. I almost fell.
> – Don't drown, I yelled behind the door.
> – Will I get a tenner if I don't? she answered.
> – And turn-turn it was turned from wood. (*KYL*, 132.)

In here, too, the "tenner" is salary – what for? For behaving nicely. As the story continues, the essential character of good-night gifts becomes increasingly commodity-like, they become a bare medium of selling and buying, since Siia understands the "gifts" as being increasingly related to money. The development is clearly visible when Siia decides that she no longer wants any more old goodies; instead, Miima should give her "say, three tenners", because then Siia could buy what she needs (*KYL*, 107). Money has value for Siia.

There are many more details that reveal the associative tie between the good-night gifts, wage, and money in Siia's mind. For instance, in her play she imagines a director of a factory, "Tson Nurmi", who has the power to tell "a thousand people when to sleep" (*KYL*, 9). In thinking about Miima's work as a dancer in a "studio", Siia concludes: "Dancing gives money [...]" Then she dreams about building a better home for herself and Miima through consumption: "[...] then we'll buy a car and a house we'll buy too, and we don't have to go in the bus or in the metro with others, as there's always some carrying" (*KYL*, 84.) In Siia's flights of fancy, the character Taija (formerly "an ordinary model", now Tson's wife and mother of two) has made a class jump compared to Miima: "Taija almost never dances. There's money." (*KYL*, 91.) In Foucauldian terms, Siia has learned to understand money as productive power. In other words, money represents something dear to her. Viikki talks about Siia's habit of rolling cigarettes for adults:

> While I was packing the bags, Siia rolled me five fags, and without the machine. Again I praised her and she said that she gets one mark a piece when she rolls for Miima. Päve paid one fifty. I said that I can pay the same as Päve. She began to press her eyes.
> – You'll puncture your eyes, I said. (*KYL*, 157–158.)

Generous pay makes Siia cry. In her associations, the wage relation or, generally, the relation of buyer and seller, and tenderness are one and the same. Siia's own narration also reveals this, as in the following:

> Then, in the evening, Viikki caught Miima [by the phone]. She had been in the studio and she had had to go to some work meeting. Viikki took me in his arms and I pushed my nose into his beard. It tickled and stung at the same time.
> – Buy skin magazines from me, I asked Viikki. – Or Mette will sell. (*KYL*, 144.)

When Viikki shows some caring for her, taking her into his arms, Siia responds by proposing to sell him porn magazines. Siia's hunger for love is articulated to the acts of selling and buying.[25] Sometimes she understands the good-night gifts quite straight-forwardly as commodities, and even capital:

> I think mothers sleep a lot.
> I opened the desk drawer and studied the good-night gifts: transparent animal sticks, fancies, nail polish, a lip salve almost full. I have a small empty bottle from Germany. They may all become valuable and rare when I'm old. (*KYL*, 85.)

The implicit deal and the promise represented by the good-night gifts have been the love and reward for behaving nicely. At this point, Siia unconsciously finds the deal unconvincing. She begins to cherish the threatened psychosocial meaningfulness of the gifts by boasting in her mind: "I have a small empty bottle from Germany." She also has to postpone the realisation of the promise of meaningfulness to the future: all the good-night gifts "may become valuable and rare when I'm old." Simultaneously, the *economic* promise of the gifts pushes aside the psychosocial promise. In other words, the commercial values, both the exchange and the surplus value, outweigh the use value. In Siia's mind, economic capital begins to act as compensation for the lack of a benign and affectionate social bond, and it veils her childish needs for love and care. This is also seen in some of her imaginative play acting about the upper class abundance of commodities. Siia makes herself believe that money or capital, indeed, will repair her reality into a better place.

That is also why she has a routine of observing economic conditions. She talks about the prices of different commodities and makes notes about buying and selling: Miima's false lashes "are thirty marks a piece." Jam jars "give money". "You get three glimmering stars for a tenner, Mette had gone to check." "Mette takes skin magazines to the boys, they pay at Nutis." (*KYL*, 17, 23, 34, 85.) On the one hand, money has a psychosocially based value: "With two big bottles and two jars you get a bag of soil"; soil with which Siia would grow plants for her mother and herself (KYL, 70). Once, when empty cans do not give any money, something makes her throat hurt, for Siia's plan has been to get a tenner to buy "soil for the cotton wool flowers and something from Tiimari" (KYL, 59). On the other hand, Siia is learning to value commercial value in itself, and only things with a commercial value in themselves: she says she does *not* collect stickers "because you can't remove them. They can't ever become valuable." (*KYL*, 29.) They do not have any exchange value or give any surplus value. For Siia, striving for money – or capital – becomes a normative rule upon which she constructs her conscious "I". If she breaks the rule, she may note: "I did *not* search his pockets because I got some coins." (*KYL*, 139; italics added.)

In these ways, Siia sees "the good-night gifts" and other material representatives of her social relations, to a great extent, in terms of exchange and surplus value. Money, Marx's "general commodity", appears to her as an "exchange value become independent" (Marx 1993, 236). Money and the market become Siia's practice of the self, a discursive skill by means of which she tries to construct her subjectivity (see Foucault 2000, 225, 290; McNay 1993, 3–4). It may give the impression of Siia's 'active' agency; in fact, at the time the novel was published many reviewers made, either ideologically or accidentally, this positive interpretation and celebrated it as a relieving counterpart to the harsh world depicted in the novel (Ojajärvi 2006, 257–267). However, Siia's subjectivity remains very fragile, even in the excerpts cited here.[26] There are hidden representations of reaching and grasping, being threatened, feeling broken apart, being eaten, having punctured one's eyes, and so on. On any larger social scale, those conditions in and alongside which Siia acts, are given: commodified, and also class- and gender-related.[27] Siia's yearning for recognition functions as a driving force in her somewhat capitalist socialisation, and the resulting subjectivity cannot resolve but only veil her problematic situation and the on-going alienation of the society in which she lives. That is to say, instead of a wishful and escapist affirmation of positive thinking in hard times, we should read Siia's character as a me-tonymical representation which makes temporarily visible the ideological reproduction of subjectivity and social relations in contemporary capital-ism (see Jameson 1977, 555; 2002, 64, 138–139, 148–149).

In the last analysis, the family relation in the novel may be interpreted as an allegory of class relation. In the 'allegorical character system' (see Jameson 2002, e.g. 148–149, 154, 245) of the novel, "Siia" is a worker who basically has nothing else except her labour to sell (as Marx defines the bare working class subject). "Siia" also tries to overcome this position by adopting the attitude of a neoliberal entrepreneurial worker (see Sennett 1998) and by collecting some rudimentary capital (empty bottles, old porn magazines, coins from pockets). The main counterpart of "Siia" is the powerful-looking and increasingly absent "Miima". At the level of this allegorical character system (though not in her own 'real' life), "Miima" represents capital – like the machine goddess "Mima" in Harry Martinson's science fiction poem *Aniara* (1956, transl. 1963, subtitled *A Review of Man in Time and Space*).

If we as readers then want to respond to this comfortless allegory of capitalism by trying to find some thematic elements which would appear as truly positive – positive in a socially-grounded and, thus, sustainable sense – we must certainly not celebrate the lone character of a defensively heroic, broken child worker. Instead, the rare utopian seeds can be found in the care, that is, in the solidarity, of some of the fellow workers, of those who are able to recognise a vulnerable position because they can imagine themselves in the same kind of position. The character Viikki is signified with such empathy and class consciousness, thanks to the care of others in the past ("There are no worthless people, you know, only worthless situations", as the good uncle said). In some of Viikki's responses to our child worker the commodification of social relations is negated:

> – Won't buy anything from you, he laughed and threw me in the air (*KYL*, 144.)

Conclusion

In this article, I have concentrated on two texts that share the motif of capitalism in the family. The motif focuses on the dialectic of the societal and the subjective, thus clearly keeping together the sometimes differentiated strands of realistic involvement.

As I mentioned in the introduction, the motif is not an entirely new one in Finnish literature. However, what is thought-provoking is that, this time, in both Westö's and Mörö's texts, it is strongly related to child characters, not just the adults in the families. Thus these 'capitalism in the family' novels posit a question about the constant expansion of capitalist and market practices: is the market colonising, more deeply than before, the 'personal', 'intimate' aspects of life?

The novels represent the situation of the family in contemporary capitalism as contradictory. On the one hand, capitalism still requires the family as a crucial means of reproducing and caring for labour power, and as a source of long-standing attachments and social empathy – dispositions which act as counter-forces to the atomistic characteristics of consumerist, neoliberal society. Yet on the other hand, the pressures of work and the overwhelming practices of consumption and commodification seem to simultaneously undermine the family. (See Fisher 2009, 33; Hochschild 2003.) Instead of long-standing empathy, they tie subjectivities inherently to consumerism, buyer–seller relationships, and even to the surplus value logic of capital accumulation. The novels by Westö and Mörö bring to light unsustainable tendencies within the family and in the ideological conditions of capitalism.

Notes

1   For a more detailed review of these themes in recent novels, see Ojajärvi 2006, 272–304.

2   See 'sociological novel' in Morner & Rausch 1991; 'thesis novel' in Cuddon 1999.

3   In naming the literary attitude this way, I am also in debt to Pertti Karkama's (1994) interpretations of the relations of Finnish literature and society.

4   Note also the echoes of Marx, for example, of the famous phrase of *The Eighteenth Brumaire of Louis Bonaparte* (1852): "Men make their own history, but they do not make it as they please; they do not make it under self-selected circumstances, but under circumstances existing already, given and transmitted from the past." On the relation of Marx and realistic attitude in literature, see Steinby 2008, 25–28.

5   On Lukács' notion of totality, cf. Pawling 2004. On the role of the 'typical' character, see "Critical Realism and Socialist Realism" in Lukács 1964.

6   A crucially representative example is obviously Väinö Linna's trilogy *Täällä Pohjantähden alla*, 1959–1962 (transl. *Under the North Star*, 2001–2003).

7   Obviously, making this argument must not dismiss the fact that the literary discourse has simultaneously grown into an assemblage of heterogeneous genres, styles, and sub-cultures.

8   Note that the dialectical social constructionism of Berger and Luckmann is earlier than the post-structuralist version of social constructionism, which is far more spatial and based on linguistic models.

9   Nor do I suppose that the position of the family would now appear in exactly the same manner as ever. The ideological function of the family may vary qualitatively as the precise mode of capitalism varies.

10 Transl. in Finnish as *Leijat Helsingin yllä* (1996). Hereafter, *DÖH* (Swedish) and *LHY* (Finnish).

11 Hereafter, *KYL*.

12 See the first chapter of *The Communist Manifesto* by Karl Marx & Friedrich Engels (1848), <http://www.marxists.org/archive/marx/works/1848/communist-manifesto/ch01.htm>.

13 Translations of Westö and Mörö by J. Ojajärvi.

14 A representative of not just romanticist but also revolutionary impulses; later on we find out that the girl is Ulrike Meinhof.

15 Textually speaking, the names of the past kings ("Henrik" and "Rickard"), as well as some allusions in the narrative to unconscious 'Oedipal' battles between 'kings', magnify the impression of estrangement between the father and his two sons (Rickard and Daniel).

16 A modification of the beginning of the novel (Henrik as a war time child in a ship).

17 In addition, an interesting detail is Henrik giving Riku a "Jim" chocolate bar; later, when Riku is driving with his own son Raj, Riku gives him *two* Jim bars, which Raj eats in a slightly beast-like manner. (*DÖH*, 46–47, 342–343; *LHY*, 54–55, 401.)

18 Some of these interpretations of commodification and Westö's novel have been outlined in an earlier article (Ojajärvi 2001).

19 See the first volume of *Capital*, Chapter 1, Section 4, <http://www.marxists.org/archive/marx/works/1867-c1/ch01.htm#S4>.

20 *The Communist Manifesto*, Chapter 1. Needless to say, the male pronoun was used for referring to all people.

21 This part of my argument is psychoanalytic and it rests on the notion that to emerge as being able to bear frustration, the 'self' needs to rest on some benign stability of the social world (see Benjamin 1995, 27–48; for my discussion on this, see Ojajärvi 2001 or Ojajärvi 2006, 52–56).

22 *The Communist Manifesto*, Chapter 1.

23 A full analysis of the novel is included in my doctoral dissertation (Ojajärvi 2006, 107–276).

24 The same prediction of caretaker eating its child may actually be hidden in the unusual names of Siia and Miima: Miima's name resembles the way the voice of a cat is described onomatopoetically in Finnish (*miu, mau*); Siia's name resembles a fish (*siika*).

25 On the general discourse of treating women and girls as commodities, on which Siia and Miima build their subjectivities, see Ojajärvi 2006, 216–225; the dissertation also considers many aspects of the psychodynamic side of the social construction of Siia's subjectivity.

26 More signs of fragility in Ojajärvi 2006, for instance 174–180, 188–194, 225–226, 252–256.

27 The intersectional intertwining of inequalities has been at the core of some recent studies on class in Finnish cultural and feminist studies, as well as of my interpretation (Ojajärvi 2006, 188–229) of the projective displacement of class relations in the narrated world of Mörö's novel.

Primary Literature

Mörö, Mari 1998: *Kiltin yön lahjat.* [Good-Night Gifts.] Helsinki: WSOY.

Westö, Kjell 1997/1996: *Leijat Helsingin yllä.* (*Drakarna över Helsingfors.*)[Kites above Helsinki.]Transl. by Arja Tuomari. 6ᵗʰ edition. Helsinki: Otava.

West, Kjell 1997/1996: *Drakarna över Helsingfors.* [Kites above Helsinki.] 5. upplagan. Helsingfors: Söderström & Co.

Secondary Literature

Canth, Minna 1985/1885: *Työmiehen vaimo. Näytelmä viidessä näytöksessä.* [The Workers' Wife. A Play in Five Acts.] Helsinki: Äidinkielen opettajain liitto.

Eskelinen, Markku 1988: *Nonstop. Trilogian muiden osien synoptinen marginaali.* [Nonstop. The Synoptic Marginal of the Other Part's of the Trilogy.] Helsinki: WSOY.

Hassinen, Pirjo 2001/2000: *Mansikoita marraskuussa*. [Strawberries in November.] 3th edition. Helsinki: Otava.

Hotakainen, Kari 1993: *Bronks*. [Bronks.] Helsinki: WSOY.

Hotakainen, Kari 1997: *Klassikko. Omaelämäkerrallinen romaani autoilevasta ja avoimesta kansasta*. [The Classic. An Autobiographical Novel about a Driving and Open Nation.] Helsinki: WSOY.

Jotuni, Maria 1981/1918: *Kultainen vasikka*. [The Golden Calf.] In: Maria Jotuni, *Näytelmät*. [Plays.] Ed. by Irmeli Niemi. Helsinki: Otava.

Krohn, Leena 2004: *Unelmakuolema*. [Dream Death.] Helsinki: Teos.

Liksom, Rosa 1985: *Yhden yön pysäkki*. [*One Night Stands*, 1993.] Helsinki: WSOY.

Linna, Väinö 1959–1962: *Täällä Pohjantähden alla 1–3*. [*Under the North Star*, 2001–2003.] Helsinki: WSOY.

Lundán, Reko 2004: *Rinnakkain*. [Side by Side.] Helsinki: WSOY.

Martinson, Harry 1963/1956: *Aniara. A Review of Man in Time and Space*. (*Aniara. En revy om människan i tid och rum*.) Transl. by Hugh MacDiarmid and Elspeth Harley Schubert. New York: Knopf.

Marttila, Hanna Marjut 2002: *Kertoi tulleensa petetyksi*. [Told He Was Betrayed.] Helsinki: Otava.

Melender, Tommi 2007: *Kunnian mies*. [Man of Honour.] Helsinki: WSOY.

Raittila, Hannu 2005: *Pamisoksen purkaus*. [The Unloading of Pamisos.] Helsinki: WSOY.

Ringbom, Henrika 1998: *Martina Dagers längtan*. [The Longing of Martina Dagers.] Helsingfors: Söderströms.

Röyhkä, Kauko 1999: *Ocean City*. [Ocean City.] Helsinki: LIKE.

Salminen, Arto 1998: *Varasto. Romaani*. [The Warehouse. A Novel.] Helsinki: WSOY.

Salminen, Arto 2005: *Kalavale. Kansalliseepos*. [An Epic Lie. The National Epic.] Helsinki: WSOY.

Seppälä, Juha 2004: *Routavuosi. Romaani*. [The Year of the Frost. A Novel.] Helsinki: WSOY.

Seppälä, Juha 2008: *Paholaisen haarukka*. [Devil's Fork.] Helsinki: WSOY.

Tuulari, Jyrki 1998: *Pyydys*. [The Trap.] Helsinki: WSOY.

Verronen, Maarit 2008: *Karsintavaihe*. [The Pruning Stage.] Helsinki: Tammi.

Vimma, Tuomas 2005: *Helsinki 12*. [Helsinki 12.] Helsinki: Otava.

Westö, Kjell 2003/2002: *Lang*. [*Lang*, 2005.] Stockholm: Nordstedts.

References

Althusser, Louis 1971/1970: *Ideology and Ideological State Apparatuses. Notes toward an Investigation*. Transl. by Ben Brewster. <http://www.marxists.org/reference/archive/althusser/1970/ideology.htm> (3.3.2011)

Annesley, James 1998: *Blank Fictions. Consumerism, Culture and Contemporary American Novel*. London: Pluto Press.

Bauman, Zygmunt 2008: *Consuming Life*. Cambridge: Polity Press.

Benjamin, Jessica 1995: *Like Subjects, Love Objects. Essays on Recognition and Sexual Difference*. New Haven and London: Yale UP.

Berger, Peter L. & Luckmann, Thomas 1984/1966: *The Social Construction of Reality. A Treatise in the Sociology of Knowledge*. Harmondsworth, Middlesex: Penguin Books.

Berman, Marshall 1988/1982: *All That Is Solid Melts Into Air. The Experience of Modernity*. Harmondsworth: Penguin Books.

Bourdieu, Pierre 1984/1979: *Distinction. A Social Critique of the Judgement of Taste*. Transl. by Richard Nice. Cambridge, Mass.: Harvard UP.

Brecht, Bertolt 1974: Against Georg Lukács. Transl. by Stuart Hood. *New Left Review* 84 (March–April): 1974, 39–53.

Burr, Vivien 2005: *Social Constructionism*. Second Edition. London–New York: Routledge.

Cuddon, J. A. 1999: *Dictionary of Literary Terms and Literary Theory*. Revised by C. E. Preston. London: Penguin Books.

Fisher, Mark 2009: *Capitalist Realism. Is There No Alternative?* Winchester, UK–Washington, USA: Zero Books.

Foucault, Michel 1994/2000: *Ethics. Subjectivity and Truth. Essential Works of Foucault 1954–1984, vol. 1*. Ed. by Paul Rabinow. Transl. by Robert Hurley & al. Harmondsworth: Penguin Books.

Hardt, Michael & Negri, Antonio 2009: *Commonwealth*. (Kindle edition.) Cambridge, Mass.: The Belknap Press of Harvard UP.

Harvey, David 2005: *A Brief History of Neoliberalism*. Oxford–New York: Oxford UP.

Heiskala, Risto & Luhtakallio, Eeva 2006: Suunnittelutaloudesta kilpailukyky-yhteiskuntaan? [From Planned Economy to the Society of Competitiveness?] In: Risto Heiskala & Eeva Luhtakallio (eds.), *Uusi jako. Miten Suomesta tuli kilpailukyky-yhteiskunta?* [New Deal. How Finland Became a Society of Competitiveness.] Helsinki: Gaudeamus, 7–13.

Hobsbawm, Eric 1999/1994: *Äärimmäisyyksien aika. Lyhyt 1900-luku (1914–1991)*. [*The Age of Extremes: The Short Twentieth Century, 1914–1991*, 1994.] Suom. Pasi Junila. Tampere: Vastapaino.

Hochschild, Arlie Russell 2003: *The Commercialization of Intimate Life. Notes from Home and Work*. Berkeley–Los Angeles–London: University of California Press.

Jameson, Fredric 1977: Ideology, Narrative Analysis, and Popular Culture. *Theory and Society* 4 (4): 1977, 543–559.

Jameson, Fredric 1979: Reification and Utopia in Mass Culture. *Social Text* 1 (Winter): 1979, 130–148.

Jameson, Fredric 1991/1999: *Postmodernism, or the Cultural Logic of Late Capitalism*. 5th printing. London–New York: Verso.

Jameson, Fredric 1981/2002: *The Political Unconscious. Narrative as a Socially Symbolic Act*. London and New York: Routledge.

Julkunen, Raija 2001: *Suunnanmuutos. 1990-luvun poliittinen reformi Suomessa*. [Change of Direction. The Political Reform in Finland in the 1990s.] Tampere: Vastapaino.

Kantokorpi, Mervi 2007: Kirjallisuus. [Literature.] In: Allan Tiitta et al. (eds.), *Maamme Suomi*. [Finland, Our Country.] Helsinki: Weilin + Göös, 296–327.

Karkama, Pertti 1994: *Kirjallisuus ja nykyaika. Suomalaisen sanataiteen teemoja ja tendenssejä*. [Literature and the Modern Era. Themes and Tendencies of Finnish Literature.] Helsinki: SKS.

Leiwo, Liinaleena 2002: Illuusiottomassa kirjallisuudessa pilkottaa valo. Eli mihin katosi pahan koulukunta. [Glimpses of Light in Disillusioned Literature, or, Where did the School of Evil Disappear.] In: Markku Soikkeli (ed.), *Kurittomat kuvitelmat. Johdatus 1990-luvun kotimaiseen kirjallisuuteen*. [Undisciplined imaginings. An introduction to Finnish literature of the 1990s.] Turku: Turun yliopisto, Taiteiden tutkimuksen laitos. Sarja A, n:o 50, 101–120.

Lukács, Georg 1964: *Realism in Our Time*. Transl. by John and Necke Mande. New York and Evanston: Harper & Row.

Löwy, Michael & Sayre, Robert 2001: *Romanticism Against the Tide of Modernity*. Transl. by Catherine Porter. Durham–London: Duke University Press.

Marx, Karl 1993/1857–1861: *Grundrisse. Foundations of the Critique of Political Economy*. Transl. and foreword by Martin Nicolaus. Harmondsworth, Middlesex: Penguin Books.

Marx, Karl 1996/1867: *Capital. Volume One. The Process of Production of Capital.* Transl. Samuel Moore and Edward Aveling, edited by Frederick Engels. <http://www.marxists.org/archive/marx/works/cw/volume35/index.htm> (26.6.2009)

Marx, Karl 1999/1952: *The Eighteenth Brumaire of Louis Bonabarte.* Several translators. <http://www.marxists.org/archive/marx/works/1852/18th-brumaire/index.htm> (26.6.2009)

Marx, Karl & Engels, Friedrich 1969/1848: *Manifesto of the Communist Party.* Transl. Samuel Moore in cooperation with Frederick Engels. <http://www.marxists.org/archive/marx/works/1848/communist-manifesto/index.htm> (26.6.2009)

McNay, Lois 1993/1992: *Foucault and Feminism: Power, Gender and the Self.* Boston: Northeastern UP.

Morner, Kathleen & Rausch, Ralph 1991: *NTC's Dictionary of Literary Terms.* Lincolnwood (Chicago), Illinois, USA: NTC Publishing Group.

Mäenpää, Pasi 2004: Kansalaisesta kuluttajaksi. [From a Citizen to a Consumer.] In: Kirsi Saarikangas, Pasi Mäenpää & Minna Sarantola-Weiss (eds.), *Suomen kulttuurihistoria 4. Koti, kylä, kaupunki.* [The Cultural History of Finland, vol. 4. Home, Village, City.] Helsinki: Tammi, 286–315.

Ojajärvi, Jussi 2001: *The Weakest Link* and the Commodification of Subjectivity by the Means of Play. *Cultural Values* (4): 2001, 477–489.

Ojajärvi, Jussi 2006: *Supermarketin valossa. Kapitalismi, subjekti ja minuus Mari Mörön romaanissa* Kiltin yön lahjat *ja Juha Seppälän novellissa "Supermarket".* [In the Light of the Supermarket. Capitalism, the Subject and the Self in Mari Mörö's *Good-Night Gifts* and Juha Seppälä's "Supermarket".] Helsinki: SKS.

Ojajärvi, Jussi 2008: Haluatko subjektiksi? Ideologinen kutsu ja yksilön uusliberalistinen hallinta: Jari Sarasvuon *Haluatko miljonääriksi?* ja Jyrki Tuularin *Pyydys.* [Who Wants to Be a Subject? Ideological ailing and the Neoliberal Governing of the Individual: Jari Sarasvuo's *Who wants to be a millionaire?* and Jyrki Tuulari's *Pyydys.*] In: Jussi Ojajärvi & Liisa Steinby (eds.), *Minä ja markkinavoimat. Yksilö, kulttuuri ja yhteiskunta uusliberalismin valtakaudella.* [The Self and the Power of the Market. Individual Subject, Culture and Society in the Era of Neoliberalism.] Helsinki: *Avain,* 135–191.

Pawling, Christopher 2004: The American Lukács? Fredric Jameson and Dialectical Thought. In: Sean Homer and Douglas Kellner (eds.), *Fredric Jameson: A Critical Reader.* Basingstoke and New York: Palgrave MacMillan, 22–41.

Peltonen, Milla 2008: *Jälkirealismin ehdoilla. Hannu Salaman* Siinä näkijä missä tekijä *ja Finlandia-sarja.* [In Terms of Post-Realism. Where the Seer, there the Maker, and the Finlandia Series by Hannu Salama.] Turku: Turun yliopisto. Sarja C, osa 272. <https://oa.doria.fi/bitstream/handle/10024/40126/C272.pdf?sequence=1> (26.6.2009)

Ruohonen, Voitto 1999: Kirjallisuus ja arvokriisi. [Literature and Value Crisis.] In: Pertti Lassila (ed.), *Suomen kirjallisuushistoria 3. Rintamakirjeistä tietoverkkoihin.* [Finnish Literary History 3. From Letters from the Front lines to Network Communications.] Helsinki: SKS, 268–279.

Rustin, Margaret & Rustin, Michael 2002: *Mirror to Nature. Drama, Psychoanalysis and Society.* London: Karnac Books.

Sassi, Ville 2009: Rahan kertoma maailma: kapitalistinen ideologia 1980-luvun suomalaisessa romaanikirjallisuudessa. [World Told by Money: Capitalist Ideology in the Finnish Novel of the 1980s.] In: Minna Ruckenstein & Timo Kallinen (eds.), *Rahan kulttuuri.* [The Culture of Money.] Helsinki: SKS, 266–278.

Sennett, Richard 1998: *The Corrosion of Character. The Personal Consequences of Work in the New Capitalism.* London: W.W. Norton.

Steinby, Liisa 2008: Ryöstelijät ammutaan. Moderni minä ja mitä sille sitten tapahtui. [Looters will be shot. The modern subject, and whatever happened to it.] In: Jussi Ojajärvi & Liisa Steinby (eds.), *Minä ja markkinavoimat. Yksilö, kulttuuri ja yhteiskunta uusliberalismin valtakaudella.* [The Self and the Power of the Market. Individual Subject, Culture and Society in the Era of Neoliberalism.] Helsinki: Avain, 25–66.

Williams, Raymond 1958: Realism and the Contemporary Novel. *Universities & Left Review* 4 (1958): Summer. <http://www.amielandmelburn.org.uk/collections/ulr/04_realism.pdf> (26.6.2009)

Williams, Raymond 1976/1977a: *Keywords. A Vocabulary of Culture and Society.* Glasgow: Fontana/Croom Helm.

Williams, Raymond 1977b: *Marxism and Literature.* Oxford: Oxford University Press.

Williams, Raymond 1989: *What I Came to Say.* Ed. by Neil Belton, Francis Mulhern and Jenny Taylor. London: Hutchinson Radius.

Ziehe, Thomas 1991/1982: *Uusi nuoriso. Epätavanomaisen oppimisen puolustus.* [Today's Youth. Defence of Unusual Learning.] Transl. Raija Sironen and Jussi Tuormaa. Tampere: Vastapaino.

Zilliacus, Clas 1999: Tunnustus, dokumentti ja raportti kirjallisuuskäsityksen avartajina. [Confession, Documentary and Report as Widening in the Conception of Literature.] Transl. Rauno Ekholm. In: Pertti Lassila (ed.), *Suomen kirjallisuushistoria 3. Rintamakirjeistä tietoverkkoihin.* [Finnish Literary History 3. From Letters from the Front lines to Network Communications.] Helsinki: SKS, 213–219.

Markku Lehtimäki

Shadows of the Past

Sofi Oksanen's *Purge* and Its Intertextual Space

[…] somewhere between the real world and the fairy-land, where the Actual and
the Imaginary may meet, and each imbue itself with the nature of the other.
– Nathaniel Hawthorne, *The Scarlet Letter* (1850)

In his book *Experiencing Fiction*, James Phelan writes that in fairy tales the
narrative itself signals which characters are good and which characters are bad,
but when we encounter more sophisticated narratives, we meet characters
for whom the simple labels of "good" and "bad" are longer adequate. We can
climb up the ladder of sophisticated narratives to look at cases in which our
moral discriminations among characters and our engagement with them
are more nuanced; and we often come across narratives that do not seem to
give sufficient signals for us to make clear and firm discriminations. (Phelan
2007, 1–2.) What interests me here is the reciprocal – and often intertextual
– relationship between fairy tales with their clear-cut figures on the one
hand and sophisticated narratives with more complex characters, events
and moral dilemmas on the other.

In this essay, I will discuss *Purge* (2008 = *P*; originally *Puhdistus*), the
internationally acclaimed novel by a young Finnish writer of Finnish-
Estonian descent, Sofi Oksanen.[1] The novel tells a story of Aliide, a somewhat sympathetic elderly woman living alone in the countryside of Western
Estonia. In her youth, Aliide has taken part (more or less voluntarily) in the
great Stalinist purification, and as a result of her decision her sister Ingel has
been sent away. In addition, Ingel's husband Hans, who is also Aliide's great
romantic love, has been hiding in Aliide's house because of his nationalist sympathies. When old Aliide meets, at the beginning of the narrative,
Ingel and Hans's young granddaughter Zara, she is forced to confront her
traumatic past again. While *Purge* deals with actual historical events and
therefore seems to lend itself easily to ideological and historicizing readings
of all kinds, it is also a literary work of art, a self-conscious design grafted
from previous fictions.[2] I will therefore read Oksanen's book side by side
with two other novels that I take to be its intertexts or, rather, subtexts: Toni
Morrison's *Beloved* (1987 = *B*), and Arundhati Roy's *The God of Small Things*
(1997 = *GST*). Each of these novels deals with the traumatic experiences of

175

a female protagonist and with histories of violence: the Soviet occupation of Estonia, the slave system in the United States, and British colonialism and caste violence in India, respectively.[3] In what follows, I will analyze one key scene of violence and trauma in each novel, but I will also have a few words to say about the beginning, the middle, and the end of *Purge* and its subtexts.

Building on Pekka Tammi's definition of *subtext*, I will try to pinpoint the novel's recurring images and plot motifs while at the same time being on the lookout for potential links to other literary texts. Combining the two facets of inquiry, Tammi argues, will help us attain a more comprehensive interpretation of the work in question. (1999, 8.) I am also making use of Brian McHale's apt concept of intertextual space. As McHale suggests, we can "picture literature as a field or, better, a network whose nodes are the actual texts of literature," and "an *intertextual space* is constituted whenever we recognize the relations among two or more texts, or between specific texts and larger categories" (1996, 56–57; my emphasis). Through its use of intertexts, *Purge* seems to map and blend together the real world of history and the Gothic worlds of fiction, in order to construct a literary world somewhere in between.

The Haunted House of Fiction

Purge is a distinctly literary novel written in the style of a dark fairy tale or Gothic romance. The home of Oksanen's protagonist Aliide is a ghost-house similar to the one inhabited by Sethe, Denver, and Paul D. in *Beloved*, and both novels partake of the tradition of Gothic romance, just like Roy's *The God of Small Things*. Ultimately, William Faulkner's most complex novel *Absalom, Absalom!* (1936) is a haunting precedent for Morrison, Roy and even Oksanen's novels. These are all haunted texts; a shadow of the past is cast upon them, whether it's the past of historical events or that of literary history. David Punter, in discussing what he calls the "postmodern Gothic," writes that "the traditional Gothic castle [or house] embodies a past that goes back behind – or beneath – the 'moment' of the subject, that asserts a different kind of continuity, even if it is one that can be known only under the sign of the secret, only in the 'shadows' of the darkened study, or in 'the shadows and the long night and the herds of the dead'" (2005, 170). The gothic is an intertextual field and space *par excellence*, and its customary imagery of lakes, forests, castles, and houses continues to provide a setting for Gothic romances, whether classic or postmodernist.

Henry James famously spoke of the "house of fiction," and as Gaston Bachelard writes in his classic study *The Poetics of Space*, "the house is one of the greatest powers of integration for […] thoughts, memories and dreams," and he consequently speaks of "the soul of the house" (1964, 6, 17). Morrison's *Beloved* begins, quite famously, with a personification of a house, which is "spiteful" and "full of a baby's venom" (*B*, 3). This "haunted house"

(*B*, 15) repeatedly interrupts the daily chores of Morrison's protagonist Sethe and her daughter Denver. The ghostly figure of Beloved also seems to exist outside Sethe's spatial and temporal experience. Obviously, besides being a character in the fictional world of the narrative, Beloved is also a self-reflexive device of novelistic discourse. As Daniel Punday puts it, "Beloved, like *Beloved*, is clearly a text to be read, a message from the past" (2003, 74). But as Phelan (2007, 58) reminds us, in Morrison's case this is not just a question of literary convention but of concrete historical shame and violence underlying the narrative.

If we look at the beginning of *Purge*, we notice that "a baby's venom" is here transformed to a "loathsome" fly that intrudes on the domestic life of Aliide, Oksanen's protagonist:

> Aliide Truu stared at the fly, and the fly stared back. Its eyes bulged and Aliide felt sick to her stomach. [...] The curtain fluttered, the lace flowers crumpled, and carnations flashed outside the window, but the fly got away and was strutting on the window frame, safely above Aliide's head. [...] Stupid fly. Stupid and loathsome. [...] the fly had beaten her in every attack, and now it was flying next to the ceiling with a greasy buzz. A disgusting bowfly from the sewer drain. She'd get it yet. (*P*, 4–5)

These two figures and motifs – the baby and the fly – are given an explanation later in the narratives, but at the beginning of *Purge* we are merely left with Aliide's frustration: "She'd get it yet." Fittingly, the first part of the novel opens with a poetic credo from Paul-Eerik Rummo: "There is an answer for everything, / if only one knew the question" (*P*, 1). Here, the dynamics of plot go hand in hand with the interpretative problems posed by the narrative as in Faulkner's *Absalom, Absalom!* where the fictional characters' attempts at understanding the world reflect the reader's attempts at understanding the novel (see Brooks 1984, 286–312; Tammi 1992, 176–177). These difficult and mysterious beginnings give us very little information about the narrative world. Thus, they are prime examples of withholding information in narrative. *Purge* is built around a mystery, which produces a suspenseful narrative drive and invites the reader's interpretation and participation.

Aliide, the mysterious heroine of *Purge*, finds a young girl called Zara from her yard in a manner reminiscent of Sethe, the protagonist of *Beloved*, finding a mysterious girl who turns out to be the ghost of her dead child. And in the beginning of *The God of Small Things*, a young woman called Rahel comes back to her childhood home, a house haunted with past memories:

> It was raining when Rahel came back to Ayemenem. Slanting silver ropes slammed into loose earth, ploughing up like gunfire. The old house on the hill wore its steep, gabled roof pulled over its ears like a low hat. The walls, streaked with moss, had grown soft, and bulged a little with dampness that seeped up from the ground. The wild, overgrown garden was full of the whisper and scurry of small lives. (*GST*, 1)

Stylistic similarities aside, the beginning of *Purge* also opens a new window into the world of history and fiction:

> Aliide straightened the drapes. The rainy yard was sniveling gray; the limbs of the birch trees trembled wet, leaves flattened by the rain, blades of grass swaying, with drops of water dripping from their tips. And there was something underneath them. A mound of something. Aliide drew away, behind the shelter of the curtain. She peeked out again, pulled the lace curtain in front of her so that she couldn't be seen from the yard, and held her breath. Her gaze bypassed the fly specks on the glass and focused on the lawn in front of the birch tree that had been split by lightning. (*P*, 5)

Through this textbook example of focalization, the story-world is gradually introduced to the reader who, for her part, becomes immersed in it. Windows may be concrete things, as it were, in fictional narratives – optical mediums through which narrators or characters see the outside world, or perhaps their own consciousness. Focalization here also functions as a way of opening an imaginary "window" into the story-world (see Jahn 2005, 175). In the case of *Purge*, this introduction to the story-world also points back towards the rich and complex literary heritage of the novel.

One of the classic motifs of gothic fiction, especially fiction written by women, is the madwoman in the attic. Upon a closer look, we see that the traditional roles of women and men are complicated and turned upside down in Oksanen's novel. In their classic feminist study, Sandra Gilbert and Susan Gubar (1979, 73–79, 338–349) bring up the "body/house" trope and the attendant binary opposition between the "angel in the house" and the "madwoman in the attic." In my view, Oksanen goes further than certain binary oppositions suggested by these early feminist literary theories. As Marleen Barr, in her "feminist topoanalysis," suggests – with reference to Charlotte Brontë's *Jane Eyre* (1847), Charlotte Perkins Gilman's "The Yellow Wallpaper" (1892), and Kate Chopin's *The Awakening* (1899) – powerful fictional women "are able to ignore yellow wallpaper, engage in women's awakening to the public world, and transcend the experience of the madwoman in the attic" (1992, 115).[4] Daniel Punday writes:

> According to Gilbert and Gubar, this traditional way of thinking about the social space allotted to women produces in literary texts a kind of duplicity. This trope implies that women are imagined either as the otherworldly "angel in the house" that conventional writing describes or the "monster" that Gilbert and Gubar insist is lurking beneath most nineteenth-century women's writing. The space of the house explicitly claims to protect the ideal angel expected by conventional thinking, but also ends up hiding the "monstrous" female identity that is suppressed by this thinking. [...] If the dominant figure of the female in the nineteenth century, the "angel in the house," is itself a metaphor developed in many different discourses, that figure nonetheless has its basis in concrete spatial arrangements that literally locate women within a domestic space. (2003, 119)

In *Purge*, Aliide's complex character, which is intimately tied to the rhythms and seasons of the earth, is neither the angel in the house – like her sister Ingel, representing the "ideal" and "traditional" woman – nor the madwoman in the attic, since this role is (ironically) reserved for the *man* in the story, the rather passive Hans whose diary writing betrays some signs of madness as time goes by and nothing ever happens. As Amy Elias suggests, in the postmodernist metahistorical romance the linkages between women and earth, nurturing, and birth may be treated as patriarchal constructions, and the idea of women's history is deftly complicated. In *Purge*, the protagonist is not content with the social and cultural role of a "good wife" but rather takes on a role usually reserved for men in society. It is true that the evocative images of nature and the everyday connect Aliide to the earth: we see her working in the garden, with its apple trees and peonies, surrounded by fields and forests, peeling onions and preserving berries in her kitchen where she is occasionally bothered by flies and worms. But in addition, she transcends the dichotomy of what may be called "patriarchal time relying on dates and history and matriarchal time based on the rhythms of the body" (2001, 89). This changing figure of a woman, situated in the traditions of historical romance and the Gothic novel and yet transcending them, is part of the decidedly feminist aesthetics of Sofi Oksanen.

If these romantic characters of the story, Ingel and Hans, with their tragic love story, appear to the reader as somewhat clichéd, this is precisely the point: they are stock characters taken from fairytales and Gothic romances, and their airy figures are in stark contrast to the more realist, modernist, and earthly characters of Aliide and Zara. Thus, the intertextual and discursive space of the novel is inhabited by distinctly *literary* devices, whether characters, plots, or motifs. It sometimes feels as if the characters themselves were living their lives within the confines of well-known cultural schemata and popular folk stories. These include the tale of the dead princess of Koluvere whose tragic story reflects the "real" story of Aliide, Ingel, and Hans. This interpretation is suggested by Zara's Little Red Riding Hood experience in the middle of a dark forest:

> Some said that the czarina had been jealous of the beautiful princess and sent her here as a prisoner. Others thought that she was brought for her own safety, to protect her from an insane husband. [...] the faces of Augusta, Aliide, and Grandmother mixed together in her mind to make one face, and she didn't dare to look to the right or the left because the trees in the forest were moving, their limbs were reaching toward her. [...] She [Zara] had to think a story to tell Aliide, too, but the only story that she could keep in her head in its entirety was the story of Augusta, the crazy, weeping princess. Maybe Zara was crazy, too, because who else but a crazy person would be running down an unknown road toward a house that she had only heard of, a house whose existence she couldn't be sure of? (*P*, 290–291)

To be sure, there are slight hints of madness in Aliide's behavior, among them her attack on the romantic marriage of Ingel and Hans, as dramatized by her way of tearing apart the colorful wedding quilt made by Ingel. In this quilt, the Ingel–Hans–Aliide relationship is spatially represented, with Aliide assigned to a marginal position:

> She found Ingel's wedding blanket in the drawer. It had a church, and a house as plump as a mushroom, and a husband and wife stitched into the red background. Aliide tore off the six-pointed stars with a pair of scissors, tore the rickrack from around the edge of that map of happiness with her fingers, and the man and wife disappeared from the picture, just like that, the cow just shreds of yarn, the cross on the church nothing but fluff! Aliide was there, too – a lamb, her namesake, was embroidered on it. [...] Martin peeked in the door, saw Aliide on her knees in a pile of yarn with the scissors in her hand, a knife beside her, her nostrils glowing red and her eyes bright. (*P*, 198)

The almost demonic tearing apart of the quilt is a sign of Aliide's rebellion against the ideal of patriarchal romance, but it is also symptomatic of a more general ideological attack against the traditional values of home, family, and church. This is a clear *mise en abyme*, a miniature picture reflecting the larger narrative and bringing out the meaning and form of the work (see Dällenbach 1989, 8). In *Purge*, the "angel in the house" is not replaced by the "madwoman in the attic," but by a third figure, a combination of earthly and spiritual aspects, as it were. In other words, the classic mirror or binary figure of gothic novels is replaced by a thinking and feeling individual who takes on an active role in the world.[5]

The Dark Cellar of History

In *Purge*, as in Morrison and Roy's novels, what happened in the past returns to haunt the present, even as these novels are "haunted" by previous literary texts. Once we recognize the mixed – and yet aesthetically organized – materials out of which Oksanen's fiction is made, it becomes more and more difficult to read the novel as a purely mimetic and referential "history" – a way of reading that is still popular among non-expert readers in Finland.

As Dominic LaCapra suggests, in striving to represent traumatizing events and traumatic experiences, fiction and history may share certain features on the narrative level, but there are still pragmatic differences with respect to truth claims. Testimonies, for instance, make truth claims about experiences or memories of those experiences. Still, as LaCapra argues, "the most difficult and moving moments of testimony involve not truth claims but experiential 'evidence' – the apparent reliving of the past, as the witness, going back to an unbearable scene, is overwhelmed by emotion and for a time unable to speak" (2004, 131). History, based on existing documents, makes truth claims about events and even about human experiences, but in trying to evoke experience, history must turn to testimony, diaries, and memoirs. Fiction makes its "claims" more indirectly and yet in a "thought-provoking, at times disconcerting manner with respect to the understanding or 'reading' of events, experience, and memory" (ibid. 132). All this is emphatically not to suggest that *Purge* is *mere* invention, but rather that fiction can provide new and sometimes deeper ways of seeing the world, opening as it does the unspoken *experiences* of history.

Indeed, in his definition of narrative, David Herman emphasizes particularity and experience related to human or human-like individuals: "Rather than focusing on general, abstract situations or trends, stories are accounts of what happened to particular people – and of what it was like for them to experience what happened – in particular circumstances and with specific consequences" (2009, 2). Whereas historical documents may only construct cold facts, it takes narrative to convey the sense how certain people felt and experienced certain things and events in given circumstances. Accordingly, James Phelan (2007, 66) suggests that *Beloved* establishes slavery not just as an abstract or historical evil but as something that continues to exert a negative influence on human beings; and the same can be said of the traumatic experiences in *The God of Small Things* and *Purge*. Consequently, what Morrison's Sethe experiences in the present time of the narrative, 1873, goes back to her experiences in the past, in 1855. Let us take a look at a key passage around the middle of the book where Sethe's violent act of killing her child in a woodshed is seen from an outside perspective, that is, through the eyes of white slave-catchers who objectify Sethe as a "nigger woman" and figure her as an animal:

> Inside two boys bled in the sawdust and dirt at the feet of a *nigger woman* holding a blood-soaked girl to her chest with one hand and an infant by the heels in the other. She did not look at them; [...]. [S]he's gone wild, due to the mishandling of the nephew who'd overbeat her and made her cut and run. Schoolteacher had chastised that nephew, telling him to think – just think – what would his own *horse* do if you beat it to beyond the point of education. [...] She was looking at him now, and if his other nephew could see that look he would learn the lesson for sure; you can't just mishandle *creatures* and expect success. (*B*, 149–150; my emphases.)

As Phelan (2007, 67) points out, here, in the middle of the narrative, Morrison provides a highly unsettling experience for the reader. Having seen Sethe from the inside or from the rather sympathetic perspective of the narrator up until now, we feel emotionally, psychologically and ethically shaken by suddenly seeing her from this alien, objectifying perspective, a perspective that sees her as a "nigger woman," a "horse," and a "creature."[6] In Phelan's view, the reader's negative judgment of the slave-catchers' vision in *Beloved* is ethically justified: as they see Sethe as an animal, we are inclined to take Sethe's side. Yet, what is very troubling in that scene, Phelan argues, is the vision of what Sethe is actually doing. While the slave-catchers' point of view may be subjective and distorted, the narrator still uses their eyes to show us Sethe's violent and murderous act toward her own baby (ibid. 67–68). Thus, while the slave-catchers' eyes are violently objectifying, Sethe is the one here who is performing actual violence. The vision provided by Morrison is disturbingly complex, also making our negative judgment of

181

Sethe possible, even though we learn later that Sethe killed her child to keep her out of slavery's violent grasp.

In *The God of Small Things*, too, there is a violent scene inviting complex emotional and ethical responses. Roy makes her child protagonists, the twins Rahel and Estha, witness a brutal and racist arrest of their romantic hero, Velutha, in a mysterious place called the History House, in the middle of the heart of darkness as the children imagine it in 1969, and this memory haunts them still in the narrative present, which is 1992:

> If they hurt Velutha more than they intended to, it was only because any kinship, any connection between themselves and him, any implication that if nothing else, at least biologically he was a fellow *creature* – had been severed long ago. They were not arresting a man, they were exorcizing *fear*. [...]
>
> Unlike the custom of rampaging religious mobs or conquering armies running riot, that morning in the Heart of Darkness the posse of Touchable Policemen acted with economy, not frenzy. Efficiency; not anarchy. Responsibility, not hysteria. They didn't tear out his hair or burn him alive. They didn't hack off his genitals and stuff them in his mouth. They didn't rape him. Or behead him.
>
> After all, they were not battling an *epidemic*. (*GST*, 309; my emphases.)

Here, "touchable" policemen almost beat to death an "untouchable" man; "untouchable" because he is too dirty and low-born to be touched, and thus he is seen through an analogy to such abstract entities as fear, or he is an "epidemic" or a "creature," just like Sethe in *Beloved*. This is a traumatic experience for the children who happen to witness a brutal mutilation of their beloved friend. As Laura Karttunen shrewdly shows, here trauma constitutes a gap in consciousness and remains inaccessible to narrative memory, and the "narrator uses disnarration, because the (narrative) memory of the beating is not available to the traumatized twins" (2008, 436). Here, as we can see, the most brutal acts of violence are actually *dis*-narrated: "*not* frenzy," "*not* anarchy," "they *didn't* hack off his genitals," "they *didn't* rape him." Roy's strategy here is effective in a rhetorical sense, since that which is negated may grow in the visual memory into a truly disturbing image; yet, at the moment it happens, the event and its meaning elude the children's understanding (see ibid. 437–438). As we read along, we realize that the children subsequently abandoned their friend Velutha at the police station because they were told that he really was a criminal – even though the reader is inclined to form a very different opinion.

Let us see, next, what happens in the middle of *Purge*. And whether we like it or not, we have to descend to a dark cellar, one of those dark cellars of human history that the title character warns us about in J. M. Coetzee's novel *Elizabeth Costello* (2003), arguing that there are things that should not happen, and at least there are things that should not be represented in fiction (see also Hyvärinen 2008; Mulhall 2009, 203–213). Similarly, Eric Berlatsky suggests that some literary texts "focus on the capacity of real events to exceed the discourse engendered to contain and explain them"; thus, for these texts, "what is real is precisely that which cannot be rendered satisfactorily in discourse, or at least in narrative" (2011, 24). In this harrowing scene, Aliide is questioned by violent, Soviet-minded interrogators, and she sees herself as an animal or inanimate object, as if seeing herself from the viewpoint of those who subject her to sexual violence. This scene is a deeply disturbing "shameful exposure," in which the experiencing subject suddenly becomes an object as seen through the eyes of others (see Bennett 2010, 316). The traumatic experience, set in 1947, obviously still haunts Aliide in the present of the narrative, which is set in 1992:

> Aliide's shirt was ripped open, the buttons flew onto the floor, against the walls – glass German buttons – and then… she became a *mouse*, in a corner of the room, a *fly* on the light that flew away, a *nail* in the plywood wall, a *rusty thumbtack*, she was a rusty thumbtack in the wall. *She was a fly* and she was walking over a *woman*'s naked breast, the woman was in the middle of a room with bag over her head, and she was walking over a fresh bruise, the blood forced up under the skin of the woman's breast, a running welt that the fly traversed, across bruises that emanated from the swollen nipple like the continents on a globe. [...] *The woman* with the bag over her head in the middle of the room was a stranger and Aliide was gone, [...]. (*P*, 151; my emphases.)

The scene is all the more disturbing because up until this point we have observed Aliide's emotions and experiences with sympathy. The picture here seems as black and white as fairy tales: she was an innocent and those monsters did bad things to her. Yet, the scene shows some complexity in terms of narrative technique, since Aliide herself adopts the objectifying gaze of her interrogators and rapists, seeing herself as another, as someone to be punished. In other words, she splits off from her body and feelings, detachedly observing her (or "the woman's") painful experience from the outside. On a closer look, the scene comes close to the narrative complexity of the scenes from Morrison's and Roy's novels.

Flies of Death, Flowers of Hope

In his classic study of literary and readerly dynamics, Menakhem Perry analyzes Faulkner's story "A Rose for Emily" (1930), in which an independent elderly woman living in her Gothic house has killed her lover and slept for years beside his decaying corpse. As Perry has it, Faulkner's Emily can be various things at the same time: a very proud woman, a hard authoritarian, an individualist, a *femme fatale*, and one who "looks down upon the cares of everyday life, upon all prosaic aspects of existence" (1979, 352). These different perspectives, given to us from the viewpoint of other people in the community, also force the reader to negotiate between them. The question is, then, whether Faulkner's Emily – or, for that matter, Oksanen's Aliide – is a madwoman or a heroine or something else, an individualist living according to her own moral code.

Only after we have read the whole narrative of *Purge* may we detect a certain disturbing quality in Aliide's reflection in the previous scene that "she was a fly." At the end of the novel, non-narrative reports and state documents

183

reveal to us that Aliide's code name as an agent was "Kärbes," meaning the "Fly," and that she probably took part in political agitation and methodically harsh interrogations herself, if only after her own traumatic experience.[7] This discovery complicates our view of the interrogation scene discussed above. The narrative never discloses the specifics of her activities as a spy. Yet the strange transition from Aliide, the victim, to the fly overlooking *a woman* being assaulted may perhaps function as a veiled reference to her future role as perpetrator.

Whereas the fly is the central traumatic figure in *Purge*, in *Beloved* we find similarly recurring images and motifs such as "little hummingbirds" that "stuck their needle beaks right through her headcloth into her hair and beat their wings" (*B*, 163). In *The God of Small Things* the protagonist is visited by the traumatic figure of "a cold moth," whose "icy legs touched her" (*GST*, 112). These motifs are examples of cold and clear images embedded in the memory of characters (cf. Hartman 1995, 357). As the characters themselves cannot give those images any solid narrative form, it becomes the task of the reader to search for some comprehensive interpretation of the story-world and of the narrative discourse. This interpretative work can be demanding, however, for trauma fictions simulate and imitate the symptoms of trauma through indirect images, recurring motifs, specific locations, and fragmentary narration as well as through intertextual allusions (see Whitehead 2004, 83–84). We can also distinguish between *external* and *internal* spaces. That is, we can pay attention to how external events in some historical and social place "intrude" upon consciousness in a traumatic way, creating an internal space (the mind), whose workings are often more difficult to interpret than those external events of history themselves (see Forter 2007, 274). As Elias characterizes *Beloved*, the novel dramatizes "the repetition compulsion of memory" (2001, 52), and, indeed, in the novel Sethe speaks of clear thought pictures floating around in the mind and the world, a kind of "*rememory* that belongs to somebody else" (*B*, 36; my emphasis).

In these novels the same things keep happening – as in *Absalom, Absalom!* where it is memorably stated that "*Maybe happen is never once*" (1990, 210) – and the past intrudes hauntingly and disturbingly on the present. Towards the end of Oksanen's novel, Aliide realizes that "certain things repeated themselves":

> Something swelled up in Aliide's brain. The curtains flapped like crazy, the clips that held them jingled, and the fabric snapped. The crackle of the fire had faded, and the tick of the clock remained, beneath the sound of the wind. Everything was repeating itself. [...] there would always be chrome-tanned boots, some new boots would arrive, the same or different, but a boot on your neck nevertheless. The foxholes had been closed up, the shell casings in the woods had tarnished, the secret dugouts had collapsed, the fallen had rotten away, but certain things repeated themselves. (*P*, 324–325)

In his analysis of Faulkner's novel, Greg Forter speaks of "the persistent planting of details whose most basic significance Faulkner withholds," thereby producing a kind of traumatic disturbance in the *reader's* mind

(2007, 278). It is as if there were too many disturbing details – such as those flies in *Purge* – and too little narrative information as to their meaning.

In their fragmented and traumatic structure, Morrison's, Roy's and Oksanen's novels present new challenges to the reader and sometimes leave them puzzled, unsatisfied, and distraught – and yet, on some level, strangely purified. These novels are dark and disturbing tales about the loss of innocence, of violence done to others, and of both mental and physical wounds that can never totally heal. As Elias says about Morrison's Sethe: "She embodies deferral: she embodies 'history that hurts,' but she also embodies the unspeakable" (2001, 66–67). In Elias's scheme, the so-called *metahistorical romance* – as opposed to the traditional historical romance – assumes the cultural construction of history; allows that the past may shape the present; asserts that all we can know about the historical past are its traces; and that all attempts to construct a historical narrative are culturally contaminated. As she defines it, "history is sublime, impossible to articulate, outside of representation, and as such leads to *ethical action* in the present" (ibid., 97; my emphasis). This ethical action, as a response to the past history's incomprehensible difficulty and cruelty, is the action taken in *Purge*.

The title of Oksanen's novel also refers to other things besides the Stalinist purification. The novel becomes a story of Aliide's personal purgatory and a story about her development into a moral and responsible human being. However, in order to purge and redeem herself, she must kill, and we learn that this is not the first time she has done so. Still, there is some hope in the ending of *Purge*, as Aliide finally decides to help Zara. She not only shoots to death two pimps and criminals who are after Zara, but she also helps her to find a more hopeful future. By doing this, she accomplishes, at least in part, the task given to her by Ingel: "'Clean your face'" (*P*, 182). As a reading experience, the novel simulates the process of traumatic experience, but it also points towards a possibility of healing. This idea is also suggested by Forter in his reading of Faulkner's novel:

> *Absalom, Absalom!* formally encodes the possibility of "working through" the trauma it transmits. To interpret the novel *is* here to metabolize the trauma inflicted by reading it. It's to move from the compulsive replication of the book's traumas that express the conditional agency of any textual interpretation. The novel's biphasic textuality in this sense contains the seeds of a hope that differentiates its imaginative designs from the movement of History within its representation – differentiates those designs, that is, from the model of history as repercussive ripples that perfectly transmit their traumatizing effects across any expanse of time and space. (2007, 280)

Forter speaks here about the specific textual form of Faulkner's novel and how it may contain "seeds of hope." We can also see that certain things – like the experience of small things in life and the natural world – continue to give hope to the characters of the novels discussed here. As one of the credos in *Purge*, taken from Paul-Eerik Rummo's poetry, has it: "Seven million years / we heard the führer's speeches, the same / seven million years / we saw the

185

apple trees bloom" (*P*, 111). Some things last and go on living; at least the land, if not people – as in the conclusion of *Beloved*, with its images of weather:

> By and by all trace is gone, and what is forgotten is not only the footprints but the water too and what is down there. The rest is weather. Not the breath of the disremembered and unaccounted for, but wind in the eaves, or spring ice thawing too quickly. Just weather. Certainly no clamor for a kiss. (*B*, 275)

Still, according to Phelan's reading of the ending of *Beloved*, we are allowed to "finish the narrative with a sense of hope rather than despair," and he even suggests that a narrative can become more readable if we can, in the end, see something positive to happen to the characters (2007, 77). And yet, to my mind, the purported hopefulness at the very end of each of the three novels becomes complicated.[8] The traces of history, its violence and shame, cannot be erased easily, nor should they be. The last phrase of Morrison's novel, "Beloved" (*B*, 275), contains in a single word the idea of love, hope for the future, and the history of racism. The last word of *The God of Small Things*, "Tomorrow" (*GST*, 340), also appears to be hopeful, and yet the reader knows that the two lovers will soon die, one of them a violent death. Pranav Jani writes:

> This juxtaposition, concluding with the chronologically earlier scene, allows Roy to discover the ordinary, the everyday resilience of popular life that cannot be completely crushed by the big – even as the "happy" ending heightens the sense of what was lost. [...] *The God of Small Things* forces the reader to find hope for the small in the midst of an invincible big that has historically never ceased to win – and yet to take that hope not as a romanticization of subaltern resistance but merely as a possibility. (2010, 213–214)

In all three novels, and explicitly in Roy's, the small things of everyday life are juxtaposed with the large and oppressive movements of national histories. Interestingly, those natural and everyday things – weather and vegetables, flies and flowers – are much more meaningful to the characters than the "big" events of the so-called official history.

As for *Purge*, a figure of hope is found in Zara who represents the new generation: "Things were going to have to change someday. [...] *Someday*" (*P*, 275). However, the last words of the novel come from the diary of her grandfather Hans, a man who was both loved and killed by Aliide. What is left is the memory of the beautiful Hans in the form of cornflowers, symbolizing both hope and suffering in Estonia. And behind the words of hope and optimism there are always those buzzing flies of history. *Purge* ends with these words:

> Although I'm not free yet, I will be soon, and my heart is as light as a swallow's. Soon the three of us will be together. (*P*, 390)

"Soon the three of us will be together." Metatextually speaking, Sofi Oksanen's novel longs to be in the same canonical category with Toni Morrison's and Arundhati Roy's great novels, and perhaps, someday, it will.

NOTES

1   This article is a revised and expanded version of an earlier essay (Lehtimäki 2010). I am grateful to Laura Karttunen for her comments on this English version.

2   In the limited scope of this essay, I will focus on *Purge*'s Anglo-American subtexts, especially those in the tradition of the English and American Gothic. Of course, we need to note Oksanen's favorite writer Marguerite Duras, especially her works such as *La Douleur* (1985) with its story of prison camps, and *Écrire* (1993) with its images of dead flies, as well as her engagement with the topic of trauma (see Knuuttila 2011). We should also recognize the influence of Finnish and Estonian fiction, folklore and culture. I'll just mention Helvi Hämäläinen's *Säädyllinen murhenäytelmä* (1941), Jaan Kross's great Faulknerian novel *Keisri hull* (1978; *The Czar's Madman*), and Tõnu Õnnepalu's *Hind* (1995) with its evocative imagery of the Estonian countryside.

3   It is crucial to note the historical, political, social, and national differences; in other words, "although globalization has at its core a profoundly economic and political set of processes, it is also everywhere a matter of cultural imaginings – often conflictual, always plural" (Chandler 2009, 3). In a similar vein, Sofi Oksanen herself has suggested that fashionable Western theories of trauma cannot fully explain the non-Western experience of the *gulag*, that is, the reality of the Soviet prison camps (2009, 15). On *gulag* narratives, see Toker 2000 and 2007.

4   Brontë's, Gilman's, and Chopin's stories would seem likely candidates for *Purge*'s intertexts as well. Barr specifically focuses on postmodern feminist fictions such as Lynne Tillman's *Haunted Houses* (1987).

5   In this vein, *Purge* is related to the Gothic tradition of *Jane Eyre* – with Aliide representing 'earth' (cf. Bertha) and Ingel, or "Angel," representing 'air' (cf. Eyre) – and to the postcolonial rewriting of Brontë's classic in Jean Rhys' *Wide Sargasso Sea* (1966), which is told from the viewpoint of the "madwoman."

6   Faulkner's *Absalom, Absalom!*, one of Morrison's subtexts, is echoed here: "[Sutpen saw] his own father and sisters and brothers as the owner, the rich man (not the nigger) must have been seeing them all the time – as cattle, creatures heavy and without grace, brutely evacuated into a world without hope or purpose for them, who would in turn spawn with brutish and vicious prolixity" (Faulkner 1990, 188; cf. Forter 2007, 274–275).

7   In an interesting book entitled *Insect Poetics* it is suggested that ever since Plato, the figure of the fly has been represented as petty and annoying, "but not without a function within the larger scheme of events as *political agitator*, everywhere 'rousing, persuading, reproving'" (Rosenstein 2006, 112; my emphasis). In the tradition of Russian literature flies and other insects play viable roles from Dostoevsky to Viktor Pelevin, in whose fiction "geographic and political borders are blurred and humans and insects become virtually interchangeable" (ibid. 113).

8   We may also note the metafictional "happy end" convention in Ian McEwan's *Atonement* (2001), a novel which bears some similarity to *Purge*. The protagonist Briony, who appears to be the writer of the narrative we are reading, tries to atone and to purge herself of a tragic misjudgment she made in her childhood. Part of that atonement and personal purification is her attempt to give in her novel happiness to those who, because of her deed, were denied it in real life. Thus,

Briony wants her novel to provide some "sense of hope or satisfaction" and "a stand against oblivion and despair," in letting the two lovers live and uniting them at the end (McEwan 2001, 350–351). See also Phelan 2007, 120–131.

References

Morrison, Toni 1998/1987: *Beloved.* [= *B.*] New York: Plume.

Oksanen, Sofi 2010/2008: *Purge.* [= *P.*] Transl. Lola Rogers. New York: Black Cat.

Roy, Arundhati 2004/1997: *The God of Small Things.* [= *GST.*] London: Harper Perennial.

Bachelard, Gaston 1964/1957: *The Poetics of Space.* Boston: Beacon Press.

Barr, Marleen S. 1992: *Feminist Fabulation. Space/Postmodern Fiction.* Iowa City: University of Iowa Press.

Bennett, Ashly 2010: Shameful Signification. Narrative and Feeling in *Jane Eyre. Narrative* 18:3, 300–323.

Berlatsky, Eric L. 2011: *The Real, the True, and the Told. Postmodern Historical Narrative and the Ethics of Representation.* Columbus: The Ohio State University Press.

Brooks, Peter 1984: *Reading for the Plot. Design and Intention in the Narrative.* New York: Knopf.

Chandler, Aaron 2009: Introduction. Imagination without Walls. In: Christian Moraru (ed.), *Postcommunism, Postmodernism, and the Global Imagination.* Boulder: East European Monographs.

Dällenbach, Lucien 1989/1977: *Mirror in the Text.* Transl. Jeremy Whiteley and Emma Hughes. Cambridge: Polity Press.

Elias, Amy J. 2001: *Sublime Desire. History and Post-1960s Fiction.* Baltimore & London: The Johns Hopkins University Press.

Faulkner, William 1990/1936: *Absalom, Absalom!* New York: Vintage.

Forter, Greg 2007: Freud, Faulkner, Caruth. Trauma and the Politics of Literary Form. *Narrative* 15(3), 259–285.

Gilbert, Sandra M., Gubar, Susan 1979: *The Madwoman in the Attic. The Woman Writer and the Nineteenth-Century Literary Imagination.* New Haven & London: Yale University Press.

Hartman, Geoffrey H. 1995: On Traumatic Knowledge and Literary Studies. *New Literary History* 26, 537–563.

Herman, David 2009: *Basic Elements of Narrative.* Malden: Wiley-Blackwell.

Hyvärinen, Matti 2008: Too Much Terror? J. M. Coetzee's *Elizabeth Costello* and the Circulation of Trauma. In: Matti Hyvärinen and Lisa Muszynski (eds.), *Terror and the Arts. Artistic, Literary, and Political Interpretations of Violence from Dostoevsky to Abu Ghraib.* New York: Palgrave Macmillan.

Jahn, Manfred 2005: Focalization. In: David Herman, Manfred Jahn and Marie-Laure Ryan (eds.), *Routledge Encyclopedia of Narrative Theory.* London and New York: Routledge.

Jani, Pranav 2010: *Decentering Rushdie. Cosmopolitanism and the Indian Novel in English.* Columbus: The Ohio State University Press.

Karttunen, Laura 2008: A Sosiostylistic Perspective on Negatives and the Disnarrated. Lahiri, Roy, Rushdie. *Partial Answers* 6(2), 419–442.

Knuuttila, Sirkka 2011: *Fictionalising Trauma. The Aesthetics of Marguerite Duras's India Cycle.* Frankfurt am Main et al.: Peter Lang.

LaCapra, Dominic 2004: *History in Transit. Experience, Identity, Critical Theory.* Ithaca & London: Cornell University Press.

Lehtimäki, Markku 2010: Sofistikoitunut kertomus ja lukemisen etiikka. [Sophisticated

Narrative and the Ethics of Reading.] *Kirjallisuudentutkimuksen aikakauslehti Avain* 2, 40–49.

McEwan, Ian 2001: *Atonement*. New York: Doubleday.

McHale, Brian 1996/1987: *Postmodernist Fiction*. London & New York: Routledge.

Mulhall, Stephen 2009: *The Wounded Animal. J. M. Coetzee and the Difficulty of Reality in Literature and Philosophy*. Princeton: Princeton University Press.

Oksanen, Sofi 2009: Johdannoksi. [Introduction.] In: Sofi Oksanen and Imbi Paju (eds.), *Kaiken takana oli pelko. Kuinka Viro menetti historiansa ja miten se saadaan takaisin*. [Fear Was Behind Everything. How Estonia Lost Its History and How to Get It Back.] Helsinki: WSOY.

Perry, Menakhem 1979: Literary Dynamics. How the Order of a Text Creates Its Meanings (with an Analysis of Faulkner's "A Rose for Emily"). *Poetics Today* 1(1–2), 35–64, 311–361.

Phelan, James 2007: *Experiencing Fiction. Judgments, Progressions, and the RhetoricalTheory of Narrative*. Columbus: The Ohio State University Press.

Punday, Daniel 2003: *Narrative Bodies. Toward a Corporeal Narratology*. New York: Palgrave Macmillan.

Punter, David 2005: *The Influence of Post-Modernism on Contemporary Writing. An Interdisciplinary Study*. Lewiston: The Edwin Mellen Press.

Rosenstein, Roy 2006: The End of Insect Imagery. From Dostoevsky to Kobo Abé via Kafka. In: Eric C. Brown (ed.), *Insect Poetics*. Minneapolis: University of Minnesota Press.

Tammi, Pekka 1992: *Kertova teksti. Esseitä narratologiasta*. [The Narrative Text. Essays on Narratology.] Helsinki: Gaudeamus.

Tammi, Pekka 1999: *Russian Subtexts in Nabokov's Fiction. Four Essays*. Tampere: Tampere University Press.

Toker, Leona 2000: *Return from the Archipelago. Narratives of Gulag Survivors*. Bloomington: Indiana University Press.

Toker, Leona 2007: Testimony and Doubt. Varlam Shalamov's "How It Began" and "Handwriting". In: Markku Lehtimäki, Simo Leisti and Marja Rytkönen (eds.), *Real Stories, Imagined Realities. Fictionality and Non-Fictionality in Literary Constructs and Historical Contexts*. Tampere: Tampere University Press.

Whitehead, Anne 2004: *Trauma Fiction*. Edinburgh: Edinburgh University Press.

Further Reading

Grönstand, Heidi 2010: Kaksi maata, kaksi kulttuuria. Sofi Oksanen suomalaisen kirjallisuuden kartalla. [Two Countries, Two Cultures. Sofi Oksanen on the Finnish Literary Map.] *Kirjallisuudentutkimuksen aikakauslehti Avain* 1/2010, 42–50.

Korhonen, Kuisma 2011: *Lukijoiden yhteisö*. [The Community of Readers.] Helsinki: Avain.

Lappalainen, Päivi 2011: Häpeä, ruumis ja väkivalta Sofi Oksasen *Puhdistuksessa*. [Shame, Body and Violence in Sofi Oksanen's *Purge*.] In: Viola Parente-Capková ja Siru Kainulainen *(eds.), Häpeä vähän! Kriittisiä tutkimuksia häpeästä*. [Shame on You! Critical Studies of Shame.] Turku: Utukirjat, 259–281.

Contributors

Mika Hallila (Ph.D.) is (acting) professor of literature at the University of Jyväskylä. He has published the study monograph "The Concept of Metafiction. Theoretical, Contextual, and Historical Study" (*Metafiktion käsite. Teoreettinen, kontekstuaalinen ja historiallinen tutkimus*, 2006). Hallila's recent research interests focus on cultural representations of tobacco in Finnish literature and the theory of the novel.
e-mail: mika.s.hallila@jyu.fi

Mari Hatavara (Ph.D.) is professor of Finnish literature at the University of Tampere, and vice director of the School of Language, Translation and Literary Studies. Her research interests include narrative theory, historical novel and intermedial relations between word and image.
e-mail: mari.hatavara@uta.fi

Päivi Heikkilä-Halttunen (Ph.D.) is a docent at the University of Tampere and independent literary scholar and critic. She regularly reviews children's and young people's literature for the leading newspaper in Finland *Helsingin Sanomat* and the *Books from Finland* periodical (www. booksfromfinland.fi). She also maintains a blog called Lastenkirjahylly (The Children's Book Shelf) at http://lastenkirjahylly.blogspot.com.

Leena Kirstinä (Ph.D.) is Emer. Professor of Finnish Literature, from the University of Jyväskylä. Her recent publication is a monograph on *Narrating Nation: Finnishness in the Prose of the 1990s* (2007). She is working with the reseach group for History of Contemporary Finnish Literature.
e-mail: leena.m.kirstina@jyu.fi

Päivi Koivisto (M.A.) is a researcher at the University of Helsinki. In her doctoral thesis (2011), she analyses and contextualises three autofictional novels by Finnish author Pirkko Saisio. At the moment she works as an publishing editor of Finnish fiction.
e-mail: paivi.koivisto@helsinki.fi

MARKKU LEHTIMÄKI (Ph.D.) is Postdoctoral Researcher at the University of Tampere and in the Academy of Finland. He is the author of *The Poetics of Norman Mailer's Nonfiction* (2005) and co-editor of *Intertextuality and Intersemiosis* (2004), *Thresholds of Interpretation* (2006), and *Real Stories, Imagined Realities* (2007). He has also written articles on narrative theory, visual culture, and American literature.
e-mail: markku.lehtimaki@uta.fi

PIRJO LYYTIKÄINEN (Ph.D.) is Professor of Finnish Literature at the University of Helsinki and Director of Finnish Doctoral Program for Literary Studies. Her main publications include three monographs on two Finnish Modernist and Romantic Authors (Volter Kilpi and Aleksis Kivi) and the Symbolist and Decadent movements in Finland. She is preparing a monograph on Leena Krohn's allegorical novels.
e-mail: pirjo.lyytikainen@helsinki.fi

KRISTINA MALMIO (Ph.D.) is Adjunct Professor, Scandinavian Literature, University of Helsinki. Her research interests concern Finland-Swedish literature in the 1910s and 1920s, contemporary Finland-Swedish prose, sociology of literature, parody, irony and metafiction.
e-mail: kristina.malmio@helsinki.fi

OUTI OJA is Ph.D. from the University of Jyväskylä. Her doctoral thesis (2009) deals with metapoetry in the Finnish lyrics in the 1990s. As postdoctoral scholar, Oja is currently working on with the research about narrative and communication in Finnish prose poetry (funded by The Finnish Literary Society).
e-mail: outi.oja@uta.fi

JUSSI OJAJÄRVI (Ph.D.) has written his article while working as a post-doc researcher in two projects funded by the Academy of Finland: "Power of Culture in Producing Common Sense" (situated at The University of Tampere, led by professor Mikko Lehtonen and docent Anu Koivunen), and "To Ignore, to Adapt Oneself, to Utilise, or to Resist?" researching the reactions of the art-world to the market-based turn in society and cultural policy (led by Professor Erkki Sevänen, University of Eastern Finland). Ojajärvi is a Lecturer in Literature at the University of Oulu (currently on leave). His main publications include the doctoral dissertation, which studies the representation of capitalism and subjectivity in contemporary Finnish literature, and several articles on the relations of culture, the self and the market in the neoliberal era (i.e. in *Avain* 2008 and other research anthologies).
e-mail: jussi.ojajarvi@oulu.fi

Index

Industry and Modernism
*Companies, Architecture and
Identity in the Nordic and
Baltic Countries during
the High-Industrial Period*
Edited by Anja Kervanto
Nevanlinna
Studia Fennica Historica 14
2007

CHARLOTTA WOLFF
Noble conceptions of politics
in eighteenth-century Sweden
(ca 1740–1790)
Studia Fennica Historica 15
2008

Sport, Recreation and Green
Space in the European City
Edited by Peter Clark,
Marjaana Niemi & Jari Niemelä
Studia Fennica Historica 16
2009

Rhetorics of Nordic
Democracy
Edited by Jussi Kurunmäki &
Johan Strang
Studia Fennica Historica 17
2010

Studia Fennica
Anthropologica

On Foreign Ground
*Moving between Countries and
Categories*
Edited by Minna Ruckenstein
& Marie-Louise Karttunen
Studia Fennica Anthropologica 1
2007

Beyond the Horizon
*Essays on Myth, History, Travel
and Society*
Edited by Clifford Sather &
Timo Kaartinen
Studia Fennica Anthropologica 2
2008

Studia Fennica Linguistica

MINNA SAARELMA-
MAUNUMAA
Edhina Ekogidho – Names
as Links
*The Encounter between African
and European Anthroponymic
Systems among the Ambo
People in Namibia*
Studia Fennica Linguistica 11
2003

Minimal reference
*The use of pronouns in Finnish
and Estonian discourse*
Edited by Ritva Laury
Studia Fennica Linguistica 12
2005

ANTTI LEINO
On Toponymic Constructions
as an Alternative to Naming
Patterns in Describing
Finnish Lake Names
Studia Fennica Linguistica 13
2007

Talk in interaction
Comparative dimensions
Edited by Markku Haakana,
Minna Laakso & Jan Lindström
Studia Fennica Linguistica 14
2009

Planning a new standard
language
*Finnic minority languages meet
the new millennium*
Edited by Helena Sulkala &
Harri Mantila
Studia Fennica Linguistica 15
2010

LOTTA WECKSTRÖM
Representations of
Finnishness in Sweden
Studia Fennica Linguistica 16
2011

Studia Fennica Litteraria

Changing Scenes
*Encounters between European
and Finnish Fin de Siècle*
Edited by Pirjo Lyytikäinen
Studia Fennica Litteraria 1
2003

Women's Voices
*Female Authors and Feminist
Criticism in the Finnish Literary
Tradition*
Edited by Lea Rojola &
Päivi Lappalainen
Studia Fennica Litteraria 2
2007

Metaliterary Layers in Finnish
Literature
Edited by Samuli Hägg, Erkki
Sevänen & Risto Turunen
Studia Fennica Litteraria 3
2009

AINO KALLAS
Negotiations with Modernity
Edited by Leena Kurvet-
Käosaar & Lea Rojola
Studia Fennica Litteraria 4
2011

The Emergence of Finnish
Book and Reading Culture
in the 1700s
Edited by Cecilia af Forselles &
Tuija Laine
Studia Fennica Litteraria 5
2011

Nodes of Contemporary
Finnish Literature
Edited by Leena Kirstinä
Studia Fennica Litteraria 6
2012